Intelligence, Sustainability, and Strategic Issues in Management

VOLUME 18 • 2016

Editorial Board

Intelligence, Sustainability, and Strategic Issues in Management

Editor: M. AFZALUR RAHIM

VOLUME 18 • 2016

CURRENT TOPICS IN MANAGEMENT

Routledge
Taylor & Francis Group

LONDON AND NEW YORK

First published 2016 by Transaction Publishers

2 Park Square, Milton Park, Abingdon, Oxon, OX14 4RN
605 Third Avenue, New York, NY 10017

Routledge is an imprint of the Taylor & Francis Group, an informa business

First issued in paperback 2020

ISSN: 1529-2088
ISBN 13: 978-1-4128-6413-8 (hbk)
ISBN 13: 978-0-367-73651-4 (pbk)

Contents

Current Topics in Management, Vol. 18, 2016, pp. 1–16

A MODEL OF LEADERS' SOCIAL INTELLIGENCE AND FOLLOWERS' SATISFACTION WITH ANNUAL EVALUATION

M. Afzalur Rahim
Western Kentucky University

Ismail Civelek
Western Kentucky University

Feng Helen Liang
Western Kentucky University

This study investigates the relationship between academic department chairs' social intelligence (SI) and faculty members' satisfaction with annual evaluation of teaching and research (SAE) at a public university in the United States. SI is defined as the ability to be aware of relevant social situations; to handle situational challenges effectively; to understand others' concerns and feelings; and to build and maintain positive relationships in social settings. We test our model with questionnaire data from 406 faculty members from 43 departments in a public university. Our data analyses with LISREL at the department level suggest that SI is positively associated with SAE. Implications for management, directions for future research, and limitations of the study are discussed.

Keywords: intelligence, social intelligence, leadership, performance evaluation

One of the most significant constructs in management and other social sciences is intelligence. Many scholars and management practitioners generally associate this construct with cognitive or academic intelligence, and IQ is used to measure it. They also assume that IQ is positively associated with one's success in life. Unfortunately, the literature on management and psychology shows that cognitive intelligence is inadequate to predict one's effective leadership or success in life (cf. Judge, Colbert, & Ilies, 2004; Rosete & Ciarrochi, 2005).

Is it possible that there are noncognitive forms of intelligence that may be associated with effective leadership? Yes, scholars have been discussing other dimensions of intelligence: emotional intelligence, social intelligence or practical intelligence, and cultural intelligence—what scholars refer to as "street smarts" (van Dyne, Ang, & Koh , 2009; Gardner, 1999; Mayer, Salovey, & Caruso, 2008a; Sternberg, 2002). The value-added contribution of our study is that it explores the relationships of academic department chairs' (DC) social intelligence (SI) components to each other and to faculty members' satisfaction with annual evaluation of teaching and research (SAE). This study attains this objective by providing a clear definition of the SI construct, collecting data with a new SI instrument, and showing to what extent department chairs' SI is associated with faculty members' SAE at a public institution in the United States.

SI is different from general, emotional, and cultural intelligence, but there are some overlaps among these constructs. Considering the research discussed in the preceding paragraph, it is hypothesized that academic leaders' social intelligence is positively associated with faculty members' satisfaction with department chairs' SAE. Next, we discuss our SI construct and the results derived from the questionnaire data collected from 406 faculty members from 43 departments at a public university in the United States.

Social Intelligence Construct

There are many definitions of SI, but the consensus among scholars is that it is the ability to interact with the environment effectively to succeed in life or in an organization. As Sternberg (2009) suggests success in career is associated with three types of intelligence: creative, analytical, and practical. Sternberg's practical intelligence is similar to social intelligence. Other scholars have investigated related concepts such as intrapersonal (emotional) and interpersonal (social) intelligence (Gardner, 1999), emotional intelligence (Goleman, 1998; Mayer, Salovey, & Caruso, 2008b), and cultural intelligence (van Dyne et al., 2009).

Although there is no agreement on the construct of SI, many scholars agree that SI is associated with one's ability to understand the thinking, feelings, and behaviors of other people; to interact with them properly; and to act effectively in various situations (Ford & Tisak, 1983; Thorndike, 1920; Kihlstrom & Cantor, 2000; Sternberg, 2002). In this study, we build on these definitions and broaden the concept of SI. We have especially adopted the definition of SI suggested by Rahim (2014) as "the ability to be aware of relevant social situational contexts; to deal with the contexts or challenges effectively; to understand others' concerns, feelings, and emotional states; and to speak in a clear and convincing manner knowing what to say, when to say it, and how to say it and to build and maintain positive relationships with others" (p. 46).

This definition consists of four categories of abilities—situational awareness, situational response, cognitive empathy, and social skills. This four-category SI nomenclature is used in the present study.

The first two abilities—situational awareness and situational response—are necessary for one's career success and effective leadership. Situational awareness refers to one's ability to collect information for the diagnosis and formulation of problem(s); situational response refers to one's ability to use this information to make effective decisions to obtain desired results. The other two abilities—cognitive empathy and social skills—refer to the abilities to understand the feelings and needs of people, to communicate with them effectively, and to build and maintain relationships. These two abilities can help a leader to remain aware of various social situational contexts, and thus improve their situational response competence. Next, we describe theoretical basis of the four SI components and interrelationships among them in detail.

Situational Awareness

This is defined as one's *competence or ability to comprehend or assess relevant social situational contexts.* This component of intelligence is also known as contextual intelligence that was first popularized by Sternberg (1985; see also Bennis & Thomas, 2002). It was described as social perceptiveness by Zaccaro, Gilbert, Thor, & Mumford (1991). This ability enables leaders in organizations to collect relevant information and diagnose situations in a timely manner and to formulate a problem correctly. The ability to diagnose a problem is very important, and shouldn't be taken for granted. Contingency theories of leadership usually neglect situational awareness, implicitly assuming that leaders understand the relevant situational variables and are able to formulate their problems correctly. But not all leaders possess the capability to make an appropriate assessment of situational variables. When leaders formulate a problem wrongly, it could lead to Type III error, defined as the probability of solving a wrong problem when one should solve the right problem (Mitroff, 1998; Mitroff & Silvers, 2010). Leaders who possess this ability are able to collect necessary information and formulate a problem correctly, thereby avoiding this error.

In case the leaders do not have adequate information on a problem or a potential business opportunity, they are likely to engage in internal and/ or external environmental scanning. In addition, the leaders may seek help from experts to gain an overall understanding of the problem. When experts have different and even contradictory assessments of a problem, it is up to the leader to decide which problem formulation reflects social reality and is to be accepted. O'Brien and O'Hare (2007) found that participants in training programs with high situational awareness performed well irrespective of the training conditions; hence, we suggest that leaders with higher situational awareness ability are better able to recognize patterns associated with their work environment. Albrecht (2007) suggested that situational awareness is one of the five components of SI, the other components being including presence, authenticity, clarity, and empathy. Albrecht defines situational awareness as the ability to read situations and comprehend social context influencing behavior, and to choose effective strategies. Mayo and Nohira (2005) suggested that a leader's ability to understand and adapt to different situational contexts is associated with leadership effectiveness.

Situational Response

This is associated with one's *competence or ability to adapt to or deal with any social situations effectively*. This is essentially the decision-making competence of leaders described by Zaccaro et al. (1991) as behavioral flexibility and by Bennis and Thomas (2002) as adaptive capacity. Most existing researches do not distinguish between situational awareness and situational response and lump them into situational awareness (Mayo & Nohira, 2005; Albrecht, 2007). In this study, we make a distinction between the two components. These two components have overlaps, but are conceptually independent. Both are essential for effective leadership. It is possible for leaders to recognize or diagnose a situation or problem correctly, but not be able to make a decision leading to desirable outcomes. In other words, it is possible for a leader to have high or low abilities associated with these two components. A high–high leader is more effective than a high–low, low–high, or low–low leader.

To illustrate this point further, consider two processes in organizational learning: *detection* and *correction* of error (Argyris & Schon, 1996), diagnosis and intervention in conflict (Rahim & Bonoma, 1979), and capabilities "to diagnose an issue and its causes" and "to decide on the best course of action" (Schmidt & Tannenbaum, 1990). The two processes—diagnosis or detection of error and intervention or correction of error—correspond with the two components of SI—assessment of and responses to situational contexts.

Existing literature on leadership has been proficient in prescribing how to match leadership styles with situational variables to improve job performance and satisfaction of followers, but so far has been inadequate in identifying the unique situations for which creative responses (leadership styles) would be needed to improve outcomes. Related to this limitation, leadership theories so far have not investigated the need for leaders to possess both situational awareness and response competencies to define the situational variables and respond to them appropriately. Even if a leader can diagnose a situation correctly, he or she may not possess the necessary competence to make an effective decision to deal with it.

Now that we have made it clear that situational awareness and situational response are two essential abilities for effective leadership, we continue to discuss, in the following sections, how the other two components—cognitive empathy and social skills—can help leaders to improve their effectiveness.

Cognitive Empathy

Empathy refers to one's ability to understand others, taking active interest in them, recognizing and responding to changes in their emotional states, and understanding their feelings (cf. Goleman, 2005; Albrecht, 2007; Ang & Goh, 2010). Empathy includes several components, cognitive, intellectual, affective, and behavioral. Specifically, cognitive empathy is associated with one's *ability to recognize the thinking, feelings, intentions, moods, and impulses of people inside and outside the organization.* Kaukiainen et al. (1999) suggested that "the cognitive component of empathy forms an essential part of social intelligence" (p. 83).

Cognitive empathy should help to improve a leader's awareness of the feelings and needs of supervisors, subordinates, and coworkers as well as people from outside the organization. This ability to connect with people should help to improve a leader's social skills. In other words, cognitive empathy should be positively associated with social skills.

Social Skills

This component is associated with *one's ability or competence to speak in a clear and convincing manner that involves knowing what to say, when to say it, and how to say it.* Social skills also involve building and maintaining positive relationships, to act properly in human relations, to deal with problems without demeaning coworkers, and to negotiate and manage conflict in a tactical and diplomatic way.

Social skills competence enables a leader to continuously collect relevant information from internal and external environments to enhance their situational awareness. Social skills ability helps leaders explain and justify their decisions to followers and motivate them so that leaders' decisions are effectively implemented. Studies by Baron and Markham (2000) and Baron and Tang (2009) suggested that entrepreneurs' social skills—competencies that help them interact effectively with others—may also play a role in their success.

In the previous section we indicated that cognitive empathy directly influences social skills, and indirectly influences situational awareness. In other words, social skills mediate the relationship between cognitive empathy and situational awareness. We also suggest that social skills are positively related to situational awareness and indirectly related to situational response. In other words, situational awareness mediates the social skills–situational response relationship.

Evaluation of Teaching and Research

The reports of teaching and research process dramatically shape the tenure decisions of tenure-track faculty members and impact merit pay increase for tenured faculty members in universities. However, the procedures and instruments that universities use to evaluate and reward faculty members vary in US higher education system (Elmore, 2008). The evaluations of teaching and research of faculty members are affected by his or her relationship with the department chair besides measurable performance metrics such as the number and quality of published articles, the number of conference presentations, and teaching evaluations by students. Therefore, the department chair's SI has a significant impact on the faculty members' satisfaction with the annual review of teaching and research.

Regarding the most efficient method of evaluating teaching and research of faculty members, there are extensive studies in OR, educational leadership, and psychology literature. Costa and Oliveira (2012) used a multicriteria optimization model to standardize annual review of teaching and research of faculty members by setting performance targets and successfully implemented in several universities in Portugal. In addition, comparative analyses of universities or departments are mostly studied in the evaluation literature of higher education (Wolansky 2001; Politis & Siskos 2004; Gimenéz & Martínez 2006; Coccia 2008).

Regarding educational scholarship, O'Meara (2005) focused on multiple types of scholarships in evaluating teaching and research of faculty members from a national study of chief academic officers of universities across the United States. Colbeck and Wharton-Michael (2006) proposed a conceptual framework to understand the factors affecting faculty members' work performance and suggested community-oriented scholarship, which should be used in annual reviews. Regarding the faculty members' beliefs on promotion and tenure decisions, Luchs et al. (2011) focused on the importance of the evaluation of service and promotion and tenure decisions. However, the present study focuses only on the reactions of faculty members to the annual review of teaching and research, not service.

Regarding educational leadership and intelligence, Sternberg (2005) proposed a model based on wisdom, intelligence, and creativity for positive educational leaders. However, his model does not include intelligence as SI for educational leaders; instead creative intelligence and practical intelligence are considered for positive leadership in education. In addition to Sternberg's seminal work, intelligence has been studied as "emotional intelligence" in educational leadership and psychology literature (Cherniss, Extein, Goleman, & Weissberg, 2006; Garner, 2010).

On the basis of previous discussion, we propose the following hypotheses:

Hypothesis 1: *Social skills mediates the relationship between cognitive empathy and situational awareness.*

Hypothesis 2: *Situational awareness mediates the relationship between social skills and situational response.*

Figure 1
A Model of Intelligent Leadership
and Satisfaction with Annual Evaluation

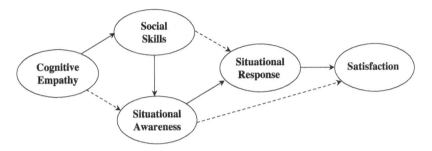

Hypothesis 3: *Situational response mediates the relationship between situational awareness and faculty members' satisfaction with annual evaluation of teaching and research.*

The relationships proposed in the hypotheses in this study are presented in Figure 1. The solid lines indicate significant relationships and broken lines indicate indirect relationships.

Method

Sample and Procedure

The data for the present study were collected from a collegiate sample of 406 faculty at a state university in the United States. Average age, teaching experience, and working experience with the present DC in years were 45.10 (*SD* = 3.82), 14.4 (*SD* = 10.99), and 4.61 (*SD* = 5.26), respectively. About 50.5% of the respondents and 35.2% of the DCs were female. About 84% of the respondents were white, 5% black, 4.8% Asian, 3.6% Hispanic, and 3.6% other. About 18.1% of the respondents were professors, 23.8% associate professors, 24.1% assistant professors, 15.9% lecturers, 11.2% adjunct professors, and 6.8% part-time professors. About 55.7% of the respondents had doctoral degrees, 38.3% had master's degrees, and 6% had other qualifications.

Measurement

Social Intelligence. The four components of supervisors' SI were measured with 28 items of the Rahim Social Intelligence Test (RSIT)—developed by and refined by Rahim (2014). The RSIT items were changed to measure faculty perceptions of their respective department chair's SI. The RSIT was designed on the basis of repeated feedback from respondents and faculty and an iterative process of exploratory and confirmatory factor analyses of various sets of items in multiple samples. Considerable attention was devoted to the study of published instruments on SI. The final revision of the instrument was made on the basis of a confirmatory factor analysis of items.

The RSIT uses a 5–point Likert scale (5 = Strongly Agree . . . 1 = Strongly Disagree) for ranking each of the items, and a higher score indicates a greater SI of a supervisor. The subscales were created by averaging responses to their respective items. Sample items are: "Our DC can size up a situation, he/she finds himself/herself in, rather quickly" (Situational awareness); "Our DC usually adapts appropriately to different situations" (Situational response); "Our DC understands people's feelings transmitted through nonverbal messages" (Cognitive empathy); and "Our DC interacts appropriately with a variety of people" (Social skills). Rahim (2014) provided evidence of internal consistency and indicator reliabilities and convergent and discriminant validities of the instrument and that it was free from social desirability response bias.

Satisfaction with Annual Evaluation of Teaching and Research (SAE). This was measured with two items developed for this study. Each item was ranked on a 5–point scale (Strongly agree = 5 . . . Strongly disagree = 1). Sample items for the scale are: "To what extent are you satisfied with DC's annual evaluation of your teaching," and "To what extent are you satisfied with DC's annual evaluation of your research." The scale was created by averaging the responses to the items, and a higher score indicated greater satisfaction with teaching and research. In the present study, the Cronbach α internal consistency reliability of this subscale was .89.

Analysis and Results

The first part of the analysis was designed to test the psychometric properties of the measures of SI and SAE. The second part of the analysis was designed to test the three study hypotheses. Data analyses were performed with SPSS 23 and LISREL 9.2 (Jöreskog & Sörbom, 1996a, 1996b) statistical packages. For LISREL analysis, the data from 406 respondents were averaged for each department, which resulted in a sample of 43 groups.

Validity Assessment (Measurement Model)

Confirmatory factor analysis of the SI and SAE items were computed. Results show excellent fit indexes for the 5-factor model (see Table 1).

The values for the Root Mean Square Error of Approximation (RMSEA) and Root Mean Square Residual (RMSR) should be ≤ .07. The values for other fit indexes, such as Normed Fit Index, Comparative Fit Index, Incremental Fit Index, and Goodness of Fit Index should be ≥ .90. As shown in Table 1, all the indexes in this group satisfied this requirement. Overall, these indexes indicate

Table 1
LISREL Summary Statistics

Statistic	Measurement Model		Structural Equations Model
	1–Factor	5–Factors	
χ^2/d	8.26	1.05	1.49
RMSEA	.42	.03	.09
Standardized RMSR	.09	.03	.04
Normed Fit Index	.91	.97	.95
Comparative Fit Index	.71	1.00	.98
Incremental Fit Index	.71	.95	.99
Relative Fit Index	.60	.95	.93

that the RSIT is a 4–dimensional measure of social intelligence and the criterion measure is a single-dimensional measure of SAE.

Common Method Variance. If the five dimensions of SI and AE were not present in the two questionnaire measures or if common method variance was present, then all the items measuring the SI and SAE will load on a single factor. If a single-factor solution fits the data well, one can conclude that common method variance is mainly responsible for explaining the relationships among the variables (Mossholder, Bennett, Kenney, & Wesolowski, 1998). Results from the one-factor solution are discussed.

The one-factor solution shows that the fit indexes, except NFI, were unsatisfactory. In other words, the single-factor model did not fit the data well and, as a result, the absence of five dimensions or the presence of common method variance in the measures should not be assumed.

Convergent Validity. The average variance extracted by all the items loading on a given factor measures convergent validity and should exceed .50 (Fornell & Larcker, 1981; Carr, 2002). These values were averaged for factors and all of the average R^2 exceeded .86, the threshold for supporting convergent validity.

This validity for the five subscales of the two instruments was also assessed by examining whether each item had a statistically significant factor loading on its specified factor (Anderson & Gerbing, 1988; Netemeyer, Johnston, & Burton, 1990). Factor loadings were highly significant, with a minimum t–ratio of 3.72 ($p < .01$). These results support the convergent validity of the subscales.

Discriminant Validity. In one test for discriminant validity the squared correlations between factors should be less than the average variance extracted for each factor (Fornell & Larcker, 1981; Carr, 2002). Results show that in each sample there is strong support for the discriminant validity between SI and SAE.

A second test for discriminant validity involves pair-wise comparisons of factors using a chi-square difference test (Anderson & Gerbing, 1988). For each pair of factors two models are developed. In one model the two factors are defined by their respective items. In the second model, the correlation between the factors is constrained to 1.00. The chi-square difference test can be applied to test if the appropriately defined two-factor model provides statistically better fit than the constrained model. In each pair-wise comparison of factors, the constrained model resulted in a significantly higher χ^2 value supporting discriminant validity. The threshold value for this chi-square difference test ($p < .05$) is a χ^2 of 3.84 with 1 degree of freedom. This test supported factor discrimination for all factors. Overall, there is adequate support for discriminant validity.

Univariate Normality. The samples exhibited a high degree of univariate normality with skewness and kurtosis statistics well within the acceptable levels of 1 and 7 for all items (Curran, West, & Finch, 1996).

Table 2 shows the means, standard deviations, Cronbach α internal consistency and indicator reliability coefficients, and variance inflation factor (VIF) of the five study variables. The internal consistency reliability coefficients of the five scales/subscales, as assessed with Cronbach α, ranged between .87 and .96. Overall, these coefficients are satisfactory (Nunnally, 1978).

Each item has a reported R^2 that measures the item's variance explained by its factor. This measure of indicator reliability should exceed .50 for each of the indicators (items) (Fornell & Larcker, 1981). The R^2s for all the items ranged between .62 and .99. These reliabilities were judged sufficient. The VIFs (ranged between 2.64 and 6.82) were lower than 10 which indicate that multicollinearity was not a problem.

Table 2
Means, Standard Deviations, Cronbach α and Indicator Reliabilities,
Pearson Correlations, and Variance Inflation Factor

Variable	M	SD	α	IR	1	2	3	4	VIF
1. Situational awareness	3.65	.95	.93	.89					4.38
2. Situational response	3.50	1.06	.93	.93	.86				5.98
3. Cognitive empathy	3.16	.82	.90	.88	.69	.74			2.64
4. Social skills	3.48	1.20	.96	.62	.85	.89	.78		6.83
5. SAE	3.66	1.01	.87	.99	.50	.51	.47	.51	

Note: $N = 406$. IR = Indicator reliability, SAE = Satisfaction with annual review of teaching and research, VIF = Variance inflation factor. All the correlations are significant at $p < .001$ (two-tailed).

Structural Equations Model

Two LISREL models were computed to test the three hypotheses. The first model tested all the relationships in Figure 1 represented by the solid and broken lines. As expected, the links represented by the broken lines were not significant, but the remaining links represented by the solid lines were all significant. In the second model only the links represented by the solid lines were tested and the results are presented in Table 3. Results provided full support for the three study hypotheses.

Hypothesis 1 was concerned with the mediation effect of social skills on the relationship between cognitive empathy and situational awareness. As shown in Table 3, the two path coefficients from cognitive empathy to social skills ($\beta = .87$) and from social skills to situational awareness ($\beta = .99$) were positive and significant. These path coefficients provided full support for Hypothesis 1.

Hypothesis 2 was concerned with the mediation effect of situational awareness on the relationship between social skills and situational response. As shown in Table 3, the two path coefficients from social skills to situational awareness ($\beta = .99$) and from situational awareness to situational response ($\beta = .99$) were positive and significant. These path coefficients provided full support for Hypothesis 2.

Hypothesis 3 was concerned with the mediation effect of situational response on the relationship between situational awareness and faculty members' satisfaction with SAE. As shown in Table 3, the path coefficient from situational awareness to situational response ($\beta = .99$) was positive and significant and the path coefficient from situational response to SAE ($\beta = .63$) was positive and significant. These path coefficients provided full support for Hypothesis 3.

As shown in Table 1, the fit indexes for the full structural equations model were satisfactory. Overall these fit indexes indicate that the model, indicated by

Table 3
Parameter Estimates for Structural Equations

Parameter Path	Statistic	z–value
CE → SS	.87	4.68***
SS → SA	.99	4.83***
SA → SR	.99	12.02***
SR → SAE	.63	5.18***

Note: Aggregated $N = 43$. These values are based on the causal model run on the covariance matrix. CE = Cognitive empathy; SS = Social skills; SA = Situational awareness; SR = Situational response; SAE = Satisfaction with the annual review of teaching and research.
*** $p < .001$.

the solid lines in Figure 1, fits well with the data. The RMSEA of .09 is greater than .07, which was probably caused by the sample size ($N = 43$) aggregated at the department level.

Discussion

The structural equations model for the study provided moderate to full support for the theoretical model presented in Figure 1. Previous studies did not test the relationships of faculty perception of the department chair's SI components to each other and to SAE. The study contributed to our understanding of the linkage between situational awareness and situational response and between situational response and SAE. It also contributed to our understanding of the relationships of cognitive empathy and social skills to situational awareness and situational response.

The study provided acceptable evidence of convergent and discriminant validities and internal consistency and indicator reliabilities of the measure of SI and SAE. Evidence from the present study provided support for construct validity of the measure of SI and SAE (cf. Bagozzi, Yi, & Philips, 1991).

Implications for Management

The department chairs need to acquire the four components of SI to improve faculty members' SAE. Interventions may be needed to enhance their SI competencies that would involve education and specific job-related training (Cherniss & Adler, 2000; Goleman, 2005). Department chairs should also be encouraged to enhance their abilities through continuous self-learning. Universities should provide positive reinforcements for learning and improving DC's essential SI competencies needed for various academic disciplines.

In the private sector, high-performing organizations now are providing opportunities to managers for continuous learning that should help to improve their use of SI. These organizations generally make appropriate changes in the organization design that involve creating flatter, decentralized, and less complex structures. They are also making appropriate changes in organizational culture that provides rewards for learning new competencies and for continuous questioning and inquiry. These changes in the organization design, culture, and positive reinforcements should encourage DCs to acquire SI competencies needed to improve faculty's SAE.

Training can help improve DC's SI but is not sufficient to fully enhance the four components of SI, which may have a positive influence on faculty members' job satisfaction and performance. Rahim's (2014) study found positive relationship between supervisors' SI and their creative performance. To enhance the effectiveness of leadership among DCs, academic institutions may have to adapt the recruiting policy of DCs so that those leaders with vision and cha-risma, that is, those who are likely to be high on SI in the first place, are hired.

Directions for Future Research

In academic institutions, further research is needed to enhance our under-standing of the relationships of SI and the effectiveness of DCs' leadership behaviors. Other criterion variables for future research should include some indicators of DCs' leadership effectiveness and faculty members' teaching and research performance, satisfaction, and organizational citizenship behavior. An important area of future research concerns carefully designing and evaluating the effects of training in SI in enhancing the aforementioned criterion variables. Field experiments are particularly useful in evaluating the effects of SI training on individual and organizational outcomes. There is also need for scenario-based and laboratory studies that control some of the extraneous variables to better understand the effects of DCs' SI. Also, it will be useful to investigate the differences in the perceptions of faculty regarding the performance of various types of academic leadership with low and high SI.

Strengths and Limitations

One of the strengths of this study is that the measures of endogenous and exogenous variables were analyzed at the department level, not individual level. This should help to overcome some of the problems of common method variance (Podsakoff, MacKenzie, Lee, & Podsakoff, 2003). Confirmatory factor analyses of the items indicated the absence of common method variance. If common method variance was present, the items of the independent and criterion mea-sures will not significantly load on the five a priori factors. Limitations of this field study should be noted. Data were collected from one public university in the southern part of the United States that might limit generalizability of the results.

References

Albrecht, K. (2007). *Social intelligence: The new science of success.* San Francisco, CA: Jossey-Bass.

Anderson, J. C., & Gerbing, D. W. (1988). Structural equation modeling in practice: A review and recommended two-step approach. *Psychological Bulletin, 103*, 411–423.

Ang, R. P., & Goh, D. H. (2010). Cyberbullying among adolescents: The role of affec-tive and cognitive empathy, and gender. *Child Psychiatry: Human Development, 41*, 387–397.

Argyris, C., & Schon, D. (1996). *Organizational learning–II.* Reading, MA: Addison-Wesley.

Baron, R. A., & Markham, G. D. (2000). Beyond social capital: How social skills can enhance entrepreneurs' success. *Academy of Management Executive, 14*, 106–116.

Baron, R. A., & Tang, J. (2009). Entrepreneurs' social skills and new venture performance: mediating mechanisms and cultural generality. *Journal of Management, 35*, 282–306.

Bagozzi, R. P., Yi, Y., & Philips, L. W. (1991). Assessing construct validity in organizational research. *Administrative Science Quarterly, 36*, 421–458.

Bennis, W. G., & Thomas, R. J. (2002). *Geeks and geezers.* Cambridge, MA: Harvard Business School Press.

Carr, C. L. (2002). A psychometric evaluation of the expectations, perceptions, and difference-scores generated by the IS–adapted SERVQUAL instrument. *Decision Sciences, 33*, 281–296.

Cherniss, C., & Adler, M. (2000). *Promoting emotional intelligence in organizations: making training in emotional intelligence effective.* Alexandria, VA: ASTD.

Cherniss, C., Extein, M., Golemen, D., & Weissberg, R. P. (2006). Emotional intelligence: What does the research really indicate? *Educational Psychologist, 41*, 239–245.

Coccia, M. 2008. Measuring scientific performance of public research units for strategic change. *Journal of Informetrics, 2*, 183–194.

Colbeck, C. L., & Wharton-Michael, P. (2006). Individual and organizational influences on faculty members' engagement in public scholarship. *New Directions for Teaching and Learning, 105*, 17–26.

Costa, C. A. B., & Oliveira, M. D. (2012). A multicriteria decision analysis model for faculty evaluation. *Omega, 40*, 424–436.

Curran, P. J., West, S. G., & Finch, J. F. (1996). The robustness of test statistics to non-normality and specification error in confirmatory factor analysis. *Psychological Methods, 1*, 16–29.

Elmore, H. W. (2008). Toward objectivity in faculty evaluation. *Academe, 94* (3), 38–40.

Ford, M. E., & Tisak, M. S. (1983). A further search for social intelligence. *Journal of Educational Psychology, 75*, 197–206.

Fornell, C., & Larcker, D. F. (1981). Evaluating structural equation models with unobservable variables and measurement error. *Journal of Marketing Research, 18*, 39–50.

Gardner, H. (1999). *Intelligence reframed.* New York: Basic Books.

Garner, P. W. (2010). Emotional competence and its influences on teaching and learning. *Educational Psychology Review, 22*, 297–321.

Gimenéz, V. M., & Martínez, J. L. (2006). Cost efficiency in the university: A departmental evaluation model. *Economics of Education Review, 25*, 543–553.

Goleman, D. (1998). *Working with emotional intelligence.* New York: Bantam Books.

Goleman, D. (2005). *Social intelligence: The new science of human relationships.* New York: Bantam Books.

Jöreskog, K. G., & Sörbom, D. (1996a). *LISREL 8: User's reference guide.* Chicago: Scientific Software International.

Jöreskog, K. G., & Sörbom, D. (1996b). *PRELIS 2: User's reference guide.* Chicago: Scientific Software International.

Judge, T. A., Colbert, A. E., & Ilies, R. (2004). Intelligence and leadership: A quantitative review and test of theoretical propositions. *Journal of Applied Psychology, 89*, 542–552.

Kaukiainen, A., Bjorkqvist, K., Lagerspetz, K., Osterman, K, Salmivalli, C., Rothberg, S., & Ahlbom, A. (1999). The relationships between social intelligence, empathy, and three types of aggression. *Aggressive Behavior, 25*, 81–89.

Kihlstrom, J. F., & Cantor, N. (2000). Social intelligence. In R. J. Sternberg (Ed.), *Handbook of intelligence* (2nd ed., pp. 359–379). Cambridge: Cambridge University Press.

Luchs, C., Seymoure, S., & Smith, W. (2011). An examination of faculty beliefs concerning P&T decisions. *Contemporary Issues in Education Research, 4* (12), 35–42.

Mayer, J. D., Salovey, P., & Caruso, D. R. (2008a). Emotional intelligence: Theory, findings, and implications. *Psychological Inquiry, 15*, 197–215.

Mayer, J. D., Salovey, P., & Caruso, D. R. (2008b). Emotional intelligence: New ability or eclectic traits? *American Psychologist, 63,* 503–517.

Mayo, A. J., & Nohria, N. (2005). *In their time: The greatest business leaders at the twentieth century.* Boston, MA: Harvard Business School Press.

Mitroff, I. I. (1998). *Smart thinking for crazy times: The art of solving the right problems.* San Francisco, CA: Berrett-Koehler.

Mitroff, I. I., & Silvers, A. (2010). *Dirty rotten strategies: How we trick ourselves and others into solving the wrong problems precisely.* Stanford, CA: Stanford University Press.

Mossholder, K. W., Bennett, N., Kemery, E. R., & Wesolowski, M. A. (1998). Relationships between bases of power and work reactions: The mediational role of procedural justice. *Journal of Management, 24,* 533–552.

Netemeyer, R. G., Johnston, M. W., & Burton, S. (1990). Analysis of role conflict and role ambiguity in a structural equations framework. *Journal of Applied Psychology, 75,* 148–157.

Nunnally, J. C. (1978). *Psychometric theory* (2nd ed.). New York: McGraw-Hill.

O'Brien, K. S., & O'Hare, D. (2007). Situational awareness ability and cognitive skills training in a complex real-world task. *Ergonomics, 50,* 1064–1091.

O'Meara, K. A. (2005). Encouraging multiple forms of scholarship in faculty reward systems: Does it make a difference? *Research in Higher Education, 46,* 479–510.

Podsakoff, P. M., MacKenzie, S. B., Lee, J. Y., & Podsakoff, N. P. (2003). Common method biases in behavioral research: A critical review of the literature and recommended remedies. *Journal of Applied Psychology, 88,* 879–903.

Polities, Y., & Siskos, Y. (2004). Multicriteria methodology for the evaluation of a Greek engineering department. *European Journal of Operational Research, 156,* 223–240.

Rahim, M. A. (2014). A structural equations model of leaders' social intelligence and creative performance. *Creativity and Innovation Management, 23* (1), 44–56.

Rosete, D., & Ciarrochi, J. (2005). Emotional intelligence and its relationship to workplace performance outcomes of leadership effectiveness. *Leadership & Organizational Development Journal, 26,* 388–399.

Rahim, M. A., & Bonoma, T. V. (1979). Managing organizational conflict: A model for diagnosis and intervention. *Psychological Reports, 44,* 1323–1344.

Schmidt, W. H., & Tannenbaum, R. (1990, November–December). Management of differences. *Harvard Business Review,* pp. 107–115.

Sternberg, R. J. (1985). *The triarchic mind: A new theory of human intelligence.* New York: Viking.

Sternberg, R. J. (2002). Successful intelligence: A new approach to leadership. In R. E. Riggio, S. E. Murphy, & F. J. Pirozzolo (Eds.), *Multiple intelligences and leadership* (pp. 9–28). Mahwah, NJ: Erlbaum.

Sternberg, R. J. (2005). WICS: A model of positive leadership comprising wisdom, intelligence, and creativity synthesized. *Educational Psychology Review, 17* (3), 191–262.

Sternberg, R. J. (2009, Fall). Wisdom, intelligence, and creativity synthesized: A new model for liberal education. *Liberal Education,* pp. 10–15.

Thorndike, R. L. (1920). Intelligence and its uses. *Harper's Magazine, 140,* 227–235.

van Dyne, L., Ang, S., & Koh, C. K. S. (2009). Cultural intelligence: Measurement and scale development. In M. A. Moodian (Ed.), *Contemporary leadership and intercultural competence: Exploring the cross-cultural dynamics within organizations* (pp. 233–254). Thousand Oaks, CA: Sage.

Wolansky, W. D. (2001). A multiple approach to faculty evaluation. Education, *Education, 97,* 8196.

Zaccaro, S. J., Gilbert, J. A., Thor, K. K., & Mumford, M. D. (1991). Leadership and social intelligence: linking social perceptiveness and behavioral flexibility to leadership effectiveness. *Leadership Quarterly, 2,* 317–342.

Biographical Notes

M. Afzalur Rahim (Ph.D., University of Pittsburgh) is a University Distinguished Professor of Management and Hays Watkins Research Fellow, Western Kentucky University. He is also the Founding Editor of *Current Topics in Management* and is the founder of the *International Journal of Organizational Analysis, International Journal of Conflict Management*, International Association for Conflict Management, International Conference on Advances in Management, International Conference on Social Intelligence, and Bangladesh Academy of Business Administration. Dr. Rahim is the author/editor of 23 books; 117 articles, book chapters, case studies, and research instruments; and 96 conference papers. His articles were published, among others, in the *Academy of Management Journal, Intelligence, Journal of Applied Psychology, Journal of Management, and Multivariate Behavioral Research.* His current research interests are in the areas of conflict management, leaders' emotional, cultural, and social intelligence. His citation index is over 7,200 in scholar.google.com. (1988mgmt@gmail.com)

Ismail Civelek is an assistant professor of management at Western Kentucky University. His areas of expertise are manufacturing and service operations management, queuing theory, simulation and revenue management. He applies queuing theory, simulation and stochastic optimization to examine decision-making by individuals and organizations in problems motivated by various industry applications. Dr. Civelek received his Ph.D. and M.S. in Operations Management and Manufacturing from Carnegie Mellon University and a B.S. in Industrial Engineering from Bilkent University. (ismail.civelek@wku.edu)

Feng Helen Liang is an assistant professor at Western Kentucky University, where she teaches strategic management, international business, and international management. Liang received her Ph.D. in business administration from University of California, Berkeley. Her research interests include technology management and innovation, multinational firm strategy, and development. (fenghelen.liang@wku.edu).

Accepted after two revisions: November 15, 2015

Current Topics in Management, Vol. 18, 2016, pp. 17–42

A NEUROCOGNITIVE MODEL OF ENTREPRENEURIAL OPPORTUNITY

Constant D. Beugré
Delaware State University

This paper introduces a neurocognitive model that explores the neural underpinnings of opportunity discovery and creation. The model emphasizes the role of brain activation in entrepreneurial opportunities and represents an attempt to unify the two conceptual frameworks of discovery and creation. It also contends that whether opportunities are discovered or created, the activation of brain structures plays an important role in their formation. The model's implications for further entrepreneurship research using neuroscientific tools and techniques and entrepreneurship education are discussed.

Keywords: creation theory, discovery theory, entrepreneurial cognitions, neurocognitive model, system 1, System 2

More than a decade ago, Gaglio and Katz (2001) note, research on entrepreneurial opportunity formation was still in its infancy and was best characterized as a scattering of descriptive studies rather than a systematic research program of theory testing and development. Since then, there has been a growing literature on entrepreneurial opportunity formation (Alvarez & Barney, 2007, 2008; Baron, 2006; Baron & Ensley, 2006; Echardt & Shane, 2003; Grégoire & Shepherd, 2012; Grégoire, Barr, & Shepherd, 2010; Haynie, Shepherd, Masakowski, & Early, 2010; Mitchell & Shepherd, 2010; Mitchell et al., 2007; Short, Ketchen, Shook, & Ireland, 2010; Vaghely & Julien, 2010). This increased interest stems from the fact that opportunity formation is an important component of the entrepreneurial process, one from which everything else follows (Baron, 2006; Baron & Ward, 2004; Gaglio & Katz, 2001; Shane & Venkataram, 2000). For this reason, understanding the opportunity formation process represents one of the core intellectual questions for the domain of entrepreneurship (Gaglio & Katz, 2001, p. 95).

Opportunity formation is an active process involving human cognition (Baron, 2007) that can be construed as the first step in the entrepreneurial process. As Shane and Venkataraman (2000) put it, "to have entrepreneurship, you must first have entrepreneurial opportunities" (p. 220). Because entrepreneurship is first and foremost a cognitively driven human behavior (Smith, 2010), such interest in entrepreneurial cognition is well guided. However, it is worth noting that although construing opportunity formation as a cognitive process has advanced our understanding of the construct, it does not acknowledge the role of neural circuitry in this process. This is astonishing because cognitive processes are substantiated by brain structures (Lieberman, 2007a). It is therefore important that any study of entrepreneurial opportunity formation recognizes the role of the neural circuitry. Thus, the purpose of this paper is to introduce a neural underpinning into research on opportunity recognition in entrepreneurship. In so doing, it fills in a gap related to the scarcity of entrepreneurship research integrating neuroscientific tools and techniques. Nicolaou and Shane (2014) note that despite the beginning of studies showing a link between the biological sciences and entrepreneurship, there is "one key dimension of the biological perspective that has been overlooked, neuroscience" (p. 98). This view is echoed by de Holan (2014) who notes that "there is as yet no published study that tries to understand any of the dimensions of entrepreneurship (e.g., opportunity recognition, entrepreneurial orientation, etc.) using neuroscientific methodologies, technologies, and tools, and the few that are relevant to our field of study were initiated by neuroscientists, psychologists, economists, or marketing scientists among others, and were obviously designed and framed with their research questions in mind" (p. 95).

This lack of emphasis on neuroscience in entrepreneurship research, in particular, entrepreneurial cognitions research, has led some authors to call for more attention in using the tools and techniques of neuroscience to uncover entrepreneurial phenomena. For example, de Holan (2014) notes that omitting neuroscience in the explanation of entrepreneurial activity is surprising given the focus of much entrepreneurship research on how entrepreneurs think and make decisions. This assumption echoes a view expressed a decade earlier by Baron and Ward (2004) who suggested the use of neuroscientific tools in research on entrepreneurial cognitions. Baron and Ward envisioned studies in which entrepreneurs and nonentrepreneurs could be asked to read descriptions of opportunities or other business situations simultaneously as their brains are being scanned. Such studies could be used to explain entrepreneurial cognitions, such as the cognitive processes underlying opportunity formation (Sarason, Dean, & Dillard, 2006; Shane, 2000, 2003; Shane & Venkataraman, 2000), knowledge structures (Baron, 2006; Baron & Ward, 2004; Shane, 2000), intuition (Mitchell, Friga, & Mitchell, 2005), entrepreneurial alertness (Busenitz, 1996; Gaglio & Katz, 2001; Yu, 2001; Tang, Kacmar, & Busenitz, 2012), entrepreneurial mindsets (Haynie et al., 2010) and many other entrepreneurial phenomena.

Thus, this paper builds on these suggestions by proposing a neurocognitive model of entrepreneurial opportunities. In so doing, it explores the neural basis of the two views of research on entrepreneurial opportunities, the *discovery view* and the *creation view*. There are at least two main reasons why a focus on opportunity creation and discovery is relevant to the analysis of the neural basis of entrepreneurial cognitions. First, entrepreneurship focuses on seeing and acting on opportunities regardless of existing resources (Stevenson & Jarillo, 1990). Second, "research on opportunity formation has coalesced around two different processes: opportunities that are formed by exogenous shocks to preexisting markets and then discovered by entrepreneurs, what we call the *discovery process* and opportunities that are created endogenously by the actions of entrepreneurs, what we call the *creation process*" (Alvarez, Barney, & Anderson, 2012, p. 303.). Thus, the discovery and creation views remain ideal candidates for early conceptualizations of the neural basis of entrepreneurial opportunities.

A neurocognitive perspective of entrepreneurial opportunities makes four contributions to the extant literature on entrepreneurial cognitions. First, as highlighted by recent developments in neuroscience, neuroeconomics, and social cognitive neuroscience, human behavior is the product of neural activation (Lieberman, 2007a; Lieberman, Jarcho, & Satpute, 2004; Lieberman, Gaunt, Gilbert, & Trope, 2002; Rilling & Sanfey, 2011; Sanfey et al., 2003). Therefore, the field of entrepreneurship cannot afford to keep ignoring the foundational micro-antecedent of human decision and action, which is the brain (de Holan, 2014). To the extent that opportunity discovery or creation is an entrepreneurial activity, understanding its neural underpinnings could inform researchers on the reasons why some people are more likely than others to generate new venture opportunities.

Second, a neurocognitive perspective not only expands the already established cognitive perspective but also offers an example of interdisciplinary research on entrepreneurial cognitions. It fits well within recent trends consisting of incorporating biological (Nicolaou, Shane, Cherkas, Hunkin, & Spector, 2008; Nicolaou, Shane, Cherkas, & Spector, 2009, Smith, 2010; Unger, Rauch, Weis, Frese, 2015; White, Thornhil, & Hampson, 2006, 2007) and neuroscientific (Beugré, 2010; Becker, Cropanzano & Sanfey, 2011; Lee, Senior, & Butler, 2012; Senior, Lee & Butler, 2011) concepts and tools into the study of entrepreneurship and/or organizational phenomena. Third, a neurocognitive perspective could allow entrepreneurship scholars to reconcile the discovery and creation views of entrepreneurial opportunity. Whether entrepreneurial opportunities are created or discovered, they involve cognitive processes that are themselves substantiated by brain structures. Such an approach could provide scientific evidence that neural structures involved in opportunity creation or discovery sometimes overlap, thus indicating that discovery and creation processes contain elements of both.

Fourth, a neurocognitive perspective could allow entrepreneurship scholars to identify the brain structures implicated in entrepreneurial opportunities. Such understanding could have practical implications insofar that one of the key elements of entrepreneurship education is to prepare students to learn how to find and act on new business or social opportunities. For example, neuroscientific evidence suggests that people who have been taught about their own brain images have better behavioral self-control than people who have not (Powell & Puccinelli, 2012). This paper is organized into three sections. The first section reviews the literature on entrepreneurial cognitions with a particular emphasis on opportunity discovery and creation. Next, it presents the neurocognitive model. The third section discusses the model's implications for research on entrepreneurship education.

Entrepreneurial Cognitions

Entrepreneurial cognitions refer to the knowledge structures that people use to make assessments, judgments, or decisions involving opportunity evaluation, venture creation, and growth (Mitchell, Busenitz, Lant et al., 2002, p. 97). The following sections briefly discuss the key assumptions of both views.

The Discovery View of Entrepreneurial Opportunity

Research on entrepreneurial cognitions can be divided into two streams, *discovery* and *creation*. Scholars emphasizing the first stream of research construes opportunities as being discovered (Baron, 2006, 2007, Grégoire, Corbett, & Murphy, 2011; Murphy, 2011; Shane, 2000), whereas the second research stream considers opportunities as being created (Krueger, 2000; Walsh, 1995). The discovery view suggests that entrepreneurial opportunities exist in the external environment waiting to be discovered, recognized, or identified by the entrepreneur. In this view, the terms, discovery, identification, and recognition are used to indicate the extent to which an entrepreneur identifies a business opportunity (Baron, 2006, 2007, Grégoire et al., 2011; Murphy, 2011; Shane, 2000). If opportunities are hidden phenomena, then, the task of the entrepreneur is to find them. Construed as such, opportunities are independent of entrepreneurs and exist regardless of whether or not they are discovered. Discovery opportunities exist even if no economic actors are aware of their existence and the fact that they are yet to be observed does not deny the reality of their existence (Alvarez et al., 2012).

The discovery view emphasizes the role of individual factors, such as entrepreneurial alertness (Baron & Ward, 2004; Gaglio & Katz, 2001; Kirzner, 1973, 1979; Tang et al., 2012) and prior knowledge (Ardichvili, Cardozo, & Ray, 2003; Baron, 2006; Corbett, 2007; Sarasvathy, 2001; Shane, 2000; Lumpkin & Lichtenstein, 2005; Shepherd & DeTienne, 2005; Ucbasaran,

Westhead, & Wright, 2009; Venkataraman, 1997) in entrepreneurial activities. Entrepreneurial alertness is construed as an individual's ability to recognize entrepreneurial opportunities that are overlooked by authors (Kirzner, 1979). Therefore, those who are entrepreneurially alert would be more likely to discover new venture opportunities compared to those who are not. The conceptualization of entrepreneurial alertness has evolved since the work of Kirzner (1973, 1979). Tang et al. (2012) conceptualize alertness as a three-dimensional construct comprising (1) *scanning and searching for new information*; (2) *connecting previously disparate information*; and (3) *evaluating whether the new information represents an opportunity*. The first dimension implies a systematic search for opportunities, while the second entails connecting the dots (Baron & Ensley, 2006). The third dimension implies making judgments about the nature of the opportunities. Such judgments are based on certain patterns that the entrepreneur perceives in the environment.

In addition to alertness, the possession of prior knowledge also facilitates the discovery of entrepreneurial opportunities. People recognize those opportunities related to information that they already possess (Venkataraman, 1997). Baron (2006) reached the same conclusion when comparing opportunity recognition to pattern recognition. As a consequence, entrepreneurs who have prior experience in a particular industry are more likely to discover opportunities for new ventures pertaining to that industry. Several empirical studies have validated this assumption. Using a sample of 630 participants from the United Kingdom, Ucbasaran et al. (2009) found that more experienced entrepreneurs identified more opportunities albeit at a diminishing rate than less experienced entrepreneurs.

Shane and Venkataraman (2000) suggest that people possess different stocks of information, and these stocks of information influence their ability to recognize particular opportunities. These stocks of information also create mental schemas, which provide a framework for recognizing opportunities (Shane & Venkataraman, 2000). Acquiring knowledge that can foster opportunity discovery mostly depends on learning (Lumpkin & Lichtenstein, 2005). Learning accumulated through experiences within industries and markets can prove useful for entrepreneurs to identify new opportunities in these markets and industries. Ardichvili et al. (2003) propose four conditions under which knowledge facilitates the discovery of new opportunities: (1) special interest knowledge and general industry knowledge; (2) prior knowledge of markets; (3) prior knowledge of customer problems; and (4) prior knowledge of ways to serve markets, which will increase the likelihood of successful opportunity recognition. In defining the constructs of causation and effectuation, Sarasvathy (2001) notes that causation relies on the individual exploiting his/her existing knowledge, whereas effectuation allows the individual to use his/her abilities to discover and exploit various contingencies. Shepherd and DeTienne (2005) found that the level of an individual's prior knowledge increased the number of opportunities identified and the innovativeness of those opportunities.

The cognitive view of opportunity discovery recognizes that linking patterns of information from various sources forms the basis of innovation and new business opportunities (Vaghely & Julien, 2010). However, evidence suggests that some opportunities are not formed by exogenous shocks to preexisting markets or industries but instead are formed endogenously by the actions of those seeking to generate economic wealth themselves (Alvarez et al. 2012). In addition, not all entrepreneurship researchers construe opportunities as objective phenomena existing in the external environment. Hence, creation theory takes a different perspective on how entrepreneurial opportunities come into existence.

The Creation View of Entrepreneurial Opportunity

Creation theory considers opportunities as being created by the actions of the entrepreneur (Alvarez & Barney, 2010; Krueger, 2000; Walsh, 1995). In the creation process, entrepreneurs are not passive participants in the formation of new opportunities because their actions are the essential source of opportunities (Alvarez & Barney, 2007, 2008). Such reasoning led Ardichvilli et al. (2003, p. 106) to suggest that "opportunities are made, not found." Research on the creation process assumes that opportunities are constructed by entrepreneurs themselves; in this sense, opportunities do not exist until entrepreneurs create them through a process of enactment (Alvarez et al. 2012). As a consequence, entrepreneurs do not search for opportunities because opportunities are not objective entities existing in the external environment. Rather, entrepreneurs generate opportunities, act, and observe how consumers and markets respond to their actions (Alvarez & Barney, 2007).

Creation theory suggests that the "seeds" of opportunities to produce new products or services do not necessarily lie in previously existing industries or markets (Alvarez & Barney, 2007). Viewed through this angle, entrepreneurial opportunities are subjective phenomena that are constructed by the entrepreneur. Hence, opportunities are very much in the eye of the beholder (Krueger, 2000) insofar that they do not exist independently of the actions taken by entrepreneurs to create them (Weick, 1979). Because the entrepreneur's actions are the source of opportunities in creation theory, Sarasvathy (2001) suggests that the entrepreneur acts as an imaginative actor who seizes contingent opportunities and exploits any and all means at hand to fulfill a plurality of current and future aspirations, many of which are shaped and created through the very process of economic decision making and are not given a priori. In other words, entrepreneurs create something with what they have at their disposal. Sarasvathy, Dew, Velamuri, and Venkataraman, (2003) differentiate creation from discovery by emphasizing the domain of application of the opportunity. They contend that when supply and demand for the product are known, the opportunity is founded. However, when neither supply nor demand is known, the opportunity is created.

Scholars advocating the creation theory contend that as the opportunity creation process begins, entrepreneurs engage in activities consistent with prior beliefs about the nature of the opportunities they might face, together with their understanding of the resources and abilities they have to eventually exploit these opportunities (Alvarez & Parker 2009; Sarasvathy 2001). These initial beliefs about opportunities and the perceptions of the resources and abilities needed to exploit them are social constructions (Alvarez et al., 2012). The creation process is also coevolutionary to the extent that opportunities evolve through the enactment process, which often changes the beliefs and assumptions of entrepreneurs creating opportunities (Alvarez et al. 2012). Despite the importance of viewing entrepreneurial opportunities through the lens of discovery theory or creation theory, it is reasonable to consider that these two views are related in several areas.

Complementarity of the Two Views

A reasonable middle ground between the two views is that some opportunities are discovered, whereas others are created (Short et al. 2010). In fact, the two streams of research can be viewed as complementary although they may use different epistemologies (Alvarez & Barney, 2010). Whether entrepreneurial opportunities are socially constructed from the subjective experiences of the individual or whether they exist in the external environment, they represent the seed of entrepreneurial action. Moreover, it may well happen that one may incorporate some aspects of the other and involve cognitive processes. Both discovery theory and creation theory assume that the goal of entrepreneurs is to form opportunities (Alvarez & Barney, 2007; Shane & Venkataraman, 2000) and recognize that opportunities exist as a result of competitive imperfections in a market or industry (Alvarez & Barney, 2007).

Alvarez and Barney (2010) acknowledge that the formation of creation opportunities need not begin with completely blind variations, thereby echoing previous assumptions by Baker and Nelson (2005) and Sarasvathy (2001) on the combination of available resources to generate something new. Likewise, Grégoire et al. (2010, p. 415) note that "the process of recognizing opportunities involves both objective and subjective dimensions. The objective reality of one's context and the subjective interpretation that one makes of this context and of one's position in it before the facts can be objectively known." To the extent that both views entail cognitive processes, they could contribute to the development of a neurocognitive model of opportunity formation. This is particularly important because research on entrepreneurial cognitions contends that opportunity formation involves cognitive processes occurring in the minds of specific people (Baron, 2006, 2007; Baron & Ensley, 2006; Grégoire et al., 2011; Loasby, 2007; Mitchell, Busenitz, Lant et al., 2002; Mitchell, Busenitz, Bird et al., 2007).

Consequently, entrepreneurs find opportunities that others may have over-looked because they possess the cognitive frameworks needed to perceive patterns among seemingly unrelated trends or events (Baron, 2006). A better analysis of cognitive processes requires a detailed study and understanding of their neural foundations, a step that current research in entrepreneurial cogni-tions has rarely taken despite repeated calls to do so (Baron & Ward, 2004; de Holan, 2014). In fact, the cognitive perspective in entrepreneurship has not integrated the concepts and tools of neuroscience in explicating the antecedents of opportunity discovery or creation. Thus, the purpose of the neurocognitive model is to address this gap.

The Neurocognitive Model of Entrepreneurial Opportunity

The neurocognitive model proposed here suggests that opportunity discovery or creation begins with the interplay between the individual and the environment as indicated by the line between the individual and the external environment (see Figure 1). This reasoning is in line with previous work on situated cognition (Smith & Semin, 2004; Haynie et al., 2010; Mitchell, Randol-Seng, & Mitchell, 2011). The notion of cognitions as situated interactive processes could be ex-tended to the study of entrepreneurial cognitions (Cornelissen & Clarke, 2010; Haynie et al., 2010; Mitchell et al., 2011). According to Smith and Semin (2004), cognition is embodied and draws from sensorimotor abilities and environments as well as brains. Even when the individual is thinking about a potential opportunity without seeing "something" in the immediate environment, this thought process is influenced by some reference to the environment. Likewise, even if opportunities exist in the environment, they must be recognized as such, thereby involving a cognitive processing from the entrepreneur. Thus, a socially situated cognition approach construes "entrepreneurial capability as much broader, emerging from a cognitive system that draws on brain, body and environment, and extends to the activities of multiple actors" (Healy & Hodgkinson, 2014, p. 778).

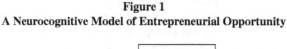

Figure 1
A Neurocognitive Model of Entrepreneurial Opportunity

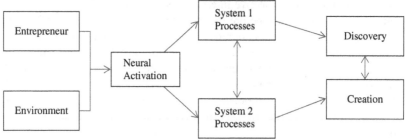

The model also contends that the activation of brain structures leads to cognitive processing. This cognitive processing relies on the X– and C–Systems (Lieberman, 2007a, 2007b) and leads to the discovery or creation of entrepreneurial opportunities. The X–System corresponds to System 1 and the C–System corresponds to System 2 (Kahneman, 2003, 2011). In this paper, I refer to System 1 or X–System and System 2 or C–System interchangeably. When brain structures underlying X–System processes are activated, the opportunity will be a discovered one. However, when brain structures involving the C–System are activated, the opportunity will be a created one. The bidirectional arrow between the X–System and the C–System indicates that the two systems interact (Lieberman, 2007b). Because of this interaction, it would probably be more accurate to suggest that although abstract reasoning requires the use of System 2, concrete contexts do not preclude its application (Evans, 1989).

Finally, the model suggests an interaction between discovery and creation processes. Representing the model as such has the advantage of indicating that considering the two systems as a dichotomy could be too simplistic because doing so would not recognize recent evidence about their overlapping nature (Lieberman, 2007b; Herring et al., 2013). Likewise, viewing discovery and creation theories as totally opposite does not acknowledge the extent to which these two views overlap. As a trend toward integrating the two systems, Herring et al. (2013) underscore the need for more nuanced theoretical perspectives that could incorporate encoding and response processes, and integrate other constructs to explain when and how these and perhaps other processes are active. One of the implications of the model is that people are prone to discover or create entrepreneurial opportunities because the brain is wired to do so. Consequently, an opportunity is an opportunity when the human brain makes sense of it.

The model raises several questions worth exploring. Could a neurocognitive perspective add to our understanding of the two views of opportunity research: the discovery view and the creation view? For instance, does discovery theory rely more on intuitive and automatic processes, whereas creation theory relies more on controlled and systematic processes? Does the model also combine elements of both systems? Hence, rather than a dichotomy, could the two systems be represented by a continuum ranging from automatic to deliberate processes? An analysis of the brain structures involved in each of these two views of entrepreneurial opportunities could provide insights in addressing these questions. It could indicate that although representing different ways of explaining entrepreneurial opportunities, the two views may be complementary and therefore could be integrated into a unified theory.

Figure 2 illustrates the two views and their corresponding neural structures. It indicates that entrepreneurial phenomena—such as prior knowledge and experience, intuition, connecting the dot, pattern recognition, and alertness—could be more influenced by X–System structures, such as the amygdala (A),

Figure 2
A Neurocognitive Model of Entrepreneurial Opportunity

Continuum from Automatic to Deliberate Processes

System 1	System 2
Brain structures involved	**Brain structures involved**
Amygdala (A)	Lateral parietal cortex (LPAC)
Basal ganglia (BG)	Lateral prefrontal cortex (LPFC)
Dorsal anterior cingulate cortex (dACC)	Medial parietal cortex (MPAC)
Lateral temporal cortex (LTC)	Medial prefrontal cortex (MPFC)
Ventromedial prefrontal cortex (VMPFC)	Medial temporal cortex (MTC)
	Rostral anterior cingulate cortex (rACC)
Entrepreneurial behaviors	**Entrepreneurial behaviors**
Use of prior knowledge	Improvisation
Use of past experiences	Effectuation
Use of intuition	Combination of several means
Connecting the dot	Reflection
Alertness	

the basal ganglia (BG), the dorsal anterior cingulate cortex (dACC), the lateral temporal cortex (LTC), and the ventromedial prefrontal cortex (VMPFC). However, improvisation, effectuation, combinations of several means to reach an end, and reflection could recruit C–System structures, such as the lateral parietal cortex (LPAC), the lateral prefrontal cortex (LPFC), the medial parietal cortex (MPAC), the medial prefrontal cortex (MPFC), the medial temporal cortex (MTL), the dorsomedial prefrontal cortex (DMPFC), and the rostral anterior cingulate cortex (rACC). Hence, the following proposition is formulated.

> *Proposition 1: Entrepreneurial opportunities that involve effectuation, bricolage, and/or improvisation would tend to activate more the brain structures implicated in System 2 than those that rely on prior knowledge, use of past experiences, intuition, connecting the dot, and/or alertness.*

> *Proposition 2: Entrepreneurial opportunities that rely on prior knowledge, use of past experiences, intuition, connecting the dot, and/or alertness would tend to activate more the brain structures implicated in System 1 than those that involve effectuation, bricolage, and/or improvisation.*

In reviewing the literature on the neural basis of automatic and controlled processes, Lieberman (2007a) found that controlled forms of social cognitions were consistently associated with activation in the lateral prefrontal cortex (LPFC), the lateral parietal cortex (LPAC), the medial prefrontal cortex (MPFC), the medial parietal cortex (MPAC), and the medial temporal cortex (MTL), whereas automatic forms of social cognition were consistently associated with activation in the amygdala (A), the ventromedial prefrontal cortex

(VMPFC), and the lateral cortex (LTC). The figure also represents the two systems as a continuum ranging from automatic to controlled processes. Recent developments in neurocognitive science advocate the view that classifying social cognitions into automatic and controlled may be too simplistic to the extent that automatic and controlled processes are intertwined mechanisms (Lieberman 2007b).

Neurocognitive Basis of Opportunity Discovery

In discovery theory, the task of the entrepreneur is to find opportunities because they exist in the external environment. In this "search and find process," entrepreneurs use their experiences and prior knowledge of the market and/or industry. This process could be construed as automatic thereby engaging the X–System (or System 1). It could influence the decision-making process of those who have expertise and prior knowledge. For example, Reyna (2004) suggests that experts acquire gist knowledge that allows them to make intuitive responses that are automatic, and effective, whereas novices need to rely on explicit analytic reasoning. If opportunities exist in the external environment, they could be construed as external stimuli to which entrepreneurs react. These reactions could be automatic for serial entrepreneurs to the extent that they rely on prior knowledge and experience to give meaning to the opportunities.

Several entrepreneurship scholars have indicated that individuals with more knowledge appear to think in a more intuitive way and make decisions in a more automatic manner rather than through a systematic process (Mitchell et al., 2005; Shepherd & DeTienne, 2005; Baron, 2006; Baron & Ensley, 2006). Entrepreneurs use prototypes as a means of identifying patterns among seemingly unrelated events or trends (Baron, 2006). Cunningham et al. (2003), Kahneman (2003, 2011), Camerer, Loewenstein, and Prelec (2005), and Lieberman (2007a) contend that automatic processes are quite well suited for processing simple valence, whereas reflection allows for tackling evaluative information at more complex levels of analysis. Although the X–System with its underlying brain structures could facilitate the discovery of entrepreneurial opportunities, it could also to some extent inhibit it. Thus, the following proposition is formulated.

Proposition 3: Serial entrepreneurs would tend to rely more on System 1 in assessing whether certain situations represent entrepreneurial opportunities compared to novice entrepreneurs.

Using the X– System could allow entrepreneurs to rely on previous experience and knowledge to point them to new opportunities. The implication is that entrepreneurs could focus more on some types of opportunities and overlook others, thereby leading to *opportunity bias*. I use the construct of opportunity bias to refer to the extent to which entrepreneurs could be inclined to focus more on some opportunities and overlook others as a result of prior experience and/or knowledge in particular markets and/or industries. For example, an entrepreneur who has knowledge and experience in the healthcare industry would be more likely to find new venture opportunities in this industry than in the automobile industry. Although the literature on biases and heuristics reveals that mental shortcuts may help individuals manage complexity, it also acknowledges that they may lead to a reduction of options (Tversky & Kahneman, 1974; Schwenk, 1986; Eisenhardt & Zbaracki. 1992). Hence, the following proposition is formulated.

Proposition 4: Reliance on System 1 may tend to lead serial entrepreneurs to experience more opportunity bias than novice entrepreneurs.

Neurocognitive Basis of Opportunity Creation

Proponents of creation theory (Sarasvathy, 2001) have focused on the role of creation or bricolage in opportunity formation. Could this process implicate the C– System more than the X– System? Could it be more conscious, deliberate, and systematic? In creation theory, opportunity creation is an iterative process, a thoughtful one that does not require that the entrepreneur relies on previous information. It could well engage the C–System, which is a symbolic processing system that produces reflective awareness (Lieberman et al., 2002). This symbolic function allows the C– System to give meaning to events. Indeed, "symbolic logic allows us to escape the limits of empiricism and move beyond the mere representation and association of events in the world and into the realms of the possible" (Lieberman et al., 2002, 221).

As illustrated in Figure 2, when opportunities are created through entrepreneurs' deliberative actions, such as improvisation, effectuation, combination of several means or reflection, they could involve the lateral and parietal cortexes (LPAC), the medial parietal cortex (MPAC), the medial prefrontal cortex (MPFC), the medial temporal cortex (MTC), the rostral anterior cingulate cortex (rACC), and the dorsomedial prefrontal cortex (DMPFC). Creation theory shows that entrepreneurs create opportunities through improvisation, effectuation, combination, and reflection (Sarasvathy, 2001; Baker & Nelson, 2005). Thus, it is likely that this creation process engages more C–System processes than X–system ones. Although C–System processes do not bear the constraints of the X–System insofar that they are not limited by prior experience or knowledge, and cognitive shortcuts, they lack the value that comes from having prior knowledge. Whether C–System processes lead entrepreneurs to create a wider set of opportunities or more innovative opportunities than X–System processes is an empirical question. Hence the following proposition is formulated.

Proposition 5: Reliance on System 2 structures would lead to the creation of more innovative entrepreneurial opportunities than reliance on System 1.

Several neuroscientific studies found that many of the brain structures identified in Figure 2 as substantiating C–System processes are involved in high-order cognitions, such as creativity (Dietrich, 2004, Howard-Jones et al., 2005). Dietrich (2004) suggests that the fact that stored knowledge and novel combinations of that knowledge are implemented in two distinct neural structures, the temporal, occipital, and parietal cortexes (TOP) and the prefrontal cortex respectively, is critical to understanding the relationship between knowledge and creativity as well as the difference between creative and noncreative behavior. In a functional magnetic resonance imaging (fMRI) study using a task that taps divergent thinking, Howard-Jones et al. (2005) found a significant activation of the right prefrontal cortex when participants were asked to create stories in response to the presentation of unrelated words.

Reconciling Discovery and Creation Theories through Neuroscience

To some extent, the neurocognitive perspective reconciles the discovery and creation theories. It suggests that regardless of the fact that opportunities are objective phenomena in the external environment waiting to be discovered, or created by entrepreneurs as a result of their actions and/or reactions, there is a neural foundation to both views. The following two scenarios support this argument. In the first scenario, an entrepreneur "sees" an opportunity as a result of market failure and decides to create a venture to exploit it. The discovery process of this opportunity involves some type of cognitive processing. The entrepreneur must have seen that there is a need for this particular product or service. However, without cognitively processing this information, the entrepreneur could not be able to consider the opportunity as a viable business opportunity. Thus, discovery theory also involves cognitions that themselves have neural foundations.

In the second scenario, an entrepreneur creates an opportunity based on his/her own actions. Although creation theory contends that entrepreneurs do not search for opportunities, we must acknowledge that human beings do not think independently of their environment. The act of creation also involves accumulation and processing of information received from the external environment. Thus, the knowledge structures that lead entrepreneurs to create new opportunities are not necessarily independent of the external environment. The concept of situated cognition embraces the notion that individual motivations and environment influence the development and selection of cognitive strategies. Smith and Semin (2004) observe that cognitions are the outcomes of dynamic processes between an agent and an environment. Kirzner (1979) acknowledges that alertness, an important factor in the discovery of entrepreneurial opportunities, entails some form of imagination and creativity.

The same is true for the concept of intuition and its role in the discovery process. For example, the construct of entrepreneurial intuition may start as a higher cognitive process but may later become a less-conscious process (Gordon, 1992; Mitchell et al., 2005). This reasoning is in line with Gordon's (1992) assumption that people becoming competent in a given domain move away from the use of symbolic or declarative knowledge and toward a reliance on perceptual, nonverbalizable procedural knowledge. Mitchell et al. (2005) note that as an individual's competence in a given domain increases, the relevant functional level of consciousness of that individual decreases. In characterizing intuition and its evolution from high-level of consciousness to low-level of consciousness, Crossan, Lane and White (1999) note that "what once required conscious, deliberate, and explicit thought no longer does. What once would have taken much deliberation and planning becomes the obvious thing to do" (p. 526).

Likewise, Stanovich (2004) argues that goals that are acquired reflectively through the C–System can, through repeated activation, be installed into rigid implicit processing mechanisms, a kind of automation of thought. In his studies on naturalistic decision making in groups, such as fire fighters and paramedics, Klein (1999) argues that very little rational decision making goes on, in the sense of deliberation between alternatives. According to Klein, what typically happens is that an expert recognizes a situation as of a kind encountered previously and rapidly retrieves a schema that provides a solution, a process he termed "recognition-primed" decision making. Although the application may involve some explicit reasoning (sometimes mental simulations to check the feasibility of solutions), the key to intelligent action is the automatic retrieval process.

It is therefore important to acknowledge that opportunity discovery and opportunity creation are recursively implicated because entrepreneurial action is both enabled and constrained by the conscious selection, imitation, and modification of business scripts by entrepreneurs (Chiasson & Saunders, 2005). Just as inception of self-awareness and self-knowledge may initially require C–System processes but may become automated overtime (Satpute & Lieberman, 2006), cognitive processes underlying opportunity discovery and/or creation may require C–System processes at the beginning. As the entrepreneur acquires more knowledge and experience, those cognitive processes may become automated. The neurocognitive perspective presents several implications for further theorizing and empirical research on entrepreneurial cognitions.

Discussion

The neurocognitive model identified specific brain structures that might be implicated in the creation and discovery processes. By doing so, the model presents implications for research and practice, particularly entrepreneurship education.

Implications for Entrepreneurship Education

The model's implications for practice would concern teaching and training programs geared toward entrepreneurship. Knowledge of brain signals improves people's capacities for self-regulation (Powell & Puccinelli, 2012). Powell and Puccinelli (2012) contend that people who have been taught about their own brain images have better behavioral self-control than people who have not. Therefore, neuroscience technology, combined with brain education and training, can improve self-control at its source in the brain, and improve experiences, expressions, and effectiveness (Powell & Puccinelli, 2012, p. 210). According to Powell and Puccinelli (2012), knowledge of brain signals improves people's capacities for self-regulation. Self-regulation can improve entrepreneurs' ability to generate ideas for new business opportunities and pursue them.

One of the goals of entrepreneurship education is to improve students' ability to discover or create business opportunities. To this end, instructors often design class assignments that require students to identify or create business opportunities. One such assignment is the scouting of business opportunities, in which students are asked to drive or walk in a neighborhood or in a particular location to identify potential business opportunities. Such an assignment can be complemented with an analysis of how the human brain works by association or "connects the dot" (Baron, 2006). For instance, entrepreneurship instructors could explain to the students how their prior life experiences or personal interests might have helped them to spot the opportunities in question. They could also explain to students what specific brain regions are implicated in this process.

In teaching creation opportunities, entrepreneurship educators could focus on providing resources, albeit limited to students and ask them to create something with the resources at their disposal—the process of effectuation (Sarasvathy, 2001) or combination (Baker & Nelson, 2005). In a follow-up class discussion, instructors could explain to the students how specific brain structures might have influenced their decisions and the type of venture opportunity created. They could use such an assignment to explain the neural foundations of creativity and how focusing on one's brain could help generate novel ideas. Despite the implications of this model for further research and entrepreneurial education, it is worth acknowledging some of its limitations.

Implications for Future Research

The five propositions formulated could pave the way for further research on the neural foundations of opportunity discovery or creation. For example, the model anticipates that entrepreneurial opportunities that involve effectuation, bricolage, and/or improvisation would tend to activate more the brain structures implicated in System 2 than those that rely on prior knowledge, use of past experiences, intuition, connecting the dot, and/or alertness. However, entrepreneurial opportunities that rely on prior knowledge, use of past experiences, intuition, connecting the dot, and/or alertness would tend to activate more the brain structures implicated in System 1 than those that involve effectuation, bricolage, and/or improvisation. It is also anticipated that serial entrepreneurs would tend to rely more on System 1 processes than novice entrepreneurs who would tend to rely more on System 2 processes. Reliance on System 2 processes may lead to the generation of more "novel" opportunities. Likewise, reliance on System 1 may tend to lead to serial entrepreneurs to experience more opportunity bias than novice entrepreneurs. Studies testing these propositions could involve participants who are entrepreneurs and nonentrepreneurs or serial and novice entrepreneurs who could be asked to imagine entrepreneurial opportunities while their brains are being scanned. Such studies could help to identify brain structures that could be more active for entrepreneurs compared to nonentrepreneurs.

Although (to the best of my knowledge) there are no neuroscientific studies of entrepreneurial opportunities to serve as guidelines, research on the neural basis of creativity, risk, and uncertainty, concepts closely related to entrepreneurship could help to shed light on the brain structures involved in entrepreneurial cognitions. Research in neurocognitive science indicates that the prefrontal cortex is involved in creativity (Dietrich 2004; Howard-Jones et al. 2005). Circuits in the prefrontal cortex perform the computation that transforms novelty into creative behavior. To that end, "prefrontal circuits are involved in making novelty fully conscious, evaluating its appropriateness, and ultimately implementing its creative expression" (Dietrich, 2004, p. 1023). The entrepreneurial process requires some forms of creativity (Gilad, 1984; Whiting, 1988; Ward, 2004; Baker & Nelson, 2005) and novel and useful ideas are the lifeblood of entrepreneurship (Ward, 2004).

Entrepreneurship scholars argue that firms create something out of nothing by "refusing to treat the resources at hand as nothing and by actively exercising their creative and combinatorial capabilities, their tolerance for ambiguity and messiness and setbacks, and their ability to improvise and take advantage of emerging resources and opportunities" (Baker & Nelson, 2005, p. 356). In her theory of effectuation, Sarasvathy argues that "the entrepreneur is an effectuator: an imaginative actor who seizes contingent opportunities and exploits any and all means at hand to fulfil a plurality of current and future aspirations, many of which are shaped and created through the very process of economic decision making and are not given *a priori*" (Sarasvathy, 2001, p. 262).

Understanding creativity and its role in the entrepreneurial process fits into the overall picture of ideation processes that characterize how entrepreneurs form opportunities. Neuroscientific evidence suggests the implication of specific brain structures in the creative process (Dietrich, 2004; Howard-Jones et al., 2005; Takeuchi et al., 2010). Creativity requires cognitive abilities—such as working memory, sustained attention, cognitive flexibility, and judgment of propriety—that are typically ascribed to the prefrontal cortex (Dietrich 2004). Understanding how these structures function could provide additional insights into the role of creativity and innovation, two concepts central to the entrepreneurial process.

Entrepreneurs operate in environments that are characterized by a high degree of uncertainty and risk (Sanfey et al., 2003; McMullen & Shepherd, 2006). Research on the neural basis of uncertainty and risk found that the orbitofrontal cortex (OFC) and the striatum are activated when people make value-based choices (Montague, King-Casas, & Cohen, 2006). Likewise, the anterior cingulate cortex (ACC) and the insula are implicated in risk prediction and probability signaling (Brown & Braver, 2005, 2007; Weller, Levin, Shiv, & Bechara, 2009; Vartanian, Mandel, & Duncan, 2011). Knoch et al. (2006) found that stimulation of the right dorsolateral prefrontal cortex (DLPFC) elicited a tendency to engage in risky behaviors. Paulus et al. (2003) also found that risk behavior leads to activation of brain structures, such as the striatum, the insula, the interior frontal gyrus, the lateral orbitofrontal cortex, and the interior cingulate cortex. To the extent that entrepreneurial action entails taking risk, this finding has important implications for research on risk taking and uncertainty in an entrepreneurial context.

Neuroscientific evidence supporting the assumptions of prospect theory indicates that choice in loss situations appears to be associated with activation in the amygdala, irrespective of an individual's tendency to take on risk, whereas OFC activation decreases with individuals' tendency to become risk-seeking with losses (Bossaerts, Preuschoff, & Hsu, 2009). Perhaps, people do not want to be risk-seeking for monetary losses; however, many people cannot overcome their tendency to become risk-seekers under adverse conditions (Bossaerts et al., 2009). Neuroscientific research suggests that the dorsolateral prefrontal cortex (DPLC) becomes more activated when people make utilitarian choices (Weber & Johnson, 2009). The evaluation and selection of entrepreneurial opportunities may be construed as a form of utilitarian choice to the extent that the entrepreneur selects and pursues the opportunity that has the potential of leading to a successful business venture. In fact, "multiple processes (some more effortful and analytic, others, automatic, associative, and often emotion-based) are put in play when a preference between risky options is constructed" (Weber & Johnson, 2009, p. 139). Selecting one opportunity over another qualifies as a risky option. Entrepreneurs do not merely retrieve information from memory when evaluating opportunities but make mental computations. Thus, an interesting research avenue could be to explore the computational models entrepreneurs use and their underlying neural regions. Such an approach could improve our understanding of the cognitive processes involved in opportunity evaluation.

A neuroscientific perspective could be expanded to the study of other factors that play an important role in opportunity discovery or creation, such as opportunity evaluation, entrepreneurial alertness, happiness, intuition, optimism, and counterfactual thinking, to name but a few. For example, previous research shows that happy individuals tend to overestimate the likelihood of positive outcomes and underestimate the likelihood of negative outcomes (Johnson & Tversky, 1983) and engage in risky behavior (Knoch et al. (2006). Could such a behavior have neural foundations? How could the identification of neural structures help to further explain the role of happiness in the entrepreneurial process? For example, opportunity evaluation entails making a choice and assigning values to the available options. Neuroscientific evidence shows that the OFC is activated when people think about gains, whereas the inferior parietal and cerebellar areas are activated when people think about losses (Dickhaut et al., 2003). Opportunities could be framed as gains or losses and such framing could affect entrepreneurs' subsequent behaviors.

The neurocognitive model could also help to explore the role of unconscious processes in opportunity discovery and creation. It is well understood that "people develop mental constructs, representations of past experiences that assist them at an unconscious level to interpret and understand new experiences and act accordingly" (Blair, 2010, pp. 60–61). Thus, it is possible that the first step in discovering or creating a business or social opportunity may even be unconscious insofar that unconscious processes are the default mode of the brain (Camerer et al., 2005). The activation of specific brain regions may lead an entrepreneur to see or imagine what the brain has already processed. For example, invoking the X–System processes could lead to an expectation that opportunity recognition could occur outside the entrepreneur's awareness to the extent that people become consciously aware of an act only after they unconsciously decide to engage in it (Dijksterhuis & Aarts, 2010).

A neurocognitive perspective could contribute to the development of experimental entrepreneurship (Schade & Burmeister-Lamp, 2009; Krueger & Welpe, 2014), an emerging field within entrepreneurship, where researchers use the experimental method to study entrepreneurial activity. "Entrepreneurship increasingly takes advantage of rigorous experimental methodologies to better understand deeper structures of entrepreneurial cognition. Neuroscience, in particular, gives us new ways to conceptualize and measure important facets of entrepreneurial decision making" (Krueger & Welpe, 2014, p. 65). Using experiments has a number of advantages, such as, causal inference, control, and replicability. Participants could be asked to imagine business opportunities in specific markets and/or industries while their brains are being scanned. Such experiments could allow researchers to pinpoint brain regions that are activated when entrepreneurs "think" about business opportunities. They could be used to study potential differences between serial entrepreneurs and novices. A research design could compare the two groups to see whether brain activations in serial entrepreneurs engage more the X–System structures, whereas those of novice entrepreneurs engage more the C–System structures. Such experiments could also incorporate situations where participants are given opportunity evaluation tasks. This could allow researchers to identify the brain regions that are activated when entrepreneurs evaluate business opportunities. By using the experimental approach, neurocognitive studies of entrepreneurship could add a naturalistic perspective to entrepreneurship research. Most research on opportunity formation is conducted after the fact, that is, after entrepreneurs have already discovered or created the opportunities.

Limitations of the Model and Conclusion

How can entrepreneurship scholars study experimentally the neuroscience of entrepreneurial cognitions? Several neuroscientific tools, such as functional magnetic resonance imaging (fMRI), repetitive transcranial magnetic stimulation (rTMS), position emission tomography (PET), and electroencephalographic technique (EEG) are available. Such tools are commonly used in the fields of neuroscience, social cognitive neuroscience, and neuroeconomics. However, a neurocognitive perspective could advance knowledge in entrepreneurship only if it could address the limitations inherent to the use of these neuroscientific tools. Lee et al. (2012, p. 922) argue that "a fundamental limitation in neuroimaging is an inability to infer complex social behavior from observations of specific activated brain regions." Another limitation is the problem of reverse inference. Reverse inference refers to the practice of reasoning backward from the presence of brain activation to the engagement of a particular cognitive function (Poldrack, 2006). Thus, it could impede a researcher's ability to attribute the activation of certain brain regions to specific cognitive processes.

Statistical correlations in neuroimaging data with performance in a task or behavioral traits do not imply that the identified areas play a causal role (Tracey & Schluppeck, 2014). However, Poldrack (2006) suggests that reverse inference can be overcome by the selectivity of a signal emanating from a particular brain region. The more selective the signal, the more likely the brain structure is directly implicated in the cognition or behavior in question. Hence, neuroscience can provide useful insights to the study of entrepreneurial opportunity. As Grégoire et al. (2010, p. 415) acknowledge, "the process of recognizing opportunities involved both objective and subjective dimensions: the objective reality of one's context and the subjective interpretations that one makes of this context and of one's position in it, before the facts can be objectively known." The use of neuroscientific tools and concepts could spur future research on the neural foundations of entrepreneurial cognitions. Despite these limitations, the neural cognitive model of entrepreneurial opportunity represents an attempt to integrate neuroscientific methods and techniques into our understanding of entrepreneurial phenomena (de Holan, 2014).

References

Alvarez, S. A., & Barney, J. B. (2007). Discovery and creation: Alternative theories of entrepreneurial action. *Strategic Entrepreneurship Journal, 1*, 11–26.

Alvarez, S. A., & Barney, J. B. (2008). Opportunities, organizations, and entrepreneurship. *Strategic Entrepreneurship Journal, 2*, 171–173.

Alvarez, S. A., & Barney, J. B. (2010). Entrepreneurship and epistemology: the philosophical underpinnings of the study of entrepreneurial opportunities. In J. P. Walsh & A. P. Brief (Eds.), *Academy of Management Annals, 4*, 557–583. Essex: Routledge.

Alvarez, S. A., & J. B. Barney, & Anderson, P. (2012). Forming and exploiting opportunities: The implications of discovery and creation processes for entrepreneurial and organizational research. *Organization Science, 24*, 301–317.

Alvarez, S. A., & Parker, S. (2009). New firm organization and the emergence of control rights: A bayesian approach. *Academy of Management Review, 34*, 209–227.

Ardichvili, A., Cardozo, R., & Ray, S. (2003). A theory of entrepreneurial opportunity identification and development. *Journal of Business Venturing, 18*, 105–123.

Baker, T., & Nelson, E. R. (2005). Creating something from nothing: Resource construction through entrepreneurial bricolage. *Administrative Science Quarterly, 50*, 329–366.

Baron, R. A. (2006). Opportunity recognition as pattern recognition: how entrepreneurs "connect the dots" to identify new business opportunities. *Academy of Management Perspectives, 20*, 104–119.

Baron, R. A. (2007). Behavioral and cognitive factors in entrepreneurship: entrepreneurs as the active elements in new venture creation. *Strategic Entrepreneurship Journal, 1* (1/2), 167–182.

Baron, R. A., & Ensley, M. D. (2006). opportunity recognition as the detection of meaningful patterns: evidence from comparisons of novice and experience entrepreneurs. *Management Science, 52*, 1331–1344.

Baron, R. A., & Ward, T. B. (2004). Expanding entrepreneurial cognition's toolbox: potential contributions from the field of cognitive science. *Entrepreneurship Theory and Practice, 1*, 553–573.

Becker, W. J., Cropanzano, R., & Sanfey, G. A. (2011). Organizational neuroscience: taking organizational theory inside the neural black box. *Journal of Management, 37*, 933–961.

Beugré, C. D. (2010). Brain and human behavior in organizations: a field of neuro-organizational behavior. In A. A. Stanton, M. Day, & I. Welpe (Eds.), *Neuroeconomics and the Firm* (pp. 289–303). Cheltenham: Elgar.

Blair, E. S. (2010). What you think is not what you think: unconsciousness and entrepreneurial behavior. In A. A. Stanton, M. Day & I. Welpe (Eds.), *Neuroeconomics and the Firm* (pp. 50–65). Cheltenham: Elgar.

Bossaerts, P., Preuschoff, K., & Hsu, M. (2009). The neural foundations of valuation in human decision making under uncertainty. In P. W. Glimcher, C. F. Camerer, E. Fehr, & R. A. Poldrack (Eds.), *Neuroeconomics: Decision Making and the Brain* (pp. 353–365). New York: Academic Press.

Brown, J. W., & Bravey, T. (2005). Learned predictions of error likelihood in the anterior cingulate cortex. *Science, 307*, 1118–1121.

Brown, J. W., & Bravey, T. (2007). Risk Prediction and Aversion by Anterior Cingulate Cortex. *Cognitive, Affective, & Behavioral Neuroscience, 7*, 266–277.

Busenitz, L. W. (1996). Research on entrepreneurial alertness. *Journal of Small Business Management, 24* (4), 35–44.

Camerer, C. L., Loewenstein, G., & Prelec, D. (2005). Neuroeconomics: How neuroscience can inform economics? *Journal of Economic Literature, 43* (1), 9–64.

Chiason, M., & Saunders, C. (2005). Reconciling diverse approaches to opportunity research using the structuration theory. *Journal of Business Venturing, 20,* 747–767.

Corbett, A. C. (2007). Learning Asymmetries and the Discovery of Entrepreneurial Opportunities. *Journal of Business Venturing, 22,* 97–118.

Cornelissen, J. P., & Clarke, J. S. (2010). Imagining and rationalizing opportunities: inductive reasoning and the creation and justification of new ventures. *Academy of Management Review, 35,* 539–557.

Crossan, M. M., Lane, H. W., & White, R. E. (1999). An organizational learning framework: from intuition to institution. *Academy of Management Review, 24,* 522–537.

Cunningham, W. A., Johnson, M. K., Gatenby, J. C., Gore, J. C., & Banaji, M. R. (2003). Neural components of social evaluation. *Journal of Personality and Social Psychology, 85,* 639–649.

de Holan, P. M. (2014). It's all in your head? Why we need neuroentrepreneurship? *Journal of Management Inquiry, 23* (1), 93–97.

Dickhaut, J. K., McCabe, J. C., Ngode, A., Rustichini, A., & Pardo, J. V. (2003). The impact of the certainty context on the process of choice. *Proceedings of the National Academy of Sciences of the United States of America, 100,* 3536–3541.

Dietrich, A. (2004). The cognitive neuroscience of creativity. *Psychonomic Bulletin & Review, 11,* 1011–1026.

Diksterhuis, A., & Aarts, H. (2010). Goals, attention, and unconsciousness. *Annual Review of Psychology, 61,* 467–490.

Eckhardt, J. T., & Shane, S. A. (2003). Opportunities and entrepreneurship. *Journal of Management, 29,* 333–349.

Eisenhardt, K. M., & Zbaracki, M. J. (1992). Strategic decision making. *Strategic Management Journal, 13* (S2), 17–37.

Evans, J. St. B. T. (1989). *Bias in human reasoning: Causes and consequences.* Brighton, UK: Erlbaum.

Gaglio, C. M., & Katz, J. A. (2001). The Psychological Basis of Opportunity Recognition: Entrepreneurial Alert. *Journal Small Business Economics, 16* (2), 95–111.

Gilad, B. (1984). Entrepreneurship: The issue of creativity in the market place. *Journal of Creative Behavior, 18,* 151–161.

Gordon, S. E. (1992). Implications of cognitive theory for knowledge acquisition. In R. R. Hoffman (Ed.), *The psychology of expertise: Cognitive research and empirical AI* (pp. 99–120). New York: Springer-Verlag.

Grégoire, D. A., Barr, P. S., & Shepherd, D. A. (2010). Cognitive processes of opportunity: the role of structural alignment. *Organization Science, 21,* 413–431.

Grégoire, D. A., Corbett, A. C., & McMullen, J. S. (2011). The cognitive perspective of entrepreneurship: An agenda for future research. *Journal of Management Studies, 48,* 1443–1477.

Grégoire, D. A., & Shepherd, D. A. (2012). Technology–market combinations and the identification of entrepreneurial opportunities: An investigation of the opportunity-individual nexus. *Academy of Management Journal, 55,* 753–785.

Haynie, J. M., Shepherd, D. A., Mosakowski, E., & Earley, C. (2010). A situated metacognitive model of the entrepreneurial mindset. *Journal of Business Venturing, 25,* 217–229.

Healy, M. P., & Hodgkinson, G. P. (2014). Rethinking the philosophical and theoretical foundations of organizational neuroscience: A critical realist alternative. *Human Relations, 67,* 765–792.

Herring, D. R., White, K. R., Jabeen, L. N., Hinojos, M., Terrazas, G., Reyes, S. M., Taylor, J. H., & Crites, S. L., Jr. (2013). On the automatic activation of attitudes: A quarter century of evaluative priming research. *Psychological Bulletin*, *139*, 1062–1089.

Howard-Jones, P. A., Blakemore, S. J., Samuel, E. A., Summers, I. R., & Claxton, G. (2005). Semantic divergence and story generation: An fMRI investigation. *Cognitive Brain Research*, *25*, 240–250.

Johnson, E., & Tversky, A. (1983). Affect, generalization, and the perception of risk. *Journal of Personality and Social Psychology*, *36*, 20–31.

Kahneman, D. (2003). Mapping bounded rationality: Psychology for behavioral economics. *American Economic Review*, *93*, 1449–1475.

Kahneman, D. (2011). *Thinking, fast and slow*. New York: Farrar, Strauss, & Giroux.

Kirzner, I. (1973). *Competition and entrepreneurship*. Chicago: University of Chicago Press.

Kirzner, I. (1979). *Perception, opportunity, and profit*. Chicago: University of Chicago Press.

Klein, G. (1999). *Sources of power*. Cambridge, MA: MIT Press.

Knoch, D. L., Gianotti, R. R., Pascual-Leone, A., Treyer, V., Regard, M., Homann, M., & Brugger, P. (2006). Disruption of right prefrontal cortex by low-frequency repetitive transcranial magnetic stimulation induces risk-taking behavior. *Journal of Neuroscience*, *26*, 6472–6469.

Krueger, N. F. (2000). The cognitive infrastructure of opportunity emergence. *Entrepreneurship Theory and Practice*, *25* (3), 5–23.

Krueger, N., & Welpe, I. (2014). Neuroentrepreneurship: What can entrepreneurship learn from neuroscience? In M. H. Morris (Ed.), *Annals of entrepreneurship education and pedagogy*. (pp. 60–90). Cheltenham: Elgar.

Lee, N., Senior, C., & Butler, J. R. M. (2012). The domain of organizational cognitive neuroscience: theoretical and empirical challenges. *Journal of Management*, *38*, 921–931.

Lieberman, M. D. (2007a). Social cognitive neuroscience: A review of core processes. *Annual Review of Psychology*, *58*, 259–289.

Lieberman, M. D. (2007b). The X– and C–systems: The neural basis of automatic and controlled social cognition. In E. Harmon-Jones & P. Winkelman (Eds.), *Fundamentals of social neuroscience* (pp. 290–315). New York: Guilford.

Lieberman, M. D., Gaunt, R., Gilbert, D. T., & Trope, Y. (2002). Reflexion and reflection: A social cognitive neuroscience approach to attributional influence. In M. P. Zanna (Ed.), *Advances in experimental social psychology* (vol. 34, pp. 199–249). New York: Academic Press.

Lieberman, M. D., Jarcho, J. M., & Satpute, A. B. (2004). Evidence-based and intuition-based self-knowledge: An fMRI study. *Journal of Personality and Social Psychology*, *7*(4), 421–435.

Loasby, B. J. (2007). A cognitive perspective on entrepreneurship and the firm. *Journal of Management Studies*, *44*, 1078–1106.

Lumpkin, G. T., & Lichtenstein, B. B. (2005). The role of organizational learning in the opportunity recognition process. *Entrepreneurship: Theory and Practice*, *29* (4), 451–472.

McMullen, J. S., & Shepherd, D. A. (2006). Entrepreneurial action and the role of uncertainty in the theory of the entrepreneur. *Academy of Management Review*, *31*, 132–152.

Mitchell, R. K., Busenitz, L., Bird, B., Gaglio, C. M., McMullen, J. S., Morse, E. A., & Smith, J. B. (2007). The central question in entrepreneurial cognition research 2007. *Entrepreneurship Theory and Practice*, *31*, 1–27.

Mitchell, R. K., Busenitz, L., Lant, T., Dougall, McP. P., Morse, E. A., & Smith, J. B. (2002). Toward a theory of entrepreneurial cognition. Rethinking the people side of entrepreneurship research. *Entrepreneurship Theory & Practice, 1*, 93–104.

Mitchell, J. R., Friga, P. N., & Mitchell, R. K. (2005). Untangling the intuition mess: Intuition as a construct in entrepreneurship research. *Entrepreneurship Theory & Practice, 29*, 653–679.

Mitchell, R. K., Randolph-Seng, B., & Mitchell, J. R. (2011). Socially situated cognition: imagining new opportunities for entrepreneurship research (Dialogue). *Academy of Management Review, 36*, 774–776.

Mitchell, R. K., & Shepherd, D. A. (2010). To thine own self be true: images of self, images of opportunity, and entrepreneurial action. *Journal of Business Venturing, 24*(1), 138–154.

Montague, P. R., King-Casas, B., & Cohen, J.D. (2006). Imaging valuation models in human choice. *Annual Review of Neurscience, 29*, 417–448.

Murphy, P. J. (2011). A 2 × 2 conceptual foundation for entrepreneurial discovery theory. *Entrepreneurship Theory and Practice, 35*, 359–374.

Nicolaou, N., Shane, S. (2014). Biology, neuroscience, and entrepreneurship. *Journal of Management Inquiry, 23* (1), 98–100.

Nicolaou, N., Shane, S., Cherkas, L., Hunkin, J., & Spector, T. D. (2008). Is the tendency to engage in entrepreneurship genetic? *Management Science, 54*, 176–179.

Nicolaou, N., Shane, S., Cherkas, L., & Spector, T. D. (2009). Opportunity recognition and the tendency to be an entrepreneur: a bivariate genetics perspective. *Organizational Behavior and Human Decision Processes, 110*, 108–117.

Paulus, M. P., Rogalsky, I. M., Simmons, A., Feinstein, J. S., & Stein, M. B. (2003). Increased activation in the right during risk-taking decision making is related to harm avoidance and neuroticism. *NeuroImage, 19*, 1439–1448.

Poldrack, R. A. (2006). Can cognitive processes be inferred from neuroimaging? *Trends in Cognitive Sciences, 10* (2), 59–63.

Powell, T. C., & Puccinelli, N. M. (2012). The brain as substitute for strategic organization. *Strategic Organization, 10*, 207–214.

Reyna, V. F. (2004). How people make decisions that involve risk: a dual–processes approach. *Current Directions in Psychological Science, 13* (2), 60–66.

Rilling, K. J., & Sanfey, G. A. (2011). The neuroscience of social decision-making. *Annual Review of Psychology, 62*, 23–48.

Sanfey, G. A., Rilling, K. J., Aronson, J. A., Nystrom, L. E., & Cohen, J. D. (2003). The neural basis of economic decision-making in the ultimate game. *Science, 300*, 1755–1758.

Sarason, Y., Dean, T., & Dillard, J. F. (2006). Entrepreneurship as the nexus of individual and opportunity: a structural view. *Journal of Business Venturing, 21*, 286–305.

Sarasvathy, S. D. (2001). Causation and effectuation: Toward a theoretical shift from economic inevitability to entrepreneurial contingency. *Academy of Management Review, 26*, 243–288.

Sarasvathy, S. D., Dew, N., Velamuri, S. R., & Venkataraman, S. (2003). Three views of entrepreneurial opportunity. In Z. J. Acs & D. B. Audretsch (Eds.), *Handbook of entrepreneurship research* (pp. 141–160). Norwell, MA: Kluwer Academic .

Satpute, A. B., & Lieberman, M. D. (2006). Integrating automatic and controlled processes into neurocognitive models of social cognition. *Brain Research, 1079*, 86–97.

Schade, C., & Burmeister-Lamp, K. (2009). Experiments on entrepreneurial decision making: a different lens through which to look at entrepreneurship. *Foundations and Trends in Entrepreneurship, 5* (2), 81–134.

Schwenk, C. H. (1986). Information, cognitive biases, and commitment to a course of action. *Academy of Management Review, 11*, 298–310.

Senior, C., Lee, N., & Butler, M. (2011). Perspective: Organizational cognitive neuroscience. *Organization Science, 22*, 804–815.

Shane, S. (2000). Prior knowledge and the discovery of entrepreneurial opportunities. *Organization Science*, 11, 448–469.

Shane, S. (2003). *A general theory of entrepreneurship: the individual-opportunity nexus*. Cheltenham: Elgar.

Shane, S., & Vankataraman, S. (2000). The promise of entrepreneurship as a field of research. *Academy of Management Review, 25*, 217–226.

Shepherd, D. A., & DeTienne, D. R. (2005). Prior knowledge, potential financial reward, and opportunity identification. *Entrepreneurship Theory and Practice, 29*, 91–112.

Short, J. C., Ketchen, D. J., Jr., Shook, C. L., & Ireland, R. D. (2010). The concept of opportunity in entrepreneurship research: past accomplishments and future challenges. *Journal of Management, 36*, 40–65.

Smith, R. (2010). Mapping neurological drivers to entrepreneurial proclivity. In A. A. Stanton, M. Day, & I. M. Welpe (Eds.), *Neuroeconomics and the firm* (pp. 193–216). Cheltenham: Elgar.

Smith, E. R., & Semin, G. R. (2004). Socially situated cognition: cognition in its social context. In M. P. Zanna (Ed.), *Advances in experimental social psychology* (vol. 36, pp. 53–117). San Diego, CA: Academic Press.

Stanovich, K. E. (2004). *The robot's rebellion: finding meaning in the age of darwin*. Chicago: Chicago University Press.

Stevenson, H., & Jarillo, J. C. (1990). A paradigm for entrepreneurship: entrepreneurial management. *Strategic Management Journal, 11*, 17–27.

Takeuchi, H., Taki, Y., Sassa, Y., Hashizume, H., Sekiguchi, A., Fukushima, A., & Kanashima, R. (2010). White matter structures associated with creativity: evidence from diffusing tensor imaging. *NeuroImage, 51*, 11–18.

Tang, J., Kacmar, K. M., & Busenitz, L. (2012). Entrepreneurial alertness in the pursuit of new opportunities. *Journal of Business Venturing*, 27, 77–94.

Tracey, P., & Schluppeck, D. (2014). Neuroentrepreneurship: "Brain pornography" or new frontier in entrepreneurship research? *Journal of Management Inquiry, 23*, 101–103.

Tversky, A., & Kahneman, D. (1974). Judgment under uncertainty: Heuristics and biases. *Science, 185*, 1124–1131.

Ucbasaran, D., Westhead, P., & Wright, M. (2009). The extent and nature of opportunity identification by experienced entrepreneurs. *Journal of Business Venturing, 24*, 99–115.

Unger, J. M., Rauch, A., Weis, S. E., & Frese, M. (2015). Biology (prenatal testosterone), psychology (achievement need) and entrepreneurial impact. *Journal of Business Venturing Insights, 4*, 1–5.

Vaghely, I. P., & Julien, P. A. (2010). Are opportunities recognized or constructed? An information perspective on entrepreneurial opportunity identification. *Journal of Business Venturing, 25*, 73–86.

Vartanian, O., Mandel, D. R., & Duncan, M. (2011). Money or life: Behavioral and neural context effects on choice under uncertainty. *Journal of Neuroscience, Psychology, and Economics, 4* (1), 25–36.

Venkataraman, S. (1997). The Distinctive domain of entrepreneurship research: an editor's perspective. In J. Katz & R. Brockhaus (Eds.), *Advances in entrepreneurship, firm emergence, and growth*, (vol. 3, pp. 119–138). Greenwich, CT: JAI Press.

Ward, B. T. (2004). Cognition, creativity, and entrepreneurship. *Journal of Business Venturing, 19*, 173–188.

Walsh, J. (1995). Managerial and organizational cognition: notes from a trip down memory lane. *Organization Science, 6*, 280–321.

Weber, E. U., & Johnson, E. J. (2009). Decisions under uncertainty: psychological, economic, and neuroeconomic explanations of risk preference. In P. W. Glimcher, C. F. Camerer, E. Fehr, & R. A. Poldrack (Eds.), *Neuroeconomics: Decision making and the brain* (pp. 127–144). New York: Academic Press.

Weller, J. A., Levin, I. P., Shiv, B., & Bechara, A. (2009). The effects of insula damage on decision-making for risky gains and losses. *Social Neuroscience, 4*, 347–358.

Weick, K. E. (1979). *The social psychology of organizing* (2nd ed.). Reading, MA: Addison-Wesley.

White, R., Thornhill, S., & Hampson, E. (2006). Entrepreneurs and evolutionary biology: The relationship between testosterone and new venture creation. *Organizational Behavior and Human Decision Processes, 100*, 21–34.

White, R., Thornhill, S., & Hampson, E. (2007). A biosocial model of entrepreneurship: The combined effects of nurture and nature. *Journal of Organizational Behavior, 28*, 451–466.

Whiting, B. G. (1988). Creativity and entrepreneurship: How do they relate? *Journal of Creative Behavior, 22*, 178–183.

Yu, T. F. L. (2001). Entrepreneurial alertness and discovery. *Review of Austrian Economics, 14* (1), 47–63.

Biographical Note

Constant D. Beugré (PhD, Rensselaer Polytechnic Institute) is a professor of management at Delaware State University, College of Business where he teaches courses in organizational behavior and strategic management at the undergraduate level and organizational leadership at the graduate level. His research interests include organizational justice, entrepreneurship, and organizational neuroscience. Dr. Beugré has published five books and more than 70 refereed journal articles and conference proceedings. His publications have appeared in academic outlets, such as *Organizational Behavior and Human Decision Processes, Decision Sciences, International Journal of Human Resource Management, International Journal of Manpower, Journal of Applied Behavioral Science, Journal of Applied Social Psychology*, and *Research in the Sociology of Organizations*. (cbeugre@desu.edu)

Current Topics in Management, Vol. 18, 2016, pp. 43–55

SUSTAINABILITY IN INVENTORY MANAGEMENT

Ismail Civelek
Western Kentucky University

In this study, we investigate the definitions of sustainability, in general, and sustainable inventory management, in particular. We also explore how companies can evaluate and implement sustainability measures and different motivations for firms to engage or invest in sustainable efforts in managing their inventories. We approach sustainable supply chains from the value chain perspective by identifying opportunities for sustainable actions and policies at different phases in the product life cycle, especially in inventory management. We review the current research literature, discuss sustainability measures in inventory management, and provide both short and long-term managerial implications for a decision maker to promote sustainability in inventory management.

Keywords: inventory management, sustainability, green supply chains

Managers in an organization have been traditionally focusing on finding ways to reduce costs and increase sales to create more value for their shareholders. However, companies have been held accountable for their performance in sustainability in terms of their impact on the environment and social welfare. Climate change, environmental disasters, like Hurricane Katrina and Sandy, and high levels of greenhouse gases increased consumer awareness about sustainability and environmental protection significantly in the past decade. While environmental sustainability is very important for consumers, our discussion in this study focuses on sustainability in the value chain. Lee (2010) emphasizes the dramatic shift in the urgency for companies to incorporate sustainability in their strategies and operations. In addition, any type of unsustainable practices in the supply chain of an organization can be public because of the Internet and social media. These global platforms can be accessed by *conscious consumers* and threaten the image of the organization. For example, Kenyon, Campbell, and Hawkey (2000) point out the public relations issue that Nike had to handle when poor working conditions in its manufacturing facilities in Southeast Asia were revealed. More recently, Greenhouse (2013) reports that three weeks after a horrific fire in one of the workshops in Bangladesh of H&M, GAP, and Zara, a deal was signed to improve working and safety conditions.

Many scholars and practitioners have recently increased their focus on awareness of sustainability in logistics and inventory management (Seuring & Muller, 2008). Specifically, auto manufacturers, including part suppliers, have major challenges in terms of environmental sustainability and pollution (Koplin, Seuring, & Mesterharm 2007). There are numerous challenges, that is, ethical and social responsibility, risks, cost increases, governmental regulations and application of green energy, that these auto manufacturers face in developing sustainable supply chains (Abbasi & Nilsson, 2012). On the contrary, pressure from regulatory institutions and stakeholders for sustainable supply chains may cause conflict between members of the supply chain (Simpson et al., 2007).

Considering the power of conscious consumers and need for sustainable practices in organizations, managers need to take sustainable strategies into account in every step. Taking the viewpoints of the value chain to define and analyze sustainability is a traditional choice since supply chain managers in a company are engaged in every step of the business process including production, logistics, inventory management, strategic planning, information systems, finance, and sales. Murphy and Poist (2003) state that supply chain managers have to understand that daily decisions incorporating sustainability have a potential positive effect on millions of shareholders. Therefore, supply chain managers should not take risks associated with sustainability due to unavoidable negative impacts in the future success of their companies. Kleindorfer, Singhal, and Van Wassenhove (2005) survey both positive and negative implications of decisions made by supply chain managers in various industries and conclude that adding sustainability throughout the supply chain of any organization provides a competitive edge to such companies against competitors to reduce overall costs and improve customer service.

Supply chain management is defined as the efficient integration of manufacturers, suppliers, warehouses, vendors, and customers to maximize value across the board by minimizing system-wide costs while satisfying customer and fill-rate requirements. Linton, Klassen, and Jayamaran (2007) define Sustainable Operations Management as the planning, coordination, and control of an organization that adds value to the customer with minimum cost, while sincerely protecting the environment. Hence, any sustainable operations strategy in a supply chain issue needs specific plans to minimize the impact on the environment. Moreover, supply chain management problems can be conveniently separated into two main categories: distribution and inventory management. In this paper, our focus is sustainability in inventory management. However, we briefly address important sustainability practices in distribution networks because major breakthroughs resulted from the distribution systems of Wal-Mart, FedEx, and UPS in the past two decades. Sustainability strategies in inventory management and distribution systems are also interrelated in supply chains. In addition, SmartWay provides a method to quantify and report the exact footprint in terms of exhaust stacks. In fact, Hewlett Packard's decision to ship all of its products with SmartWay carriers has placed a tremendous focus on lowering the carbon footprint throughout the distribution networks (Campbell, 2014).

Our main objective is to investigate how organizations evaluate and implement sustainability practices in managing their inventories. We approach sustainable supply chains from the value chain perspective by identifying opportunities for sustainable actions and policies at different phases in the product life cycle, especially in inventory management. In this study, we also review current operations management literature and discuss sustainability measures in inventory management. Our main contribution in this study is to provide both short- and long-term managerial strategies for a decision maker to promote sustainability in inventory management. In the organization of our paper, first we review sustainability measures in supply chains from distribution systems to inventory management. Afterward, we focus on current topics in inventory management in regard to sustainability practices. We conclude our paper with a discussion on managerial implications, new research directions, and limitations of the study.

Sustainability in Supply Chains

Sustainable supply chain management is defined as the planning, coordination, and control of a company's supply chain that creates value to its customers with minimum cost, while genuinely protecting the environment (Linton et al. 2007). Thus, embracing sustainability in supply chains implies that managing supply chains should not only target cost reductions as the sole objective, but should also focus in protecting the environment and minimizing carbon emissions through reverse logistics, green supply chain measures, and remanufacturing. Sustainability and cost/profit optimization should not have conflicting objectives for a supply chain decision maker.

Now, we review sustainability issues in supply chain management and separate the supply chain into three categories: green supply chains, distribution systems, and inventory management. Green supply chains refer to any measure that reduces waste, carbon emissions, and damage to the environment in managing supply chains. On the contrary, distribution systems focus on transportation of goods in supply chains and inventory management including warehousing, replenishing stocks, and forecasting in organizations. Before we investigate contemporary problems in inventory management related to sustainability and present managerial implications, we provide a comprehensive review of sustainability in the area of supply chain management.

Green Supply Chains

Green supply chain management is defined by adding "green" dimension into the definition of supply chain management. Thus, green supply chain management takes positive and negative effects of supply chain management into account. Moreover, green supply chain management can arise from inside an organization to respond to preferences of environmentally conscious customers. In fact, in practice, green supply chain management has become both a strategic and operational decision-making tool for numerous manufacturing and service companies.

Regarding the performance measures for green supply chain management, Hervani, Helms, and Sarkis (2005) propose a performance measure to define green supply chain management as "Green Purchasing + Green Manufacturing/ Materials Management + Green Distribution/Marketing + Reverse Logistics." In this formal definition of green supply chain management, Hervani et al., (2005) put "green" into each step of the supply chain management from procurement to transportation and close the supply chain loop via reverse logistics.

In light of successful implementation of green supply chain management, organizations require strong leadership to promote interorganizational sharing of environment responsibility. There are various tools in the managerial arsenal for decision makers to promote sustainability like the design for environment, product stewardship, and the life cycle assessment. Out of these techniques and philosophies, the life cycle assessment is very crucial to provide a structural approach in defining and evaluating the total environmental impact in producing a good or providing a service to customers. The life cycle assessment includes environmental impacts of procurement, distribution, warehousing, marketing, and information systems. Bowen, Cousins, Lamming, and Faruk (2001) assert that a dynamic corporate environmental stance and a strategic supply chain management approach are necessary to develop appropriate capabilities for a green supply chain. Levinson (2009), in his historical data analysis of US manufacturing firms, reports that the total pollution emitted by US manufacturers declined over the past 30 years by about 60% while manufacturing output increased by 70%. Even though the majority of the reduction of pollution has been achieved by the adoption of new technologies, outsourcing direct and indirect pollution, mainly to China, has been an important supply chain strategy to improve firms' performance in the area of sustainability.

Regarding the performance metrics and measures in green supply chain management, we provide a sample of general metrics used in practice to promote sustainable supply chains: costs associated with environmental compliance, total fuel use, total energy use, total water use, liabilities under environmental regulations, ratio of remanufacturable products, and nonpoint and point air emissions. There are, in fact, numerous performance metrics related to sustainability in supply chains depending on the company, market, and regulations set by the government. Thus, organizations need to choose and implement a sample of these performance measures to increase their efforts in promoting sustainability in their supply chain management.

Distribution Systems

Companies have been implementing sustainability measures throughout the entire supply chain, especially within distribution activities. These key activities are very crucial to all organizations and contribute the most to the total cost of logistics. In such distribution systems, transportation, inventory management, warehousing, purchasing, environmentally friendly packaging design, preventive maintenance, and information technology are all included. Hence, sustainability measures should be considered in each step of these distribution activities.

Transportation of goods, raw materials, and finished goods require a large amount of fossil fuels that can cause a major negative impact on the environment and human health. The two major strategies companies follow to improve sustainability in transportation networks are hybrid fleets and choice of rail or water freight. Dey, LaGuardia, and Srinivasan (2011) discuss that FedEx and Wal-Mart have already been transforming their trucks into hybrid diesel transporters that, indeed, both lower the carbon emissions and overall distribution costs. Specifically, Wal-Mart increased the efficiency of its vehicle fleet by 25% from 2005 to 2008; eliminated 30% of the energy used in stores, and reduced its solid waste from US stores by 25% (Dey et al., 2011). Moreover, companies with the ability to ship their goods and raw materials via water and rail freights for long distances lower their freight costs and the risk of supply chain disruptions.

Inventory Management

The main goal of inventory management in an organization is to reduce the cost of activities in a supply chain without sacrificing the service level by improving the efficiency or productivity of the supply chain. Regarding sustainability measures in a supply chain, decision makers need to consider inventory policies that minimize cost and negative impact to the environment. Since the carrying costs associated with owning and moving inventory are very significant in traditional supply chain management, decision makers have been implementing various techniques such as reducing demand variability and lead-time, improving forecast accuracy, aggregating different sources of risk in supply chains and strengthening relationships with suppliers and vendors. Most of these tools, in fact, are also used to improve sustainability in inventory management by reducing carbon emissions. For example, companies can minimize waste or excess inventory by implementing better inventory replenishment policies and information technology. This kind of operational improvement in managing inventories will translate into less energy used in heating, cooling, and material movement for raw materials, work-in-progress inventory, and finished goods.

Within specific supply chains, that is, healthcare supply chains, material and warehousing costs are very significant and can outweigh labor costs in some cases. Reducing costs motivates the need for better inventory management policies in supply chain management. That is generally the main goal of a company. Dekker, van Asperen, Ochtman, and Kusters (2009) show that if companies send their shipments to intermodal terminals, they can improve their inventory costs significantly. Hence, sustainability measures in inventory management should coincide with cost-cutting measures. Any sustainability proposal in managing inventories should decrease procurement or distribution costs, too. Because of cost reduction goals in a supply chain, integrating sustainability in inventory management has been a very complex managerial problem for decision makers.

Considering current research on sustainable inventory management, Bouchery, Ghaffari, Jemai, and Dallery (2012) conclude that frequent deliveries of small batches can increase the carbon emissions in the supply chain if transportation distances are significant and the carbon footprint associated with the storage of goods that require refrigeration can outweigh the advantages of full truckload deliveries. Moreover, Toptal, Özlü, and Konur (2014) extend the traditional economic order quantity model to consider carbon emissions reduction investment availability under carbon cap, cap, and cap-and-trade policies. Their results indicate that when a company can invest in carbon emission reduction, compared to a given tax policy, a cap policy that will lower costs and not increase carbon emissions is feasible. In addition, their recent study shows that for any given cap policy, there exists a cap-and-trade policy that will lower costs and the carbon footprint of the supply chain.

Current Issues in Sustainable Inventory Management

The main goal of inventory management gains another dimension by incorporating sustainability in inventory policies; however, it is still centered on reducing the cost of managing inventories without sacrificing service by improving the efficiency or productivity of inventory replenishment systems in a supply chain. Majority of the techniques used by inventory managers have also had a positive impact on the carbon emissions of a company. These managerial measures include reducing demand variability, improving forecasting models and supplier reliability, reducing manufacturing and supplier lead times. Using these techniques to minimize cost in inventory management can lead to improvements in the sustainability of the supply chain. For example, carrying a lower amount of inventory will prompt the need for a smaller warehouse and less number of material handling equipment. This then will translate into less energy spent in cooling/heating the warehouse area for raw materials, work-in-progress and finished goods, and movements of material handling tools.

Healthcare

Now, we discuss current sustainability issues in inventory management. We first emphasize the impact of sustainable inventory management in healthcare operations; then, we investigate the applications of reverse logistics in different industries. Civelek (2012) reviews current research streams in operations management including strategic, tactical, and operational decision making and provides a classification of healthcare management research to investigate new research directions in practice. In addition, Civelek, Karaesmen, and Scheller-Wolf (2015) focus on the recent issues in blood inventories to provide new policies in managing inventories of blood platelets. Since the mid-1990s, developments in healthcare operations include vertical and horizontal integration in the healthcare supply chain, managed care pressures, changes in federal reimbursement, the rise of e-commerce following advancements in information technology, and the recent implementation of the Affordable Care Act in 2014.

Healthcare supply chains typically include a complex network of manufacturers, purchasers, and healthcare providers. Manufacturers make the products and distributors buy in bulks in an attempt to take advantage of economies of scale while funding their operations through administrative fees. The hospitals, as healthcare providers, consume the products to provide patient care. The drugs, medical devices, and blood products are transported, stored, and transformed into healthcare services for the patient at the end of the supply chain.

Considering hospital systems and health insurance companies, new vertically integrated organizations, called Health Maintenance Organization (HMO), have been created in the healthcare industry. The main reason for the rise of HMOs is integration of downstream toward the patients to capture a greater market share in patient flow and insurance premiums. In addition to the downstream, hospital systems have to integrate upstream with the wholesalers and distributors to improve their revenue position. Because of these consolidations between health providers and insurance companies, there are significant improvements in capacity utilization and inventory management in healthcare operations. This has positive impacts on sustainability, like reduction in carbon emissions and inventories in healthcare supply chains.

In discussions about the trends in healthcare inventory management, Burns and Pauly (2002) claim that the horizontal and vertical integrations in healthcare industry are generally counterproductive and that merging into a larger organization, such as a HMO, fails to compensate for the increased paperwork and poor restructuring. They instead suggest focusing on information technology improvements and better handling of high-cost medical care. On the contrary, Williams (2004) asserts that preventive maintenance, reducing demand variability, using automated inventory replenishments, and tracking inventories with barcodes would improve managing inventories for healthcare providers. Van Berkel, Fujita, Hashimoto, and Geng (2009) analyze the "eco-town" model in Japan between 1999 and 2006 and conclude that ambitious recycling legislation enforcing disinfection of hospital wastes into bricks, which are used in furnaces to melt steel, helped to increase the level of environmental sustainability.

In light of current issues in sustainable inventory management, decision makers need to recognize the increasing role of the green supply chain in new product development, improving forecasting accuracy and dynamic demand management. The introduction of new technology due to sustainability initiatives introduces a number of supply chain management issues such as controlling costs, lowering variation in patient care, diversification of distribution network choices, and minimizing the adoption period through training providers. For example, the introduction of new "green" technology may cause the price/value of items already in inventory to change. Planning for such a change should be an important factor in evaluating current technology versus new sustainable technology offered by the manufacturers.

Reverse Logistics

Logistics managers traditionally focus on organizing forward distribution, which includes transportation, warehousing, packaging, and managing inventories of goods. With the introduction of sustainable initiatives in supply chains, environmental considerations have become important for decision makers to increase the level of recycling, disposal, and remanufacturability. Carter and Ellram (1998) state that reverse logistics is a process whereby companies can become more environmentally efficient through recycling, remanufacturing/reusing products, and reducing the amount of materials used. Supply chain managers are eager to adopt reverse logistics activities because of competition and changes toward sustainability in the corporate culture. Furthermore, Barker and Zabinsky (2010) assert that there are three major driving forces for decision makers to incorporate reverse logistics into their operations: government regulations, significant economic value of a used product, and compliance to environmentally conscious customers.

Although reverse logistics provide significant benefits to any supply chain, its implementation is typically very difficult and the economical benefit is often overcome by the cost of application of reverse logistics activities. For example, a company's distribution system is commonly designed for efficient forward flow due to many years of experience building relationships with suppliers and vendors; however, introducing reverse logistics activities can be very costly and inefficient. Even if there are high costs associated with reverse logistics, decision makers still want to incorporate such activities through designing recycling and reusing materials in the supply chain. For example, supply chain and inventory managers consider reverse logistics activities in sorting, testing, collecting, and reprocessing through each step of the supply chain.

Discussion

In this section of our study, we provide managerial measures to decision makers in supply chain management on how to promote sustainability in inventory management, distributions, and other operational activities. In order to make sustainability efforts successful in supply chain management, environmental and financial goals have to be aligned. Besides sustainable measures being economical, companies need strong leadership and continuous improvement in every step of "green" transformation. For example, FedEx teamed up with the Environmental Defense Fund to transform their midsize truck fleet into hybrid diesel vehicles in 2005. The hybrid trucks improved the fuel economy by 42% and reduced green gas emissions by 25%. Therefore, any sustainable measure has to make sense economically. Otherwise, decision makers are reluctant to implement any sustainable measures in supply chains unless there is an enforcing governmental regulation. Our main contribution in this paper is to provide inventory managers in supply chains a review and road map in successfully implementing sustainability measures. Throughout our study, we provided examples of why sustainability is an important dimension of supply chains, especially inventory management, and showed strategies to successfully implement such sustainability measures. Even if some of the benefits of sustainability in supply chains are not always quantifiable, managers in supply chains can unlock a great deal of business potential by reduced costs, improved business relationships with customers, lower consumption of natural resources and energy, better brand recognition, decreased safety risks, and employee motivation. These benefits will result in better product quality and customer service that translates into better stock prices for the company's shareholders.

Implications for Management

The implications of this study suggest that decision makers in inventory management need to implement sustainability measures urgently but with consideration of cost savings. We provide both short-term and long-term actions decision makers can take to improve sustainability in their supply chains. For short-term actions, managers should act immediately by starting simple. There are numerous simple measures that can be implemented immediately without any substantial cost or time. For example, managers should calculate their inventory turnover immediately and start tracking that measure to realize when the company is not turning its inventories fast or slow. Moreover, any sustainability implementation requires strong leadership and dedication from top management due to the need for resources and organizational commitment. Therefore, the top management in an organization must provide support in creating standards and measures that are enforceable without significant friction among employees. Managers should benchmark each area of inventory management against other firms, particularly industry leaders. This will help in providing a sense of measurability, which can be analyzed and compared with the benchmark.

As for long-term recommendations, managers need to set measurable carbon emission goals and monitor the progress of their company continuously. This will allow decision makers to create measurable goals to encourage reductions in the carbon footprint of supply chains. Furthermore, managers should stay ahead of government regulations because these enforcements can hurt operations and marketing of their products and services. Hence, companies need to start measuring the carbon footprint for each of their product and service to increase their flexibility in responding any change in regulations. This definitely helps firms to differentiate themselves from their competitors, reduce costs, increase employee satisfaction, and improve customer service.

Limitations

Most studies in sustainability lack real industry data with correct benchmarks due to regulations and confidentiality. However, this limitation is fading away following strong dedication from decision makers in implementing sustainability measures. In addition to lack of data in sustainability problems in inventory management, introducing new objectives, like reducing carbon emissions, or new constraints, such as government policies, unfortunately limits building tractable analytical models to find an optimal inventory replenishment policy.

Directions for New Research

The concept of sustainability in supply chains, especially inventory management, has been a relatively new and popular research area in both literature and practice. There are still numerous unanswered questions about implementation of sustainability measures in inventory management. For example, there is currently no structural operations research model that quantifies the value of "green" initiatives, such as reverse logistics in managing inventories. Moreover, the relationship between traditional inventory models, carbon emissions, and government regulations, like cap-and-trade, has not been investigated thoroughly in the operations management literature. A full-scale analysis of sustainable lot sizing policy for multiproduct inventory policy is still an open problem. Therefore, we believe that future research in sustainable inventory management should focus on developing analytical models considering the economic and environmental parameters and variables for the optimal "green" inventory replenishment policy.

References

Abbasi, M., & Nilsson, F. (2012). Themes and challenges in making supply chains environmentally sustainable. *Supply Chain Management: An International Journal, 17*, 517–530.

Barker, T. J., & Zabinsky, Z. B. (2010). Designing for recovery. *Industrial Engineer, 42* (4), 38–43.

Bouchery, Y., Ghaffari, A., Jemai, Z., & Dallery, Y. (2012). Including sustainability criteria in inventory models. *European Journal of Operational Research, 222*, 229–240.

Bowen, F. E., Cousins, P. D., Lamming, R. C., & Faruk, A. C. (2001). The role of supply management capabilities in green supply. *Production and Operations Management, 10*, 174–189.

Burns, L. R., & Pauly, M. V. (2002). Integrated delivery networks: A detour on the road to integrated healthcare? *Health Affairs, 21* (4), 128–143.

Campbell, A. (2014). *Rethinking logistics and supply chains: What's the buzz?* http://www.greenbiz.com/article/rethinking-logistics-and-supply-chain-verge, accessed on November 6, 2014.

Carter, C. R., & Ellram, L. M. (1998). Reverse logistics: A review of the literature and framework for future investigation. *Journal of Business Logistics, 19* (1), 85–102.

Civelek, I. (2012). Healthcare management: Operations and strategy. *Current Topics in Management, 16*, 167–179.

Civelek, I., Karaesmen, I., & Scheller-Wolf, A. (2015). Blood platelet inventory management with protection levels. *European Journal of Operational Research, 243*, 826–838.

Dekker, R., van Asperen, E., Ochtman, G., & Kusters, W. (2009). Floating stocks in FMCG supply chains: Using intermodal transport to facilitate advance deployment. *International Journal of Physical Distribution & Logistics Management, 39*, 632–648.

Dey, A., LaGuardia, P., & Srinivasan, M. (2011). Building sustainability in logistics operations: a research agenda. *Management Research Review, 34*, 1237–1259.

Greenhouse, S. (2013, May 13). Major retailers join bangladesh safety plan. *New York Times*, http://www.nytimes.com/2013/05/14/business/global/hm-agrees-to-bangladesh-safety-plan.html?_r=0, accessed on November 6, 2014.

Hervani, A. A., Helms, M. M., & Sarkis, J. (2005). Performance measurement for green supply chain management. *Benchmarking: An International Journal, 12*, 330–353.

Kenyon, P., Campbell, F., & Hawkey E. (2000, January 15). Gap and nike: No sweat. *BBC News*.

Kleindorfer, P. R., Singhal, K., & van Wassenhove, L. N. (2005). Sustainable Operations Management. *Production and Operations Management, 14*, 482–492.

Koplin, J., Seuring, S., & Mesterharm, M. (2007). Incorporating sustainability into supply management in the automotive industry: the case of the volkswagen AG. *Journal of Cleaner Production, 15*, 1053–1062.

Lee, H. L. (2010). Don't tweak your supply chain – rethink it end to end. *Harvard Business Review, 88* (10), 62–69.

Levinson, A. (2009). Technology, international trade, and pollution from us manufacturing. *Economic Review, 99*, 2177–2192.

Linton, J. D., Klassen, R., & Jayaraman, V. (2007). Sustainable supply chains: An introduction. *Journal of Operations Management, 25*, 1075–1082.

Murphy, P. R., & Poist, R. F. (2003). Green Perspectives and Practices: A Comparative Logistics Study Patterns. *Supply Chain Management, 8*, 122–131.

Seuring, S., & Muller, M. (2008). From a literature review to a conceptual framework for sustainable supply chain management. *Journal of Cleaner Production, 16*, 1699–1710.

Simpson, D., Power, D., & Samson, D. (2007). Greening the automotive supply chain: A relationship perspective. *International Journal of Operations & Production Management, 27* (1), 28–48.

Toptal, A., Özlü, H., & Konur, D. (2014). Joint decisions on inventory replenishment and emission reduction investment under different emission regulations. *International Journal of Production Research, 52*, 243–269.

Van Berkel, R., Fujita, T., Hashimoto, S., & Geng, Y. (2009). Industrial and urban symbiosis in japan: analysis of the eco-town program 1997–2006. *Journal of Environmental Management, 90*, 1544–1556.

Williams, M. (2004). Materials management and logistics in the emergency department. *Emergency Medicine Clinics of North America, 22* (1), 195–215.

Biographical Note

Ismail Civelek is an assistant professor of management at Western Kentucky University. His areas of expertise are manufacturing and service operations management, queuing theory, simulation, and revenue management. He applies queuing theory, simulation, and stochastic optimization to examine decision making by individuals and organizations in problems motivated by various industry applications. Dr. Civelek received his PhD and MS in Operations Management and Manufacturing from Carnegie Mellon University and a BS in Industrial Engineering from Bilkent University. (ismail.civelek@wku.edu)

Accepted after two revisions: December 28, 2015

Current Topics in Management, Vol. 18, 2016, pp. 57–79

HOME COUNTRY, INDUSTRY, AND OWNERSHIP DILUTION: SIGNALING DURING INTERNATIONAL IPOS

Yi Karnes
California State University, East Bay

Mona Makhija
The Ohio State University

Mike W.Peng
University of Texas at Dallas

This study examines international firms issuing initial public offering (IPO) in the United States. Drawing from agency theory and signaling theory, we analyze the precedent and consequence of governance decisions in international IPO firms. Analyzing data from 410 international and US domestic IPO firms, we find that US firms have more managerial ownership dilution than international firms during IPO. We also find that cultural distance between the home country of the international firms and the United States affects managerial ownership structure change. We recognize managerial ownership dilution, home country political risk, and industry risk as signals to investors that affect valuation of IPOs.

Keywords: initial public offering (IPO), cultural distance, managerial ownership

Note: The authors thank two anonymous reviewers for their comments on the paper and Helen Liang for her feedback on an earlier version of the paper.

Although there is growing literature on the impact and consequence of international firms' entry into the US market, few studies have examined the characteristics of international firms raising capital for the first time in the United States. Increasing numbers of international firms have made first offers of equity in the United States. An initial public offering (IPO) is one of the most critical junctures in the development of a firm (Daily, Certo, & Dalton, 2003). The decision to enter the US market through an IPO presents many exciting opportunities for the continued growth and prosperity of international firms. On the contrary, international firms also face the challenge of adverse selection from potential investors. The US market for IPOs provides an important context to study the key players of corporate governance including investors and managers (Beatty & Zajac, 1994; Carpenter, Pollock, & Leary, 2003). Drawing from agency theory and signaling theory, the goal of this paper is twofold: first, to examine international firms' governance mechanisms during IPO; second, to investigate how the characteristics of the firm, the industry, and the home country affect the valuation of international IPOs.

A firm's cost of capital depends crucially on the firm's governance, which is defined broadly as the set of mechanisms that affect how information flows and agency costs are handled, and therefore, how they impact firm value (Stulz 1999). Firms with poor governance are those where information asymmetry and agency cost problems concern investors. Such firms find it more expensive to raise funds for an IPO since it is difficult to signal the quality of management to the market. Information problems and adverse selection might stem from the fact that, though management has good information about the projected cash flows, it cannot credibly signal investors (Stulz, 1999). Adverse selection may be more severe in international IPO firms in the United States since the US investors are not familiar with the firms. Influential studies on principal–agent problems, beginning with Jensen and Meckling (1976), often tout the benefits of corporate governance mechanisms in reducing information asymmetry between investors (principals) and managers (agents). IPO literature has recognized such governance mechanisms including underwriter reputation (Carter & Manaster, 1990), top management team legitimacy (Cohen & Dean, 2005), and board structures (Certo, Covin, Daily, & Dalton, 2001; Peng, 2004; Sundaramurthy, Pukthuanthong, & Kor, 2014). In addition, literature on international IPOs has identified country-level factors that affect information asymmetry including a country's regulatory environment (Moore , Payne, Bell, & Davis, 2015), economic freedom (Bell, Moore, & Al-Shammari, 2008), and corruption (Payne, Moore, Bell, & Zachary, 2013). Although these studies emphasized the impact of firm-level practices and country-level differences that affect IPO valuation, what is missing is an investigation of the interplay of country differences and firm practices. Do IPO firms respond to prevailing country factors? If they do, why and how? The purpose of this paper therefore is to answer these questions and fill the theoretical gap in understanding the relationship between country characteristics and governance mechanisms of IPO firms.

Research on corporate governance is being criticized for ignoring the endogeneity problem of firms' governance mechanisms (Beatty & Zajac, 1994; Filatotchev & Bishop, 2002; Iyengar & Zampelli, 2009). We address this problem by investigating a firm's strategic decision of governance structures and linking the decision with the valuation of an IPO. By empirically addressing the endogenous choice of managers, this study contributes to the growing body of knowledge on corporate governance and provides a broad picture of the precedent and consequence of governance decisions in international IPO firms.

Boulton, Smart, and Zutter (2010) started to investigate the relationship between IPO firms' governance mechanisms and country factors. Moore et al. (2015) suggested that companies seeking investments from foreign countries should try to minimize cultural differences. In response to Moore et al 's (2015) suggestion, and extending the research by Boulton et al. (2010), we study the important issues pertaining to international IPOs and contribute to the literature by validating the interplay of country-level differences and firm-level practices. Three research questions arise in our study: (1) Are there valuation differences between US domestic IPOs and international IPOs? (2) What corporate governance mechanisms affect valuation of international IPOs? (3) How do international firms compensate for information asymmetry in the United States?

Valuation of IPOs and Underpricing

Among firms that transition from private to public ownership, the original investors sell equity to an investment banker who then sells the stock to first-day investors (Certo et al. 2001). The investors bear a wider range of risk when choosing to invest in an IPO firm instead of an established firm (Beatty & Zajac, 1994; Larraza-Kintana, Wiersema, Gomez-Mejia, & Welbourne, 2007) and require premiums to bear this risk. These premiums manifest as underpricing: the wealth that the first-day investors accrue when the initial offer price is less than the first-day stock closing price. Underpricing represents both wealth creation for first-day investors who purchase stock at the initial issue price and un-retained wealth for the original investors who sold their equity to the investment banker at a price below where it is valued by the investor market (Certo et al., 2001). The presence of underpricing is effectively capital uncollected by the IPO firm due to undervaluation of the firm. The extent of underpricing can be reduced by a number of governance-related signals that may potentially enhance firm value. Previous studies identifying signals that reduce underpricing (Carter & Manaster, 1990; Certo et al., 2001; Cohen & Dean, 2005; Hsu & Ziedonis, 2013; Sundaramurthy et al., 2014) often treated governance-related signals as exogenous firm characteristics. However, in the context of IPOs, it would be natural to suggest that the governance mechanisms may be an outcome of the IPO firm's strategic decisions (Beatty & Zajac, 1994; Filatotchev & Bishop, 2002). As Hermalin and Weisbach (2003) point out, the question of governance choice and function must be answered simultaneously. By treating the firm's governance mechanism as an endogenous factor, we investigate how governance structure might be an outcome of the international firm's strategic decision, and how this decision would affect the valuation of an international IPO in the United States.

Home Country and Managerial Ownership Structure Change

Home country plays a crucial role in firm strategies (Roth & Romeo, 1992). Much of the research on international management has studied home country differences in subsidiary strategies and structures (Hennart & Larimo, 1998). To identify traits of the home country that are theoretically relevant for the purpose of explaining differences of corporate governance mechanisms, one should understand the determinants of ownership and control (La Porta, Lopez-de-Silanes, & Shleifer, 1999). The choice of ownership levels is tied to the issue of how much control the firm desires (Anderson & Gatingnon, 1986). Firms that desire greater control over its foreign operations seek a greater degree of subsidiary ownership (Erramilli, 1996). In a manner similar to that of Erramilli (1996), who argues that high uncertainty avoidance and power distance should lead to a greater propensity for high control, we propose how much control managers of IPO firms desire is a function of the extent of differences in values, customs, and behavior between managers and potential public investors. Compared with US domestic firms, principal–agent conflicts in international IPO firms may be more severe since the managers in international firms are more likely to have different values and customs from public investors in the United States. Thus, managers of international firms may tend to search for ways to obtain control during IPO.

Studies show that ownership and control systems, which are observed corporate governance characteristics, may be a result of endogenous strategic decisions (Beatty & Zajac, 1994; Mark & Li, 2001; Filatotchev & Bishop, 2002). Private firms usually have a high managerial ownership prior to an IPO. When going from private to public, firms make a strategic decision to reduce managerial ownership share and introduce more capital via the stock market. IPO firms are in great need of capital and issue new equity results in diluted managerial ownership. However, because of *ex post* agency conflicts between managers and potential investors, managers worry that ownership dilution may decrease their control of the firm. Managers in international firms are likely to maintain more shares when they foresee the diverging interests of US investors.

Traditional foreign entry literature recognizes the liability of foreignness when firms enter foreign markets (Hymer, 1976) and proposes that firms need to develop strategies to overcome this form of liability (Zaheer, 1995). Cultural distance, the difference between the cultural characteristics of the home country and of the target countries, intensifies the liability of foreignness proportionally since information about the firms becomes more difficult to obtain (Roth & O'Donnell, 1996). Agency theory recognizes information asymmetry and divergent interests between managers and investors (Jensen & Meckling, 1976). The greater the cultural distance, the more likely that values and interests differ between foreign managers and US investors. International IPO firms from culturally distant countries need to develop strategies to overcome this liability to raise capital in the United States.

Signaling theory (Spence, 1973; Certo et al., 2001; Cohen & Dean, 2005) proposes that firms may employ certain signals that help align interests and overcome negative perceptions with potential investors. Upper echelon research (Hambrick & Mason, 1984) and its extension (Filatotchev & Bishop, 2002; Higgins & Gulati, 2003; Higgins & Gulati, 2006; Zhang & Wiersema, 2009) focus on the evaluation of management quality based on various characteristics of top managers. These characteristics are utilized as signals by investors to gauge the economic value of the IPO firm (Cohen & Dean, 2005). The quality of management, although not easily observed, may be revealed in the governance structure of managerial ownership. Managerial ownership share signals the market how confident the managers are about the future performance of the firm. Managers' risk of not getting the desired return on their stock options is partially a function of their personal efforts and talents (Sanders & Boivie, 2004). Accordingly, the risk associated with stock-based financial incentives is lower for a high-quality manager than it is for a low-quality manager (Wiseman & Gomez-Mejia, 1998). If managerial ownership is reduced in a large scale during an IPO, it signals to investors that the managerial quality is poor or the managers are not willing to risk their personal wealth. On the contrary, less managerial ownership dilution is a governance mechanism that signals aligned interests between managers and investors since management is confident to tie personal wealth to the firm's future performance. Hence, international firms from culturally distant countries can compensate for the liability of foreignness by employing a less diluted managerial ownership structure during IPO.

On the basis of our theoretical discussion, two hypotheses are formulated. These were as follows:

Hypothesis 1a: *International firms are likely to have less managerial ownership dilution than U.S. firms during IPO.*

Hypothesis 1b: *International firms based in more culturally distant countries from the U.S. are likely to have less managerial ownership dilution during IPO.*

Managerial Ownership Structure Change and Underpricing

In the process of an IPO, the firm is subjected to a set of agency relationships that are related to information asymmetry concerning the "true" value of the firm (Filatotchev & Bishop, 2002). The condition of information asymmetry between managers and potential investors creates a context wherein the governance mechanism is an important consideration in investors' valuation of IPOs. When firms raise new equity capital, they must reveal certain information about their ventures, such as the size of the venture, the line of business in which it is involved, and the evidence of past performance. These observable characteristics of the venture are used by outsiders to assess uncertainty associated with their investment (Downes & Heinkel, 1982). Other characteristics of the firm, such as quality of management, are hard for potential investors to observe. It is therefore possible that a firm is unable to finance good projects because its managers cannot convince investors that these projects are worthwhile (Stulz, 1990).

Roll (1986) suggests that managers driven by hubris may overestimate the value of a firm. This may be the case in international IPOs, since entering into the US market often indicates that these non-US firms have "made it." It is then possible that these managers retain more ownership during IPO since they overestimate the firm's future growth potential. Nevertheless, stock options indicate managers' expected return based on *ex ante* quality of management and give managers incentive to improve firm performance in the future. Smith and Stulz (1985) argue that investors can reduce the likelihood of managers passing up valuable projects by increasing the relationship between managers' wealth and firm performance. Since managerial ownership increases the sensitivity of managerial wealth to firm performance (Guay, 1999), it works as a mechanism to align the objectives of managers and investors and reduce uncertainty related to IPOs. Less dilution of managerial ownership out of total stock signals to potential investors that the uncertainty associated with principal–agent problems may be reduced.

Since information asymmetry between investors and managers may be greater in international firms than in domestic firms, international firms may present higher uncertainty (Burgman 1996). Investors anticipate the higher uncertainty in international firms and require a premium to make these relatively risky investments. Several information asymmetry-based explanations (Leland & Pyle, 1977; Rock, 1986) suggest a positive relationship between the uncertainty surrounding an IPO and subsequent underpricing since that is the premium for investors to bear the risk of the economic activities of investing in the firms. To reduce agency costs and to communicate their expected value to potential investors, IPO firms may seek signals that are difficult for lower-quality firms to imitate (Filatotchev & Bishop, 2002; Zhang & Wiersema, 2009). Even when managers do not substantially improve organizational practices, they may signal to prospective investors and influence the perception of uncertainty in capital markets (Zajac & Westphal, 2004). Stock-based incentives are observable corporate governance mechanisms that vary across firms (Sanders & Boivie, 2004). Managers with less ownership dilution signal tremendous confidence in their firm before the IPO and their aligned objectives with investors after the IPO. These signals compensate for information asymmetry between the principal and agents in international IPO firms, which reduces IPO underpricing. This leads to the following hypothesis:

Hypothesis 2: *Managerial ownership dilution is positively related to international firms' IPO underpricing.*

Home Country Political Risk and Underpricing

Studying international firms issuing IPO in the United States, Kadiyala and Subrahmanyam (2002) argue that if the home country of an international firm has nontransparent accounting standards, it may be difficult for US investors to ascertain the true value of the firm even when a public price is available from the home market. However, they did not find differences in firm valuation for issuers from emerging markets and for issuers from developed markets. It is likely that a foreign country's accounting standards are not as strong signals to investors as other factors native to the firm's country of origin. A more refined examination of the home country effect by explicitly looking at the political risk may advance our understanding of international IPO valuation.

Although the economic impact of political institutions is generally accepted, the question of which institutions matter and how they influence business decisions are only beginning to be unpacked (Henisz 2000). Research has studied the risks associated with home countries (Burgman, 1996) and host countries (Ghoshal, 1987; Kogut, 1989; Dunning, 1998) that influence decisions of international portfolio diversification. One of the important risks under consideration is political risk. Political risk is the risk of adverse consequences arising from political events (Kobrin, 1979). Countries with weak control on corruption, less stable governments, or weak protections against expropriation of investments have higher political risks that reduce the capital available to the market (Lesmond, 2005). Political risk is an important signal to investors since it indicates how the likelihood of sovereign governments unexpectedly changing the "rules of the game" may significantly influence the value of a firm (Butler & Joaquin, 1998).

Explaining why underpricing exists, Rock (1986) argues that uninformed investors face adverse selection because informed investors do not subscribe to a new issue that they suspect is overpriced, leaving the entire issue to uninformed investors. Hence the typical share must be offered at a discount in order for uninformed investors to earn a return. Signaling hypothesis would predict a higher risk premium for firms from countries with higher political risk since the high risk sends a negative signal to US investors evaluating international IPOs. The less stable government and weaker protection against expropriation associated with home environments may increase uncertainty for the future performance of international firms. Thus, home countries' political risk may discount the offering of shares (Brewer 1993), and higher underpricing is required to attract investors.

Hypothesis 3: *Home countries' political risk is positively related to international firms' IPO underpricing.*

Industry Risk and Underpricing

International IPOs already face significant risk. The nature of the high-technology sector adds another layer of risk to international firms. High-tech industries' product cycles are of relatively short duration. Risk is inherent when firms are required to quickly establish a market position (Carpenter et al., 2003). Values of human capital and intangible assets are not adequately reflected in codified forms like financial statements in high-tech industries (Reuer, Shenkar, & Ragozzino, 2004). These intangible assets therefore create tremendous information asymmetry between insiders and new investors (Espenlaub, Goergen, & Khurshed, 2001) and result in great uncertainty in the value of the firm. The issuer in high-tech industries offers shares at a discount to overcome information asymmetry associated with these industries. These discounted shares signal the true value of the firm. Thus, international firms in high-tech industries are likely to underprice during their IPOs.

Proposing different corporate governance mechanisms as a bundle, Rediker and Seth (1995) suggest that the impact of one factor might be insufficient to affect the valuation of firm performance. There may be factors at the firm level that interact with industry risks and influence IPO valuation. The risky nature of high-tech industry may increase the likelihood that firm governance will include a particular type of investor: the venture capitalists (VCs) (Carpenter et al. 2003). VCs are financial intermediaries specializing in raising capital from a variety of institutional and private investors to invest in high-risk, but high-potential firms. VC-backed firms are better positioned to signal quality at IPO (Hsu & Ziedonis, 2013). Unlike other intermediaries, VCs also actively mold the company and its strategy through participation in strategic decision making, placement of directors on the board, and mobilization of other valuable resources via their network of contacts (Fried, Burton, & Hisrich, 1998; Van den Berghe, 2002; Gulati & Higgins, 2003). These participations are value-adding activities (Fitza, Matusik, & Elaine, 2009) that reduce the risks associated with high-tech industries. Therefore, firms in high-tech industries and backed by VCs signal the market that they are likely to grow rapidly and have high potentials, and reduce risks inherent with these industries. Two hypotheses were formulated:

Hypothesis 4a: *International firms in high-tech industries have higher IPO underpricing than those in non-high-tech industries.*

Hypothesis 4b: *The positive relationship between high-tech industries and underpricing is weaker when international firms are backed by venture capitalists.*

Method

Data

The IPO data for this study were obtained from Securities Data Corporation (SDC) from 1992 through 2005. Study of IPOs in a single target country controls for any host country effect that could obscure the home country factors that are of interest to this study. During this time period, 556 international IPOs occurred in the United States. Of these firms, 299 contained incomplete information on managerial ownership and were not included in this study. We obtained firm assets, debt, and sales from COMPUSTAT and further excluded firms that had not shared these variables. As a result, our sample contained 205 international IPOs from 34 countries. Israel, with 46 IPOs, has the largest number of firms in our sample. We examined the deleted data and found no significant difference in underpricing between the omitted and included firm data. Ignoring firms with incomplete data is not likely to cause bias in our analysis.

We follow Chaplinsky and Ramchand (2000) to match international IPOs with US domestic IPOs by time and industry. We first match the US firms on the same date of IPO issuance with each international firm, then match by industry. If there is no matching US IPO on the same issuance date, we find one with the closest date. There are 205 matched US domestic IPOs in this sample.

The Model

We first make a univariate analysis to compare international IPOs with matched US domestic IPOs, and then turn to a multivariate analysis. The hypotheses are tested using the sample of 205 international IPO firms and the sample of 410 firms combining international IPO firms and matched domestic IPO firms respectively. In the combined sample, a dummy variable is included indicating whether the IPO is international or US domestic.

To avoid inconsistent coefficient estimates, we use two-stage least squares (2SLS) regression instead of ordinary least squares (OLS) regression (Greene, 1997; Hoetker & Mellewigt, 2009) to examine the valuation of IPOs. We estimate managerial ownership structure change in the first stage of the regression. On the basis of the theoretical argument that home country and cultural distance plays a critical role in ownership decisions of international firms (Roth & Romeo, 1992; Hennart & Larimo, 1998), we use cultural distance as an instrumental variable. Cultural distance is treated as an exogenous factor, affecting managerial ownership structure change during IPO. The estimated value of managerial ownership dilution from the first stage regression is then fit into the second stage regression in each sample to predict underpricing. We cluster IPO firms according to different exchanges they are listed, which are American Exchange, Nasdaq, New York Stock Exchange, Over-the-counter, and Small market capitalization.

Measurement

Dependent Variable. IPO underpricing is calculated as the difference between the closing price on the first day of trading and the offer price, expressed as a percentage of the offer price.

Independent Variables. Hofestede's cultural indices are of particular interest to this study. They have been used extensively in international business research (Kogut & Singh, 1988; Agarwal & Ramaswami, 1992; Erramilli, 1996) and adopted in Kogut and Singh (1988)'s measurement of cultural distance. We follow Kogut and Singh (1988) to measure cultural distance between the home country and the United States.

Managerial ownership dilution is measured as managerial ownership share before IPOs minus managerial share after IPOs. The mean of managerial ownership dilution out of total share is 17.99% in the combined sample and 15.63% in the international IPO sample. The maximum is 99.19% and the minimum is −33.3% in both samples.

We acquired political risk indices from Euromoney. The indices range from 8.09 (Russian Federation) to 25 (Switzerland). We multiply this number by −1 so that a bigger number indicates higher political risk.

High-tech industries, such as pharmaceutical, Biotech instrument, software/ communication are recognized by SDC. We code high-tech industries as 1 and non-high-tech industries as 0. VC-backed firms are coded as 1 and non-VC-backed firms are coded as 0.

Control Variables. Observable characteristics of the international firms are used by outsiders to assess uncertainty associated with their investment (Downes & Heinkel, 1982). To control for these firm characteristics, we include firm assets, debt, and sales (in thousand dollars) at the year of the IPO in the control variables.

The "hotness" of the IPO counts the number of IPOs that occur in the focal firm's industry sector. This measure captures the legitimacy of the industry sector. Ritter (1984) finds that same industry groups of stock are overvalued (hot issues) during certain periods. To control for the industry effect, we include the number of IPOs in the same industry in the issuing year in the United States. We also control for the industry variation, measured by standard deviation of underpricing of IPOs in the same industry and same year.

There are possible confounding effects between industries and exchanges. If high-technology stocks tend to list on Nasdaq, then differences across exchanges may actually be the result of differences across industries (Foerster & Karolyi, 1993). Both industry and exchange dummies are included in the analysis.

We control for home country economic factors at the year of IPO. Both logarithm of of GDP and market capitalization as the percentage of GDP are included as control variables. Home countries are categorized into 12 geographic regions, and 11 region dummies are included.

Other firm effects included are offer price, logarithm of share size, whether the IPO is an American depository receipt (ADR) or a common share, and whether the firm is issuing IPO simultaneously outside of the United States.

Results

Table 1 shows the univariate comparison between international data and matched US domestic data. There is no significant difference between the two groups in terms of underpricing, refuting the perception that international firms have more uncertainty than domestic firms and should have more underpricing. However, this may be explained by market signals of international IPO firms such as less managerial ownership dilution out of total shares shown in Table 3. International firms may compensate for higher uncertainty by managerial ownership structure change that indicates higher management quality. This can be further supported in the multivariate analysis.

Table 2 provides the correlation matrix and descriptive statistics for the variables. Table 3 shows the first stage regression, and Table 4 shows the second stage regression on underpricing using the predicted value of managerial ownership dilution from the first stage regression.

In Model 1 of Table 3, the dummy variable of international firm is significant and negatively related with managerial ownership dilution, suggesting that international firms have less managerial ownership dilution during IPO, supporting Hypothesis 1a. The cultural distance variable is significant in Model 2 and Model 3, and is negatively related to managerial ownership dilution. This indicates that firms from more culturally distant nations tend to have less managerial ownership dilution when issuing IPO in the United States, supporting Hypothesis 1b.

Table 1
Comparison of International IPOs and Matched US Domestic IPOs

	International IPOs Mean (SD)	Domestic IPOs Mean (SD)	Difference
Managerial ownership dilution	15.63 (14.35)	19.57 (13.91)	3.94**
Total assets (MM$)	117.07 (22.06)	832.50 (252.89)	715.43**
Long term debt (MM$)	30.78 (9.43)	90.92 (26.96)	60.14*
Sales (MM$)	94.22 (18.44)	281.57 (59.37)	187.35**

Note: $N = 205$ in the International IPOs sample and $N = 205$ in the Domestic IPOs sample.
* $p < .05$. ** $p < .01$.

Table 2
Means, Standard Deviations, and Correlation Matrix in International Sample

Variables	Mean	SD	1	2	3	4	5	6	7	8
1. Underpricing	16.73	36.35								
2. Cultural distance	1.36	1.26	-.05							
3. Mgr owner dilution	15.63	14.35	-.07	-.11						
4. Political risk	19.99	3.88	-.03	.72	-.09					
5. High-tech industry	.58	.50	.16	-.18	-.09	-.04				
6. VC	.11	.31	-.08	.07	-.07	.09	.11			
7. Log GDP	9.51	.89	.06	-.61	.165	-.57	.08	-.29		
8. Smlt offering	.18	.38	.05	.08	-.15	.06	-.1	.01	-.20	
9. Assets	.83	3.62	-.04	.02	-.25	-.00	-.15	-.03	-.12	.21
10. Debt	.09	.39	-.07	.01	-.25	.01	-.21	.00	-.24	.30
11. Sales	.28	.85	-.04	.01	-.28	.02	-.19	-.01	-.15	.33
12. Offer price	12.17	5.86	.15	.10	-.19	.03	-.14	.04	-.28	.38
13. Log size	14.95	.83	-.05	.08	-.18	.01	-.08	.26	-.24	.12
14. No. of mgrs	2.72	1.65	-.09	-.09	-.31	-.09	-.07	.25	-.2	.25
15. ADR	.31	.47	-.12	.20	-.15	-.06	-.08	.14	-.45	.24
16. No. industry	79.62	59.21	.12	-.16	.036	.11	.31	-.18	.28	-.06
17. SD. industry	33.29	25.21	.34	-.09	-.07	-.01	.34	-.00	.21	.08
18. No. listed home	1039.1	860.8	.05	-.53	-.04	-.45	.13	.06	.13	-.17
19. Mkt cap of GDP	92.41	67.6	.23	-.08	.035	.34	-.12	-.12	.34	-.11

(Continued)

Table 2 (Continued)

Variables	9	10	11	12	13	14	15	16	17	18	19
10. Debt	.73										
11. Sales	.62	.66									
12. Offer price	.27	.40	.40								
13. Log size	.20	.21	.32	.44							
14. No. of mgrs	.43	.56	.50	.50	.65						
15. ADR	-.02	.04	.12	.32	.10	.08					
16. No. industry	-.11	-.13	-.14	-.08	-.21	-.17	-.07				
17. SD. industry	-.10	-.14	-.00	.02	-.06	-.01	-.14	.49			
18. No. listed home	.06	-.03	-.00	-.08	.25	.20	-.04	-.12	-.09		
19. Mkt cap of GDP	-.09	-.11	-.08	-.08	-.09	-.09	-.07	.12	.09	.15	

Table 3
First Stage Regression on Managerial Ownership Dilution

	Model 1 (Combined Sample)	Model 2 (International Sample)	Model 3 (International Sample)
International firm	−6.05*		
Cultural distance	−4.15*	−4.60*	−4.88*
Political risk		−1.41	−1.49
High-tech industry	−5.30**	−7.68**	−9.31**
VC	−4.92**	−4.18	−13.80*
High-tech × VC			14.18*
Log GDP	−3.27	−4.79	−4.53
Simultaneous offering	−.62	−.63	.48
Asset	−.28	.18	.16
Debt	−1.90	−7.90	−7.73
Sales	−3.10*	−2.07	−1.54
Offer price	−.07	.10	.12
Log size	3.29*	.98	1.59
No. of managers	−2.79***	−1.96	−2.29*
ADR	−3.80	−6.14	−6.35
No. industry	.01	.02	.02
SD. industry	−.03	−.04	−.05
No. listed home		−.00	−.00
Mkt cap of GDP		−.02	−.02
Constant	29.41	31.82	25.29
R^2	.18	.18	.19
F	20.70***	18.43***	28.15***

Note: $N = 410$ (Model 1) and 205 (Model 2 and Model 3). Control variables Industry and Exchange are included in Model 1, 2, and 3. Control variable Geographic Region is included in Model 2 and 3.
* $p < .05$. ** $p < .01$. *** $p < .001$.

To test the effect of governance structure on underpricing, the estimated variable from first stage—managerial ownership dilution—is fitted into the second stage regression models in Table 4. Managerial ownership dilution is positively related to underpricing in Model 4 and Model 5, supporting Hypothesis 2 and the results from our univariate analysis: international firms compensate for

Table 4
Second Stage Regression on Underpricing

	Model 4 (Combined Sample)	Model 5 (International Sample)	Model 6 (International Sample)
International firm	8.73		
Managerial ownership dilution (predicted)	.71***	1.14*	.97*
Political risk		3.45*	3.44*
High-tech industry	6.98*	17.49	20.74*
VC	−1.86	−4.48	21.69**
High-tech × VC			−39.59**
Log GDP	2.77	.59	−.95
Simultaneous offering	3.75	2.95	3.48
Asset	.93	.76	.84
Debt	−18.86**	1.89	−3.68
Sales	3.29	.62	−1.22
Offer price	2.44*	2.85	2.8*
Log share size	−.42	3.23	2.85
No. of managers	−.34	−1.98	−1.40
ADR	−15.90*	−7.33	−7.81
No. industry	.02	−.07	−.08
SD. Industry	.39**	.47**	.49**
No. listed home		0.00	0.00
Mkt cap of GDP		.18	.18
Constant	−83.32	−66.54	−42.37
R^2	.14	.19	.26
F	15.35***	17.59***	28.32***

Note: $N = 410$ (Model 4) and 205 (Model 5 and Model 6). Control variables, Industry and Exchange, are included in Model 4, 5, and 6. Control variable, Geographic Region, is included in Model 5 and 6.
* $p < .05$. ** $p < .01$. *** $p < .001$.

high uncertainty by having less managerial ownership dilution. Model 5 shows that an international firm's home country political risk is positively related to international IPO underpricing, supporting Hypothesis 3. Whether or not the

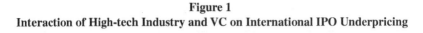

Figure 1
Interaction of High-tech Industry and VC on International IPO Underpricing

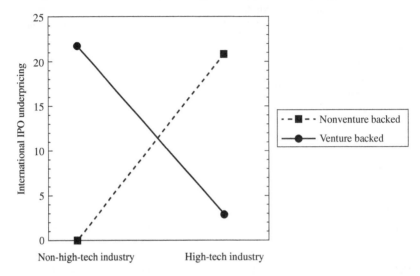

firm is in the high-technology sector is not significantly related to international IPO underpricing in Model 5. Hypothesis 4a is not supported. Hypothesis 4b is supported in Model 6 of Table 4 and portrayed in Figure 1. The interaction term of high-tech industry and VC is significantly negative, indicating that venture capitalists have a moderating effect in regard to the relationship between high-tech industry and IPO underpricing. Furthermore, Figure 1 illustrates that high-tech industry has opposite effects on international IPO underpricing among VC-backed firms and non-VC-backed firms, which explains why the variable of high-tech industry is not significant in Model 5.

It is difficult in many strategy data sets to find instrumental variables that affect strategy choice but not performance (Hamilton & Nickerson, 2003). Instrumental variables should be predetermined to control for the endogenous choice of firms (Liang, 2015) and satisfy two requirements: it should be correlated with the endogenous variable and orthogonal to the error process (Baum, Schaffer, & Stillman, 2003). We used STATA's ivreg2 command, which utilizes Kleibergen-Paap and Anderson-Rubin tests for weak instruments and tested that the instrumental variable is valid and relevant (Baum, Schaffer, & Stillman, 2007).

Studies have tried to control for firm capital structure using ratios of firm assets and debts. Controlling for the ratio of firm assets and debts instead of including firm assets and debts variables does not change the results of our findings.

Discussion

Our study of international IPOs from country-, industry-, and firm-level provides an extensive view of corporate governance. Rediker and Seth (1995) criticize the single-level analysis of corporate governance and propose how different governance mechanisms may interact with each other. We extend previous research that mainly focuses on a single viewpoint of corporate governance by studying international IPOs from multiple levels. Our findings regarding the impact of home country on firm-level governance structures and of venture capitalist on industry-level risks support the interaction of different governance factors and enrich research on corporate governance from various perspectives.

There are signals at the country-level and industry-level that affect the valuation of international IPOs. Home country political risk and industry risk create uncertainty in future firm performance. Both risks are embedded in the international firms' environments. Investors bear these risks by requiring a premium (manifested as underpricing) to invest in firms with high country-level and industry-level risks. We find that risks associated with high-tech industry may be reduced when the IPO firms are backed by venture capitalists. Venture capitalists provide corporate governance mechanisms that increase the quality of management (Van den Berghe, 2002), thus affecting the relationship between industry risk and IPO valuation.

Implications for Management

Earlier research on governance mechanisms and their effect on IPO ignored the endogeneity problem inherent when firms self-select governance mechanisms (Beatty & Zajac, 1994; Filatotchev & Bishop, 2002). Our study finds that an IPO firm adopts certain governance mechanisms and signal to prospective investors. These results explain the incentives behind international IPO managers' choices of governance mechanisms and the associated consequences. Our findings refute the view that international firms are more underpriced than US firms. We confirm that managers of international firms can employ governance mechanisms that affect the perception of uncertainty related to international IPOs.

The positive relationship between managerial ownership dilution and underpricing suggests that higher managerial ownership dilution signals higher risk to the market. When managers choose to maintain their ownership during an IPO, they signal high firm quality and aligned interests with potential investors. Managers of international firms may adopt this corporate governance mechanism to compensate for the inherent uncertainty associated with international IPOs.

International firms from culturally distant countries compensate for the liability of foreignness through firm-level practices. Our study validates the interplay of country characteristics and firm strategies. Managers of international firms from culturally distant countries may adjust firm strategies accordingly to signal their values and interests in a foreign country. Our findings provide guidance to managers of international firms by demonstrating how managers may respond to prevailing country factors and signal their firm value to potential investors.

Limitations

Some international firms were excluded in our sample due to missing information. We compared the omitted data with our sample and found no serious bias, although omission of data limits our sample size. We have a relatively smaller dataset from 1992 to 2005. Similar research using larger datasets may provide robust tests of our hypotheses and results.

Although a large number of control variables were included in our analysis, a dataset with more firm information may provide additional understanding of the IPO firms. The age of firms may signal information to potential investors. Previous studies on international IPO found that information of international firm age may be difficult to obtain (Chaplinsky & Ramchand, 2000). Controlling for firm age significantly reduces our data size due to the missing data of international firms, hence firm age is not included in the control variables.

Alternatives to Kogut and Singh's cultural distance may be considered, such as Ronen and Shenkar (1985)'s "cultural blocs." Since our present study controls for geographic areas of the foreign firms, using Ronen and Shenkar's cultural blocs measure would result in too many dummy variables, leading to multicollinearity.

Directions for Future Research

In addition to managerial ownership structure change, there are other firm-level governance mechanisms that may affect uncertainty and information asymmetry associated with international IPOs. Future research that includes more firm-level governance mechanisms, such as selection of underwriters and structure of board of directors, will further our understanding of how firms self-select corporate governance mechanisms and how this affects the valuation of an IPO. Future research that implements alternative measures of cultural distance may also provide detailed insight into a given country's effect on managerial decisions.

References

Agarwal, S., & Ramaswami, S. (1992). Choice of foreign market entry mode: Impact of ownership, location and internalization factors. *Journal of International Business Studies, 23*, 1–27.

Anderson, E., & Gatingnon, H. (1986). Modes of foreign entry: A transactions cost analysis and propositions. *Journal of International Business Studies*, *17*, 1–26.

Baum, C. F., Schaffer, M. E., & Stillman, S. (2003). Instrumental variables and GMM: estimation and testing. *Stata Journal*, *3*, 1–31.

Baum, C. F., Schaffer, M. E., & Stillman, S. (2007). Enhanced routines for instrumental variables/gneralized method of moments estimation and testing. *Stata Journal*, 7, 465–506.

Beatty, R. P., & Zajac, E. J. (1994). Managerial incentives, monitoring, and risk bearing: A study of executive compensation, ownership, and board structure in initial public offerings. *Administrative Science Quarterly*, *39*, 313–335.

Bell, G. R., Moore, C. B. & Al-Shammari, H. A. (2008). Country of origin and foreign ipo legitimacy: understanding the role of geographic scope and insider ownership. *Entrepreneurship Theory and Practice*, *32*, 185–202.

Boulton, T. J., S. B. Smart, & C. J. Zutter 2010. IPO Underpricing and International Corporate Governance. *Journal of International Business Studies*, *41*, 206–222.

Brewer, T. (1993). Government policies, market imperfections, and foreign direct investment. *Journal of International Business Studies*, *24*, 101–120.

Burgman, T. A. (1996). An empirical examination of multinational corporate capital structure. *Journal of International Business Studies*, *27*, 553–570.

Butler, C., & Joaquin, C. (1998). A note on political risk and the required return on foreign direct investment. *Journal of International Business Studies*, *29*, 599–607.

Carpenter, M. A., Pollock, T. G., & Leary, M. M. (2003). Testing a model of reasoned risk-taking: governance, the experience of principals and agents, and global strategy in high-technology IPO firms. *Strategic Management Journal*, *24*, 803–820.

Carter, R., & Manaster, S. (1990). Initial public offerings and underwriter reputation. *Journal of Finance*, *45*, 1045–1067.

Certo, S. T., Covin, J. G., Daily, C. M., & Dalton, D. R. (2001). Wealth and the effects of founder management among IPO-stage new ventures. *Strategic Management Journal*, *22*, 641–658.

Chaplinsky, S., & Ramchand, L. (2000). The impact of global equity offerings. *Journal of Finance*, *55*, 2767–2789.

Cohen, B. D., & Dean, T. J. (2005). Information asymmetry and investor valuation of IPOs: Top management team legitimacy as a capital market signal. *Strategic Management Journal*, *26*, 683–690.

Daily, C. M., Certo, S. T., & Dalton, D. R. (2003). Investment bankers and IPO pricing: does prospectus information matter? *Journal of Business Venturing*, *20*, 93–111.

Downes, D. H., & Heinkel, R. (1982). Signaling and the Valuation of Unseasoned New Issues. *Journal of Finance*, *37*, 1–10.

Dunning, J. H. (1998). Location and the multinational enterprise: A neglected factor? *Journal of International Business Studies*, *29*, 45–66.

Erramilli, M. K. (1996). Nationality and subsidiary ownership patterns in multinational corporations. *Journal of International Business Studies*, *27*, 225–248.

Espenlaub, S., Goergen, M., & Khurshed, A. (2001). IPO lock-in agreements in the UK. *Journal of Business Finance and Accounting*, *28*, 1235–1278.

Filatotchev, I., & Bishop, K. (2002). Board composition, share ownersip, and "underpricing" of U.K. IPO firms. *Strategic Management Journal*, *23*, 941–955.

Fitza, M., Matusik, S. F., & Elaine, M. (2009). Do VCs matter? The importance of owners on performance variance in start-up firms. *Strategic Management Journal*, *30*, 387–404.

Foerster, S. R., & Karolyi, G. A. (1993). International listings of stocks: The case of Canada and the U.S. *Journal of International Business Studies*, *24*, 763–784.

Fried, V. H., Burton, G., & Hisrich, R. (1998). Strategy and the Board of Directors in Venture Capital-Backed Firms. *Journal of Business Venturing, 13*, 496–503.

Ghoshal, S. (1987). Global strategy: An organizing framework. *Strategic Management Journal, 8*, 425–440.

Greene, W. H. (1997). *Econometric Analysis*. Upper Saddle River, NJ: Prentice Hall.

Guay, W. (1999). The sensitivity of CEO wealth to equity risk: An analysis of the magnitude and determinants. *Journal of Financial Economics, 53*, 43–71.

Gulati, R., & Higgins, M. C. (2003). Which ties matter when? the contingent effects of interorganizational partnerships on IPO success. *Strategic Management Journal, 24*, 127.

Hambrick, D. C., & Mason, P. A. (1984). Upper echelons: the organization as a reflection of its top managers. *Academy of Management Review, 9*, 193–206.

Hamilton, B. A., & Nickerson, J. A. (2003). Correcting for Endogeneity in Strategic Management Research. *Strategic Organization, 1* (1), 51–78.

Henisz, W. J. (2000). The institutional environment for economic growth. *Economics & Politics, 12* (1), 1–31.

Hennart, J. F., & Larimo, J. (1998). The impact of culture on the strategy of multinational enterprises: Does national origin affect ownership decisions? *Journal of International Business Studies, 29*, 515–538.

Hermalin, B. E., & Weisbach, M. S. (2003). Boards of directors as an endogenously determined institution: A survey of the economic literature. *Economic Policy Review 9* (1), 7–26.

Higgins, M. C., & Gulati, R. (2003). Getting off to a good start: The effects of upper echelon affiliations on underwriter prestige. *Organization Science, 14*, 244–263.

Higgins, M. C., & Gulati, R. (2006). Stacking the deck: The effects of top management backgrounds on shareholder decisions. *Strategic Management Journal, 27*, 1–25.

Hoetker, G., & Mellewigt, T. (2009). Choice and performance of governance mechanisms: matching alliance governance to asset type. *Strategic Management Journal, 30*, 1025–1044.

Hsu, D. H., & Ziedonis, R. H. (2013). Resources as dual sources of advantage: Implications for valuing entrepreneurial-firm patents. *Strategic Management Journal, 34*, 761–781.

Hymer, S. H. (1976). *The international operations of national firms: A study of direct foreign investment*. Cambridge, MA: MIT.

Iyengar, R. J., & Zampelli, E. M. (2009). Self-selection, endogeneity, and the relationship between ceo duality and firm performance. *Strategic Management Journal, 30*, 1092–1112.

Jensen, M. C., & Meckling, W. F. (1976). Theory of the firm: Managerial behavior, agency costs, and ownership structure. *Journal of Financial Economics, 3*, 305–360.

Kadiyala, P., & Subrahmanyam, A. (2002). Foreign firms issuing equity on us exchanges: an empirical investigation of IPOs and SEOs. *International Review of Finance, 3*, 27–51.

Kobrin, S. (1979). Political risk: A review and reconsideration. *Journal of International Business Studies, 10*, 67–80.

Kogut, B. (1989). A note on global strategies. *Strategic Management Journal, 10*, 383–389.

Kogut, B., & Singh, H. (1988). The effect of national culture on the choice of entry mode. *Journal of International Business Studies, 19*, 411–432.

La Porta, R., Lopez-de-Silanes, F., & Shleifer, A. (1999). Corporate ownership around the world. *Journal of Finance, 54*, 471–518.

Larraza–Kintana, M., Wiersema, R. M., Gomez-Mejia, L. R., & Welbourne, T. M. (2007). Disentangling compensation and employment risks using the behavioral agency model. *Strategic Management Journal, 28*, 1001–1019.

Leland, H., & Pyle, D. (1977). Information asymmetries, financial structure, and financial intermediation. *Journal of Finance, 32*, 371–387.

Lesmond, D. A. (2005). Liquidity of emerging markets. *Journal of Financial Economics, 77*, 411–452.

Liang, F. (2015). Does foreign direct investment harm the host country's environment? Evidence from China. *Current Topics of Management, 17*, 105–121.

Mark, Y. T., & Y. Li 2001. Determinants of Corporate Ownership and Board Structure: Evidence from Singapore. *Journal of Corporate Finance, 7*, 235–256.

Moore, C. B., Payne, T. G., Bell, G. R., & Davis, J. L. (2015). Institutional distance and cross-border venture capital investment flows. *Journal of Small Business Management, 53*, 482–500.

Payne, T. G., Moore, C. B., Bell, G. R., & Zachary, M. A. (2013). Signaling organizational virtue: An examination of virtue rhetoric, country-level corruption, and performance of foreign IPOs from emerging and developed economies. *Strategic Management Journal, 7*, 230–251.

Peng, M. W. (2004). Outside directors and firm performance during institutional transitions. *Strategic Management Journal, 25*, 453–471.

Rediker, K. J., & Seth, A. (1995). Boards of directors and substitution effects of alternative governance mechanisms. *Strategic Management Journal, 16*, 85–99.

Reuer, J., Shenkar, O. & Ragozzino, R. (2004). Mitigating risk in international mergers and acquisitions: The role of contingent payouts. *Journal of International Business Studies, 35*(1), 19–32.

Ritter, J. R. (1984). The hot issue market of 1980. *Journal of Business, 57*, 215–240.

Rock, K. (1986). Why new issues are underpriced. *Journal of Financial Economics, 15*, 187–212.

Roll, R. (1986). The hubris hypothesis of corporate takeovers. *Journal of Business, 59*, 197–216.

Ronen, S., & Shenkar, O. (1985). Clustering countries on attitudinal dimensions: A review and synthesis. *Academy of Management Review, 10*, 435–454.

Roth, K., & O'Donnell, S. (1996). Foreign subsidiary compensation: An agency theory perspective. *Academy of Management Journal, 3*, 678–703.

Roth, M., & Romeo, J. (1992). Matching product category and country image perceptions: a framework for managing country of origin effects. *Journal of International Business Studies, 23*, 477–498.

Sanders, W. M. G., & Boivie, S. (2004). Sorting things out: valuation of new firms in uncertain markets. *Strategic Management Journal, 25*, 167–186.

Smith, C., & Stulz, R. M. (1985). The determinants of firms' hedging policies. *Journal of Financial and Quantitative Analysis, 20*, 391–406.

Spence, M. (1973). Job market signalling. *Quarterly Journal of Economics, 87*, 355–374.

Stulz, R. M. (1990). Managerial discretion and optimal financing policies. *Journal of Financial Economics, 26*, 3–27.

Stulz, R. M. (1999). Globalization, corporate finance, and the cost of capital. *Journal of Applied Corporate Finance, 12*, 8–25.

Sundaramurthy, C., Pukthuanthong, K. & Kor, Y. (2014). Positive and negative synergies between the CEO's and the corporate board's human and social capital: A study of biotechnology firms. *Strategic Management Journal, 35*, 845–868.

Van den Berghe, L. (2002). The Role of Venture Capitalist as Monitor of the Company: A Corporate Governance Perspective. *Corporate Governance: An International Review, 10*, 124–135.

Wiseman, R. M., & Gomez-Mejia, L. R. (1998). A behavioral agency model of managerial risk taking. *Academy of Management Review*, *23*, 133–153.

Zaheer, S. (1995). Overcoming the liability of foreignness. *Academy of Management Journal*, *38*(2), 341–363.

Zajac, E. J., & Westphal, J. D. (2004). The social construction of market value: institutionalization and learning perspectives on stock market reactions. *American Sociological Review*, *69*, 433–457.

Zhang, Y., & Wiersema, M. F. (2009). Stock market reaction to CEO certification: The signaling role of CEO background. *Strategic Management Journal*, *30*, 693–710.

Biographical Notes

Dr. Yi Karnes is an associate professor of management at California State University, East Bay. She received PhD in Strategy and International Business from the Ohio State University. She has published in journals such as *Journal of International Business Studies, Journal of Management Studies, Journal of World Business* and *Asia Pacific Journal of Management*. Her research and teaching interests are in the areas of international business and strategic management. (yi.karnes@csueastbay.edu)

Dr. Mona Makhija is a professor of management and human resources at the Fisher College of Business, Ohio State University. She has published in journals such as *Academy of Management Review, Strategic Management Journal, Journal of International Business Studies,* and *Organization Science.* She has presented her research at top academic and professional meetings and teaches courses in international business, international strategy, and institutions. (makhija.2@osu.edu)

Dr. Mike W. Peng is a professor of organizations, strategy and international management at the University of Texas at Dallas. He has published in journals such as *Academy of Management Review, Journal of Management Studies, Strategic Management Journal, Journal of International Business Studies,* and *Journal of World Business.* His area of research expertise is global strategy, international business, competition in emerging economies, and institution-based view. (mikepeng@utdallas.edu)

Accepted after three revisions: August 15, 2015

Current Topics in Management, Vol. 18, 2016, pp. 81–100

THE ROLE OF STATUS IN IMITATIVE BEHAVIOR: THE INFLUENCE OF ALL-AMERICAN SECURITY ANALYSTS ON THEIR PEERS

Joshua S. Hernsberger
Western Kentucky University

M. Shane Spiller
Western Kentucky University

Imitation is a common response to decision making under uncertainty, but what explains which actors are likely to be imitated? Prior research has focused on observable economic attributes, and has given far less attention to the role of status in imitation. The social hierarchical nature of status makes it especially relevant to understanding imitative behavior. Individuals who desire the approval and respect of their peers, and who are anxious not to diminish their own social standing, may be more likely to imitate those they perceive as having prestige. We look at the case of security analysts, who face uncertainty and ambiguity in making their earnings forecasts and stock recommendations. We propose that because they are concerned about how they are evaluated by others within the investment community, security analysts are likely to imitate their high-status peers – those certified by *Institutional Investor's* All-America Research Team. We find that the recommendations issued by All-American analysts lead to subsequent changes in the stock recommendations issued by other analysts, and that this effect is moderated by the analyst's firm-specific experience. Our study provides insight into the role of status in imitative behavior at the individual level and suggests that distinctions between individuals based on perceived prestige influence decision making under uncertainty.

Keywords: decision-making, imitation, status, security analysts

Management scholars have shown great interest in understanding imitation since it has been found to be a common response to decision making under uncertainty (Lieberman & Asaba, 2006). Because individuals are boundedly rational and lack complete information (Cyert & March, 1963; Milliken, 1987), they "cannot assess connections between actions and outcomes with great confidence" (Lieberman & Asaba, 2006, p. 368), and as a result imitate the behavior of others. Consequently, when faced with conditions of uncertainty, managers look to others to ascertain the right course of action. Researchers posit that an actor's observable attributes, as well as assessments from others, are used in evaluating the appropriateness of the actor's behavior (Bikhchandani, Hirshleifer, & Welch, 1992; Dimaggio & Powell, 1983). Thus, researchers argue that actors are likely to be imitated when they have observable signals of expertise, power, or legitimacy (Bikhchandani, Hirshleifer, & Welch, 1998; Deephouse, 1996; Dimaggio & Powell, 1983). Empirical research has largely focused on objective characteristics of the firm that managers are associated with when examining imitation. This research has generally found that firm size, and firm profitability, are positively associated with imitation (Han, 1994; Haunschild & Miner, 1997). Managers from large and/or profitable firms are likely to be imitated by their peers in smaller and/or less profitable firms. Although this prior research has proved insightful in the role of objective firm-level factors in imitation, we know little about how a manager's personal, subjective attributes influence imitation.

This study seeks to address the gap in our understanding of imitation by focusing on one particular subjective attribute, a manager's status, and the role it plays in imitation, since "status issues permeate social and organizational life" (Chen, Peterson, Phillips, Podolny, & Ridgeway, 2012, p. 299), and thus it is likely to be an important factor in managerial decision making under uncertainty. Our understanding of the role of status in imitation is quite limited. The results from extant empirical research on status and imitation have been inconclusive. Although most studies hypothesize a positive relationship between status and imitation (i.e., those with higher status are more likely to be imitated), several studies have found that status is not statistically related to imitation (e.g., Rao, Greve, & Davis, 2001; Soda, Zaheer, & Carlone, 2008), or is negatively related to imitation (e.g., Kraatz & Zajac, 1996). Furthermore, several papers have not operationalized status appropriately, but instead have relied on observable characteristics such as firm size or its network centrality to confer status (Davis & Greve, 1997; Han, 1994). These are not appropriate indicators (Pearce, 2011) since status exists in the context of a social hierarchy where one's ranking is determined by "the amount of esteem, respect, or approval" granted by others (Goode, 1978, p. 7), which is based on the aggregation of many subjective and objective factors (Lynn, Podolny, & Powell, 2009). Further confusion exists because many of the studies examining imitation (e.g., Haunschild & Miner, 1997) utilize traits such as firm size and success but do not claim to show that high-status actors are imitated. Unfortunately these studies are later interpreted as providing evidence that there is "imitation of prestigious firms" (Still & Strang, 2009, p. 65), and that "high status actors tend to be targets of imitation" (Wry, Lounsbury, & Greenwood, 2011, p. 155), and "that as high status actors adopt a behavior others follow suit" (Rao et al., 2001, p. 507). In summary, we lack an understanding of the role that status plays in imitation due to (1) inconclusive empirical findings; (2) inappropriate operationalization of the concept of status; and (3) misinterpretations of extant findings.

In this study, we propose that status plays an important role in imitation because of the influence that an individual's position in a social hierarchy can have on others in the social group, as well as on stakeholders within the broader social context. Since high-status individuals are afforded respect and esteem, and are perceived to be competent, they serve as a key referent in the "assessments of others" (Belliveau, O'Reilly, & Wade, 1996, p. 1572). In addition, high-status individuals may benefit from being perceived as having legitimacy, which is known to lead to imitation. Given that individuals are "deeply concerned with social evaluation and esteem" (Chen et al., 2012, p. 299), the socially constructed determination of status makes it especially relevant to understanding imitative behavior.

In this study, we extend our understanding of decision making under uncertainty by examining the role of status in imitative behavior. In examining the role of status in imitative behavior, we focused on security analysts, who are employed by investment banks and brokerage houses to issue earnings forecasts and stock recommendations on companies. Analysts face a complex task because of the uncertainty surrounding the factors that affect a firm's future performance (Zhang, 2006). Analyst stock recommendations are made throughout the year, and are highly visible and observable since they are disseminated to clients and available through the *Institutional Brokers' Estimate System* (IBES) dataset. Because analyst forecasts and recommendations are widely known to other security analysts and throughout the investment community, analysts are concerned about making accurate forecasts (Hong, Kubik, & Solomon, 2000; Welch, 2000). The uncertainty associated with forecasting a firm's earnings and concerns over accuracy provide an environment likely to lead to imitation. In addition, status can be operationalized within this setting since *Institutional Investor* magazine provides an annual ranking of analysts in the industry. This certification contest is based on experts' subjective evaluations that are influenced by social factors, and is therefore likely to be highly indicative of an analyst's status (Phillips & Zuckerman, 2001). Thus, security analysts provide an appropriate context for examining whether status plays a role in imitation.

Our model, as shown in Figure 1, shows that, for a given firm, an analyst's stock recommendation is influenced by the recommendation made by a high-status (All-American) analyst. This relationship is moderated by the level of uncertainty concerning the firm's future performance, as well as by the number

Figure 1
Model: The Influence of All-American Security Analysts'
Stock Recommendation on Non-all-American Analysts' Stock Recommendations

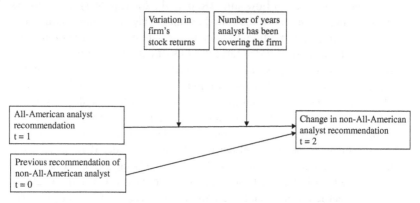

Note: At time t = 0 a non-All-American analyst issues a stock recommendation for a given firm. At time t = 1 an All-American stock analyst issues a recommendation for that firm. At time t = 2 the non-All-American issues a stock recommendation, which has been influenced by the All-American analyst's recommendation. In addition, because stock recommendations are bounded at the high end as well as the low end, the non-All-American's recommendation is influenced by his/her recommendation at t = 0.

of years the analyst has been covering the firm. In addition, due to the bounded scale used to classify stock recommendations, an analyst's recommendation will also be influenced by his/her previous recommendation.

Theory and Hypotheses Development

Status has been an important concept in the study of social science since the beginning of the 20th century, when Max Weber identified the privileges that accrue to high-status actors. Weber defines status as an "effective claim to social esteem in terms of positive or negative privileges" (Weber, 1978, p. 305), which occurs largely outside of the economic sphere. Sociologists interpret status as a prestige hierarchy and study it by comparing groups or individuals who are "ranked vis-à-vis one another on the basis of subjective evaluation" (Omodei, 1982, p. 196). Accordingly, in this paper, we define status as a hierarchical ranking of an actor based on the actor's prestige (Haug, 1977), where prestige is defined as a subjective evaluation based on "the amount of esteem, respect, or approval that is granted by an individual or group" (Goode, 1978, p. 7). Status enables comparison among actors, where a high-status actor is given more respect and deference than actors who rank lower on the social hierarchy (Anderson, John, Keltner, & Kring, 2001). This hierarchical definition is consistent with its utilization in both the sociology (e.g., Gould, 2002; Lynn et al.,

2009; Phillips & Zuckerman, 2001) and management literatures (e.g., Jensen, 2006; Jensen & Roy, 2008; Washington & Zajac, 2005).

Many researchers conflate an actor's status with their underlying capabilities (Washington & Zajac, 2005), and thus assume those actors with high status also have the greatest capabilities. However, an actor's status may not be indicative of the actor's underlying quality since status is based on a subjective evaluation of one's esteem, respect, or approval (Podolny, 1993, 2001). The social cues by which individuals are judged can amplify small differences in "observable individual qualities" into large differences in status (Gould, 2002, p. 1170), or entirely decouple an actor's status from the actor's underlying quality (Lynn et al., 2009). Consequently, an actor of low quality can have higher status than an actor of high quality. Indeed, there is a "long sociological tradition in asserting that an actor's status is often weakly related to her ability" (Phillips & Zuckerman, 2001, p. 9).

Since status is determined by position in a social hierarchy; it may deviate from a ranking based on objective characteristics (Pearce, 2011). For example, an individual's status in an organization can differ from his or her formal position in the organization (Pearce, 2011). Similarly, a firm's status is not a reflection of its size (Phillips & Zuckerman, 2001) or financial performance (Washington & Zajac, 2005). Accordingly, many researchers rely on subjective indicators of prestige to measure status, rather than objective criteria. For example, Podolny (1993) evaluates the status of investment banks by using a bank's relative position in tombstone advertisements for public offerings. He surmises that banks with high status are grouped in a higher bracket while those with lower status are grouped in a lower bracket. Managers at investment banks are "extremely conscious of the status ordering" (Podolny, 1993, p. 854) and banks have been known to withdraw from profitable deals when lower-status banks are placed above them (Podolny, 1993).

Another measurement approach looks at reputable third-party evaluations, such as certification contests in which "actors in a given domain are ranked based on performance criteria that are accepted by key stakeholders as being credible and legitimate" (Wade, Porac, Pollock, & Graffin, 2006, p. 644). Certification contests provide an indicator of status because the criteria chosen to evaluate performance "are themselves the outcomes of institutional processes" (Rao, 1994, p. 32). Most certification contests aggregate the evaluations of a group of experts into a single rank, and thus enable "summary comparisons of rated actors" (Wade et al., 2006, p. 644). In addition, because certification contests are generally well publicized, they can provide a useful indicator of the status hierarchy within a field, which may otherwise be unobservable (Graffin, Wade, Porac, & McNamee, 2008).

In this paper, we focus on security analysts in order to better understand the role of status in imitation. Security analysts are specialists who analyze the performance and future prospects of companies, and disseminate their evaluations to investors through the issuance of research reports and stock recommendations (Michaely & Womack, 1999). An important indicator of status within the security analyst community is *Institutional Investor*'s All-America Research Team (Hayward & Boeker, 1998; Westphal & Clement, 2008). The All-America Research Team is a list of analysts compiled annually by *Institutional Investor* from a survey that asks over 2,000 professional money managers, such as hedge fund managers and mutual fund managers, to rank analysts based on how helpful they were to the respondent over the previous year (Bagnoli, Watts, & Zhang, 2008; Groysberg, Lee, & Nanda, 2008). *Institutional Investor* uses the survey results to rank analysts first through third, as well as several honorable mentions, in various industry sectors, such as Chemicals/Commodity and Packaging.

The All-America Research Team can be considered a certification contest that measures status because it is based on experts' subjective evaluations, not objective measures (Groysberg & Lee, 2008), and because it aggregates the opinions of multiple experts into a single hierarchical ranking. These types of certification contests are strongly influenced by social factors, such as the perceived respect and esteem that is afforded an actor by others, and are thus likely to be highly indicative of an actor's status (Wade et al., 2006). Empirical research has shown that the All-America Research Team differs significantly from rankings based on objective measures of past performance, such as *The Wall Street Journal's* Best on the Street, an annual ranking of analysts based on the profitability of their stock recommendations (formerly known as All-Star Analysts) (Emery & Li, 2009). These differences indicate that social factors play a large role in the All-America Research Team rankings (Emery & Li, 2009). Consequently, the All-America Research Team provides a measure that can be used to ascertain status among security analysts not directly indicative of underlying abilities (Groysberg & Lee, 2010; Phillips & Zuckerman, 2001).

Given the uncertainty associated with making earnings forecasts and stock recommendations, and given that analysts are concerned about how they are evaluated by various stakeholders within the investment community, we propose that analysts are likely to imitate their high-status peers—All-American analysts. Owing to their high status, All-American analysts are afforded greater respect and esteem (Emery & Li, 2009), which sets them apart from others (Devers, Dewett, Mishina, & Belsito, 2009). This distinction means that the stock recommendations issued by All-American analysts for a given firm are likely to influence how the stock recommendations issued by other analysts within the industry sector are likely to be assessed. We know from prior research that investors and employers rate the performance of an analyst relative to other analysts within the industry sector, and not on an absolute scale (Hong & Kubik, 2003). As a result, analysts are highly sensitive to how their recommendations compare to those of their peers. For example, in advising investors on asset allocation, analysts in charge of investment newsletters have been found to imitate the asset allocation recommendations made by the *Value Line* newsletter, the market leader of newsletters (Graham, 1999). Analysts at *Value Line* influence other analysts because investors use *Value Line* recommendations "as a benchmark against which they compare the advice of other newsletters" (Graham, 1999, p. 250). These findings, that analysts are likely to imitate the market leader, provide support for a status model of imitation.

Because high-status individuals serve as an important source of comparison that serves as the basis for how others within the broader context are likely to assess individuals within the group, status is likely to play an important role in imitation. By imitating their high-status peers, analysts diminish the risk of deviating from recommendations made by analysts who are highly esteemed in their industry sector, and thus appearing out of line. Moreover, in highly uncertain environments, the quest for legitimacy can serve as a motivating factor for imitation. Legitimacy is a "social judgment of appropriateness, acceptance, and/ or desirability" (Zimmerman & Zeitz, 2002, p. 416). Accordingly, legitimacy evaluations are based on social justification using normative rationality, which differs from justification based on economic rationality (Oliver, 1997). Security analysts are embedded in a social world (Fogarty & Rogers, 2005), and rely on social approval from executives of the firms they provide coverage for, investors who rely on their reports and stock recommendations, and other analysts (Groysberg & Lee, 2008, 2010; Westphal & Clement, 2008). All-American analysts have high social approval, and their legitimacy is generally unquestioned (Phillips & Zuckerman, 2001). Since legitimate actors are perceived as making appropriate decisions (Suchman, 1995), analysts seeking to appear legitimate will imitate the behavior of these legitimate actors. This process of "mimetic isomorphism can be viewed as rational imitation" (Lieberman & Asaba, 2006, p. 372). Thus, we propose that concerns over how they will be evaluated by others, and the impact that these assessments may have on their careers, can lead non-All-American analysts to imitate their high-status peers, the All-American analysts.

Hypothesis 1: *All-American analyst stock recommendations will be positively related to changes in the stock recommendations subsequently issued by other analysts for a given firm.*

The Moderating Role of Uncertainty

The job of a security analyst is more difficult when the firm's industry is characterized by greater instability and dynamism. Analysts may be unsure how to model the future performance of firms in industries that are undergoing discontinuous technological change (Beunza & Garud, 2007). In addition, broader economic factors as well as changes in buyer behavior and preferences can have a significant impact on a firm's business model, in turn leading to greater uncertainty about a firm's future prospects.

Firms differ in the amount of information they provide to analysts concerning their future performance, which can significantly impact analysts' forecasts of future performance. For example, firms differ in whether they provide earnings guidance prior to their filing of financial documents with the SEC. Firms that do release guidance about their future prospects provide analysts and investors with additional information, which decreases the uncertainty associated with forecasting a firm's future performance (Cotter, Tuna, & Wysocki, 2006). There is also considerable variation among firms in the information disclosed in their financial statements (Lang & Lundholm, 1996). Given that imitation is influenced by the degree of uncertainty (Lieberman & Asaba, 2006), we propose that the greater uncertainty analysts have about the future prospects of the firm, either due to the nature of the industry or to the amount of information provided by the firm, the more likely they will be to imitate the stock recommendations made by their high-status peers.

Hypothesis 2: *The effect of All-American analyst stock recommendations on changes in the stock recommendations subsequently issued by other analysts is greater when there is more uncertainty associated with the future performance of a given firm.*

The Moderating Role of Analyst Experience

Analysts are not able to incorporate all of the available information about a firm in their earnings forecasts and stock recommendations (Abarbanell & Bushee, 1997) because the information may be difficult and time consuming to interpret (Maines, McDaniel, & Harris, 1997; Plumlee, 2003). However, the longer an analyst has been covering a firm, the more adept he/she becomes in analyzing the future prospects of the firm (Mikhail, Walther, & Willis, 1997), since firms have idiosyncratic characteristics that can be learned only through experience providing coverage for that specific firm (Clement, 1999). Moreover, analysts with greater experience covering the firm are likely to be more efficient at finding relevant information about the firm and its industry, have greater access to firm insiders, and have a better understanding of the factors that influence the firm's future earnings (Clement, 1999; Mikhail et al., 1997). As a result, an analyst's experience analyzing a particular firm reduces the uncertainty associated with forecasting the firm's future prospects, giving the analyst greater confidence in his/her stock recommendations. In turn, the analyst becomes less likely to be influenced by the recommendations issued by high-status analysts for a given firm.

Hypothesis 3: *The effect of All-American stock recommendations on the change in the stock recommendation subsequently issued by other analysts is less when the analyst has more experience covering a given firm.*

Method

Sample

To test our hypotheses, we identified a sample of firms that have coverage by one or more All-American analyst as listed in *Institutional Investor's* All-America Research Team in 2004. For 2004, 333 different analysts in 70 different industry sectors were identified as All-American analysts. We were able to identify 260 of the 333 All-American analysts in the IBES database. The sample consists of the 1,070 firms for which an All-American analyst issued a stock recommendation in 2005.

For the sample of 1,070 firms with All-American analyst coverage, we collected all stock recommendations issued by other analysts (those not listed on the 2004 All-America Research Team). To capture a change in a given analyst's recommendation, each analyst had to have at least two research reports for a given firm—one issued prior to and one after the issuance of an All-American analyst research report for a given firm. The elimination of analysts with only one research report resulted in a final sample of 617 firms.

The final sample includes a paired set of 2,078 stock recommendations (2 recommendations per analyst per firm for a total of 4,156 stock recommendations) issued by 959 analysts for 617 firms. Consistent with prior research (e.g., Welch 2000), our sample of stock recommendations included more strong buy-and-buy recommendations (1,858) than sell-and-underperform recommendations.

Dependent Variable

Change in Analyst Recommendation. Analyst recommendation data was collected from the IBES database that uses a 5-point scale, from 1 (strong buy) to 5 (sell), to code analyst recommendations. To make the measure more intuitive, we reverse coded the recommendations so that 5 represents a Strong Buy, whereas 1 represents a Sell. A change in analyst recommendations is calculated by subtracting the initial analyst recommendation (issued prior to the All-American analyst recommendation) from the recommendation made after the All-American analyst recommendation. Thus, a 0 value would indicate no change occurred in the analyst stock recommendation, while a positive value indicates a more favorable stock recommendation, and a negative value indicates a less favorable stock recommendation. For our sample, the change in analyst recommendation has a mean of .02, with a range of -4 to $+4$.

Independent Variables

All-American Analyst Recommendation. For each of the 2,078 pairs of analyst recommendations, we identified one All-American analyst recommendation that served as the explanatory variable. Given that some firms have coverage by multiple All-American analysts, we utilized the most recent All-American recommendation, since research has shown that the most recent recommendation has more influence on analysts than other recommendations (Welch 2000). For our sample, the All-American analyst recommendation has a mean of 3.26, with a range of 1–5.

Variation in Stock Return. In order to capture the uncertainty surrounding a firm's future performance we used the standard deviation of a firm's excess stock returns, defined as the difference between a firm's stock returns and a value-weighted market return (Lim, 2001; Zhang, 2006). The standard deviation in a firm's excess stock returns is a measure of information uncertainty that captures the "ambiguity with respect to the implications of new information for a firm's value, which potentially stems from two sources: the volatility of a firm's underlying fundamentals and poor information" (Zhang, 2006, p. 105). Thus, the standard deviation in a firm's excess stock returns captures both external and internal sources of uncertainty in the firm's future earnings. We follow Zhang (2006) and utilize the standard deviation of a firm's *weekly* excess stock returns over the firm's prior quarter to measure the variation in a firm's stock return. We collected the excess stock return data from the *Center for Research in Security Prices* (CRSP) *Daily Stock* database. For our sample, variation in stock return has a mean of .04 with a range of 0–.12.

Years Covering the Firm Years covering the firm capture the amount of experience that an analyst has in providing coverage for a given firm up to 2005. In our sample, the variable years covering the firm has a mean of 2.81 with a range of 0–12.

Control Variables

Firm Size. Research has shown that a firm's size can affect an analyst's recommendations because larger firms may be able to influence an analyst's employer (Westphal & Clement, 2008). We measured firm size as the logarithm of the firm's total sales in 2004, which ranged from $15.94 million to $26.38 million, with a mean of $21.92 million.

Firm Performance. By controlling for firm performance, the models include the effect that the firm's quarterly performance may have on an analyst's stock recommendation (Biggs, 1984). We measured firm performance as the firm's return on assets (ROA) in the quarter preceding the quarter in which the analyst issued a recommendation. In our sample, firm performance ranged from –.28 to .22, with a mean of .02.

Analyst Prior Recommendation. Research has shown that an analyst's stock recommendation for a firm is highly dependent on the analyst's prior recommendation (Welch, 2000). Analyst prior recommendation is the initial recommendation used in the calculation of the dependent variable, change in analyst recommendation. For our sample, analyst prior recommendation ranges from 1 to 5, with a mean of 3.50.

Analysis

In this study, we examined how All-American analyst recommendations may affect the change in recommendations issued by other security analysts. We estimated the change in analyst recommendation using ordinary least squares (OLS). Although the dependent variable, the change in analyst recommendation, is a categorical variable on an ordinal scale, OLS is the proper statistical technique to analyze the data because there are more than five categories (Menard, 2002).

The dependent measure, change in analyst recommendation, is a change measure that captures the difference in an analyst's stock recommendation for a given firm. Researchers have noted that change scores can be problematic because they exhibit a regression to the mean effect (Bergh & Fairbank, 2002; Cohen, Cohen, West, & Aiken, 2003). As a result, one would expect that a recommendation with a high value, such as a strong buy (5), would likely be followed by a recommendation with a lower value, such as a buy (4), and thus result in a negative value for the change in the analyst recommendation variable. In order to control for the regression to the mean effect, we included the analyst's prior recommendation as a control variable in the models.

Results

Table 1 presents the means, standard deviations, and correlations for the full dataset. Table 2 presents the multiple regression results for change in analyst recommendation, the dependent variable, regressed on the explanatory and control variables. Model 1 includes control variables only. As expected, the coefficient for analyst prior recommendation ($b = -1.00$, $p < .01$) is negative and statistically significant, which indicates that an analyst's prior recommendation influences change in analyst recommendation, which is consistent with the expectations of a regression to the mean effect. In our models, analyst prior recommendation captures all of the objective factors that are likely to influence the stock recommendation.

Model 2 includes the control variables, variation in stock returns, years covering the firm, and the explanatory variable, the All-American analyst recommendation. As shown in Model 2, the coefficient for All-American analyst recommendation is positive and statistically significant ($b = .08, p < .01$). These

Table 1

Descriptive Statistics and Correlations

Variable	Mean	SD	1	2	3	4	5	6	7
1. Change in analyst recommendation	.02	1.44	1.00						
2. Firm size	21.92	1.62	.04	1.00					
3. Firm performance	.02	.03	.03	.01	1.00				
4. Analyst prior recommendation	3.50	1.04	-.72	-.03	.06	1.00			
5. Variation in stock returns	.04	.02	-.03	-.51	-.02	-.01	1.00		
6. Years covering the firm	2.81	2.87	.03	.11	.00	.02	-.12	1.00	
7. All-American analyst recommendation	3.26	.83	.02	.01	.07	.04	-.05	.03	1.00

$N = 2078$. Correlations larger than .04 are significant at $p < .05$ level and those larger than .05 are significant $p < .01$ level.

Table 2
Results of Regression Analyses for Predicting
Change in Analyst Recommendation

Variable	Model 1	Model 2	Model 3
Constant	3.12**	3.22**	3.20**
	(.31)	(.39)	(.39)
Firm size	.01	.00	.00
	(.01)	(.02)	(.02)
Firm performance	3.79**	3.61**	3.64*
	(.84)	(.84)	(.84)
Analyst prior recommendation	−1.00**	−1.00**	−1.00**
	(.02)	(.02)	(.02)
Variation in stock returns		−1.82	−1.77
		(1.38)	(1.39)
Years covering the firm		.02*	.02*
		(.01)	(.01)
All-American analyst recommendation		.08**	.08**
		(.03)	(.03)
All-American analyst recommendation × Variation in stock returns			−.15
			(1.61)
All-American analyst recommendation × Years covering the firm			−.02*
			(.01)
Adjusted R^2	.52	.52	.52
ΔR^2		.004**	.001*
F-value	742.72**	377.07**	284.25**

Note: $N = 2078$ † $p < .10.$ * $p < .05.$ ** $p < .01.$
Standard errors are reported in parentheses.

results support Hypothesis 1, that All-American analyst stock recommendations will be positively related to changes in the stock recommendations subsequently issued by other analysts for a given firm.

Model 3 includes the interaction terms of All-American analyst recommendation and variation in stock returns, and All-American analyst recommendation and years covering the firm. The variables were mean–centered prior to the creation of the interaction term (Aiken & West, 1991). As shown in Model 3, the coefficient for the interaction term of All-American analyst recommendation and the variation in a firm's *weekly* stock returns is not statistically significant ($b = -2.00$, ns) . We also examined the moderating

Figure 2
Interaction of All-American Analyst Recommendation
and Years Covering the Firm

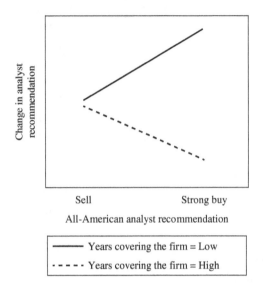

effect of the variation in a firm's *daily* and *quarterly* excess stock returns. The results were consistent, with no statistical significance. Thus, Hypothesis 2, that the effect of All-American analyst stock recommendations on changes in the stock recommendations subsequently issued by other analysts is greater when there is more uncertainty associated with the future performance of a given firm, is not supported.

As shown in Model 3 the coefficient for the interaction term of All-American analyst recommendation and years covering the firm is negative and statistically significant ($b = -.02$, $p < .01$). In order to more fully analyze the significance and direction of the moderating effect of years covering the firm, we analyzed the value and statistical significance of the explanatory variable's total effect at low (0) and high (5.5) values of the moderator variable (i.e., years covering the firm) using the variable's mean plus or minus one standard deviation (Aiken & West, 1991). As shown in Figure 2, when an analyst has no prior experience covering the firm (low value), the All-American analyst's recommendation has a positive and statistically significant influence on the analyst's recommendation ($b = .08$, $p < .01$). When an analyst has extensive experience (e.g., more than 5 years) covering the firm, the All-American analyst's recommendation has a negative and statistically significant influence ($b = -.06$, $p < .01$). These results provide support for Hypothesis 3, that the effect of All-American stock recommendations on the change in the stock recommendation subsequently issued by other analysts is less when the analyst has more experience covering a given firm.

Discussion

This study sought to understand the role of status in imitation under conditions of uncertainty. We investigated the role of status by examining security analysts, who face high levels of uncertainty in making their earnings forecasts and stock recommendations. We found that high-status analysts—those certified by *Institutional Investor's* All-America Research Team—do indeed influence their peers. Specifically, the stock recommendations made by All-American analysts for a given firm lead to subsequent changes in the stock recommendations issued by other analysts for that firm. In addition, we found that the influence of All-American analysts is moderated by experience. Analysts with more years of providing coverage for a given firm are less likely to be influenced by the recommendations issued by their high-status peers. Our findings indicate that as analysts develop expertise about specific firms, they are less likely to ignore their private information and imitate their high-status peers. We did not find evidence that the extent of uncertainty in predicting a firm's future earnings is a significant moderator of the influence of high-status analysts on their peers. We investigated the moderating role of uncertainty further by segregating the sample based on firm size, financial performance, and the amount of analyst coverage. This additional analysis revealed that, even accounting for differences in firm context, the extent of uncertainty about the future prospects of a firm did not moderate the influence that high-status analysts had on their peers.

This study provides greater clarity on both the concept of status and its role in imitation. Prior research findings that large and successful firms are imitated (e.g., Haunschild & Miner, 1997) have been interpreted as evidence that there is "imitation of prestigious firms" (Still & Strang, 2009, p. 65), that "high status actors tend to be targets of imitation" (Wry et al., 2011, p. 155), and "that as high status actors adopt a behavior others follow suit" (Rao et al., 2001, p. 507). However, since status is socially constructed, it may be unrelated to economic-based attributes such as size or financial performance (Gould, 2002; Lynn et al., 2009; Phillips & Zuckerman, 2001).

Implications for Management

Recent research has found that executives spend a great deal of time and resources trying to influence analysts (Westphal & Clement, 2008), as well as trying to make decisions that analysts will find appropriate (Benner & Ranganathan, 2012; Westphal & Graebner, 2010). Several studies have conjectured that high-status analysts may have more influence than their peers (Hayward & Boeker, 1998; Wiersema & Zhang, 2011), but this has not been tested empirically. This study, by differentiating between analysts, provides evidence that All-American analysts may indeed be more influential than their peers. Thus, on the basis of the results of this study, we suggest that executives focus their limited time and resources on high- status analysts (i.e., All-American analysts), since their assessments will have a significant impact on their colleagues.

Strengths and Limitations

One of the strengths of this study is the research setting. By focusing on security analysts, we were able to identify high-status actors using a socially constructed measure, which allowed us to clarify its role in imitative behavior under conditions of uncertainty. Furthermore, by examining imitative behavior at the individual rather than at the firm level, and by examining decisions that are made relatively frequently, this study contributes to the imitation literature by providing "a broader set of domains where imitation processes arise" (Lieberman & Asaba, 2006, p. 381).

As with all empirical research, this study has several limitations. It finds that high-status security analysts' stock recommendations are imitated by their peers. These stock recommendations are unambiguous, and thus it is not clear how low-status actors respond to their high-status peers in decisions that involve a great deal of ambiguity. In addition, the security analyst industry provides a clear demarcation of status. Analysts who have been designated by *Institutional Investor* as All-American analysts have high status, while other analysts do not. It is likely that in other industries status is more contested, and thus the results of this study may not be generalizable to those industries. Finally, this study relies on a single year of data, since All-American analysts are chosen annually. Future research may seek to examine what impact security analysts who have been selected as All-American analysts in multiple years have on their peers.

Directions for Future Research

Although we find evidence that high-status analysts can influence the recommendations issued by other security analysts, there may be other factors that are important to consider. Analysts who work at the top investment banks (e.g., Goldman Sachs, Morgan Stanley), or analysts who are frequently mentioned in the business press, may also have greater influence among their peers. As such, further work could benefit by accounting for variation in the reputation and prestige of analysts' employers and variation in analysts' visibility within the financial community.

References

Abarbanell, J. S., & Bushee, B. J. (1997). Fundamental analysis, future earnings, and stock prices. *Journal of Accounting Research, 35*, 1–24.

Aiken, L. S., & West, S. G. (1991). *Multiple regression: Testing and interpreting interactions*. Newbury Park, CA: Sage.

Anderson, C., John, O.P., D. Keltner, & Kring, A. M. (2001). Who attains social status? Effects of personality and physical attractiveness in social groups. *Journal of Personality and Social Psychology, 81*, 116–132.

Bagnoli, M., Watts, S. G., & Zhang, Y. (2008). Reg-FD and the competitiveness of all-star analysts. *Journal of Accounting and Public Policy, 27*, 295–316.

Belliveau, M. A., O'Reilly III, C. A., & Wade, J. B. (1996). Social capital at the top: effects of social similarity and status on CEO compensation. *Academy of Management Journal, 39*, 1568–1593.

Benner, M. J., & Ranganathan, R. (2012). Offsetting illegitimacy? How pressures from securities analysts influence incumbents in the face of new technologies. *Academy of Management Journal, 55*, 213–233.

Bergh, D. D., & Fairbank, J. F. (2002). Measuring and testing change in strategic management research. *Strategic Management Journal, 23*, 359–366.

Beunza, D., & Garud, R. (2007). Calculators, lemmings or frame-makers? The intermediary role of securities analysts. *Sociological Review, 55*, 13–39.

Biggs, S.F. (1984). Financial analysts' information search in the assessment of corporate earning power. *Accounting, Organizations and Society, 9*, 313–323.

Bikhchandani, S., Hirshleifer, D., & Welch, I. (1992). A theory of fads, fashion, custom, and cultural change as informational cascades. *Journal of Political Economy, 100*, 992–1026.

Bikhchandani, S., Hirshleifer, D., & Welch, I. (1998). Learning from the behavior of others: Conformity, fads and informational cascades. *Journal of Economic Perspectives, 12*, 151–170.

Chen, Y. R., Peterson, R. S., Phillips, D. J., Podolny, J. M., & Ridgeway, C. L. (2012). Introduction to the special issue: Bringing status to the table – attaining, maintaining, and experiencing status in organizations and markets. *Organization Science, 23*, 299–307.

Clement, M. B. (1999). Analyst forecast accuracy: Do ability, resources, and portfolio complexity matter? *Journal of Accounting and Economics, 27*, 285–303.

Cohen, J. C., Cohen, P., West, S. G., & Aiken, L. S. (2003). *Applied multiple regression/correlation analysis for the behavioral sciences*. Mahwah, NJ: Erlbaum.

Cotter, J., Tuna, I., & Wysocki, P. D. (2006). Expectations management and beatable targets: how do analysts react to explicit earnings guidance? *Contemporary Accounting Research, 23*, 593–624.

Cyert, R. M., & March, J. G. (1963). *A Behavioral theory of the firm*. Cambridge, MA: Wiley-Blackwell.

Davis, G. F., & Greve, H. R. (1997). Corporate elite networks and governance changes in the 1980s. *American Journal of Sociology, 103*, 1–37.

Deephouse, D. L. (1996). Does isomorphism legitimate? *Academy of Management Journal, 39*, 1024–1039.

Devers, C. E., Dewett, T., Mishina, Y., & Belsito, C. A. (2009). A general theory of organizational stigma. *Organization Science, 20*, 154–171.

Dimaggio, P. J., & Powell, W. W. (1983). The iron cage revisited: institutional isomorphism and collective rationality in organizational fields. *American Sociological Review, 48*, 147–160.

Emery, D. R., & Li, X. (2009). Are the Wall Street analyst rankings popularity contests? *Journal of Financial Quantitative Analysis, 44*, 411–437.

Fogarty, T. J., & Rogers, R. K. (2005). Financial analysts' reports: an extended institutional theory evaluation. *Accounting, Organizations and Society, 30*, 331–356.

Goode, W. J. (1978). *The celebration of heroes: prestige as a control system.* Berkeley, CA: University of California Press.

Gould, R. V. (2002). The origins of status hierarchies: a formal theory and empirical test. *American Journal of Sociology, 107*, 1143–1178.

Graffin, S. D., Wade, J. B., Porac, J. F., & McNamee, R. C. (2008). The impact of CEO status diffusion on the economic outcomes of other senior managers. *Organization Science, 19*, 457–474.

Graham, J. R. (1999). Herding among investment newsletters: Theory and evidence. *Journal of Finance, 54*, 237–268.

Groysberg, B., & Lee, L. (2008). The effect of colleague quality on top performance: The case of security analysts. *Journal of Organizational Behavior, 29*, 1123–1144.

Groysberg, B., & Lee, L. (2010). Star power: Colleague quality and turnover. *Industrial and Corporate Change, 19*, 741–765.

Groysberg, B., Lee, L., & Nanda, A. (2008). Can they take it with them? The portability of star knowledge workers' performance. *Management Science, 54*, 1213–1230.

Han, S. (1994). Mimetic isomorphism and its effect on the audit services market. *Social Forces, 73*, 637–640.

Haug, M. R. (1977). Measurement in social stratification. *Annual Review of Sociology, 3*, 51–77.

Haunschild, P. R., & Miner, A. S. (1997). Modes of interorganizational imitation: The effects of outcome salience and uncertainty. *Administrative Science Quarterly, 42*, 472–500.

Hayward, M. L. A., & Boeker, W. (1998). Power and conflicts of interest in professional firms: Evidence from investment banking. *Administrative Science Quarterly, 43*, 1–22.

Hong, H., & Kubik, J. D. (2003). Analyzing the analysts: career concerns and biased earnings forecasts. *Journal of Finance, 58*, 313–351.

Hong, H., Kubik, J. D., & Solomon, A. (2000). Security analysts' career concerns and herding of earnings forecasts. *RAND Journal of Economics, 31*, 121–144.

Jensen, M. (2006). Should we stay or should we go? Accountability, status anxiety, and client defections. *Administrative Science Quarterly, 51*, 97–128.

Jensen, M., & Roy, A. (2008). Staging exchange partner choices: When do status and reputation matter? *Academy of Management Journal, 51*, 495–516.

Kraatz, M. S., & Zajac, E. J. (1996). Exploring the limits of the new institutionalism: the causes and consequences of illegitimate organizational change. *American Sociological Review, 61*, 812–836.

Lang, M. H., & Lundholm, R. J., (1996). Corporate disclosure policy and analyst behavior. *Accounting Review, 71*, 467–492.

Lieberman, M. B., & Asaba, S. (2006). Why do firms imitate each other? *Academy of Management Review, 31*, 366–385.

Lim, T. (2001). Rationality and analysts' forecast bias. *Journal of Finance, 56*, 369–385.

Lynn, F. B., Podolny, J. M., & Tao, L. (2009). A sociological (de)construction of the relationship between status and quality. *American Journal of Sociology, 115*, 755–804.

Maines, L. A., McDaniel, L. S., & Harris, M. S. (1997). Implications of proposed segment reporting standards for financial analysts' investment judgments. *Journal of Accounting Research, 35*, 1–24.

Menard, S. (2002). *Applied logistic regression analysis.* London: Sage.

Michaely, R., & Womack, K. L. (1999). Conflict of interest and the credibility of underwriter analyst recommendations. *Review of Financial Studies, 12*, 653–686.

Mikhail, M. B., Walther, B. R., & Willis, R. H. (1997). Do security analysts improve their performance with experience? *Journal of Accounting Research, 35*, 131–157.

Milliken, F. J. (1987). Three types of perceived uncertainty about the environment: State, effect, and response uncertainty. *Academy of Management Review, 12*, 133–143.

Oliver, C. (1997). Sustainable competitive advantage: Combining institutional and resource-based views. *Strategic Management Journal, 18*, 697–713.

Omodei, R. A. (1982). Beyond the neo-Weberian concept of status. *Journal of Sociology, 18*, 196–213.

Pearce, J. L. (2011). Introduction: The power of status. In J. L. Pearce (Ed.), *Status in management and organizations*. Cambridge: Cambridge University Press.

Phillips, D. J., & Zuckerman, E. W. (2001). Middle-status conformity: Theoretical restatement and empirical demonstration in two markets. *American Journal of Sociology, 107*, 379–429.

Plumlee, M. A. (2003). The effect of information complexity on analysts' use of that information. *Accounting Review, 78*, 275–296.

Podolny, J. M. (1993). A status-based model of market competition. *American Journal of Sociology, 98*, 829–872.

Podolny, J. M. (2001). Networks as the pipes and prisms of the market. *American Journal of Sociology, 107*, 33–60.

Rao, H. (1994). The social construction of reputation: certification contests, legitimation, and the survival of organizations in the American automobile industry: 1895–1912. *Strategic Management Journal, 15*, 29–44.

Rao, H., Greve, H. R., & Davis, G. F. (2001). Fool's gold: Social proof in the initiation and abandonment of coverage by Wall Street analysts. *Administrative Science Quarterly, 46*, 502–526.

Soda, G., Zaheer, A., & Carlone, A. (2008). Imitative behavior: Network antecedents and performance consequences. *Advances in Strategic Management, 25*, 531–560.

Still, M. C., & Strang, D. (2009). Who does an elite organization emulate? *Administrative Science Quarterly, 54*, 58–89.

Suchman, M. C. (1995). Managing legitimacy: Strategic and institutional approaches. *Academy of Management Review, 20*, 571–610.

Wade, J. B., Porac, J. F., Pollock, T. G., & Graffin, S. D. (2006). The burden of celebrity: The impact of CEO certification contests on CEO pay and performance. *Academy of Management Journal, 49*, 643–660.

Washington, M., & Zajac, E. J. (2005). Status evolution and competition: Theory and evidence. *Academy of Management Journal, 48*, 282–296.

Weber, M. (1978). *Economy and society.* Berkeley, CA: University of California Press.

Welch, I. (2000). Herding among security analysts. *Journal of Financial Economics, 58*, 369–396.

Westphal, J. D., & Clement, M. B. (2008). Sociopolitical dynamics in relations between top managers and security analysts: Favor rendering, reciprocity, and analyst stock recommendations. *Academy of Management Journal, 51*, 873–897.

Westphal, J. D., & Graebner, M. E. (2010). A matter of appearances: How corporate leaders manage the impressions of financial analysts about the conduct of their boards. *Academy of Management Journal, 53*, 15–44.

Wiersema, M. F., & Zhang, Y. (2011). CEO dismissal: The role of investment analysts. *Strategic Management Journal, 32*, 1161–1182.

Wry, T., Lounsbury, M., & Greenwood, R. (2011). The cultural context of status: Generating important knowledge in nanotechnology. In J. L. Pearce (Ed.), *Status in management and organizations* (pp. 155–190). Cambridge: Cambridge University Press.

Zhang, X. F. (2006). Information uncertainty and stock returns. *Journal of Finance, 61*, 105–136.

Zimmerman, M. A., & Zeitz, G. J. (2002). Beyond survival: Achieving new venture growth by building legitimacy. *Academy of Management Review, 27*, 414–431.

Accepted after two revisions: September 10, 2015

Biographical Notes

Joshua S. Hernsberger is an assistant professor of management at Western Kentucky University. His research focuses on how social evaluations influence firms' strategic decisions, with a particular emphasis on top management teams and capital markets. His research has been presented at conferences such as the Academy of Management, Strategic Management Society, and the International Conference on Advances in Management. (joshua.hernsberger@wku.edu)

M. Shane Spiller is an associate professor of management of the Gordon Ford College of Business, Western Kentucky University where he is a Hays Watkins Teaching Fellow. His research interests include motivation, leadership, and ethics with numerous articles published in a wide range of academic journals including the *Journal of Business Ethics* and *Journal of Management Issues*. (shane.spiller@wku.edu)

Accepted after two revisions: September 10, 2015

Current Topics in Management, Vol. 18, 2016, pp. 101–122

THE NEGATIVE IMPACTS OF EMBEDDEDNESS: EVIDENCE FROM CHINA

Lei Xu
Texas Tech University

Qinglian Lu
Stanford University

This study discusses the negative impact of relational embeddedness on entrepreneurship in a transitional economy. Using national as well as urban data from China, we examine how and when embeddedness influences entrepreneurial processes. The results show that embeddedness in kinship networks negatively affects self-employment. As such, we suggest that entrepreneurs in transitional economies, such as China, may consider developing their skills in management as well as undertaking high-tech ventures because kinship networks are not as beneficial as expected. Even though we could not find support for the contingent value of political affiliation, we encourage entrepreneurs not to ignore the role of political connections as they may entail potential business opportunities and political benefits. Taking the institutional context into account substantially contributes to our understanding of the role of embeddedness.

Keywords: embeddedness in kinship, political affiliation, self-employment

> *As a new social order settles, it is likely that those who are on the top will find themselves able to maintain that position, and those at the bottom will end up on staying there as well. Change is the exception and reproduction the rule of social orders, be they communist or capitalist.*

> Ivan Szelenyi and Eric Kostello (1996, 1095)

Resources and information are important to entrepreneurs across societies. However, the means to achieve the end may vary in different institutional contexts and cultures (Yiu & Lau, 2008). The significance of embeddedness in obtaining resources and information has been highlighted in existing entrepreneurship literature. It has been argued that embedded ties are a double-edged sword that facilitates entrepreneurial processes as well as derails beyond certain threshold because cohesive ties transmit resources and identities but lead to information redundancy (Granovetter, 1985; Portes, 1998; Portes & Sensenbrenner, 1993; Uzzi, 1996, 1997, 1999). For example, Newbert and Tornikoski (2013) suggest that both relational and structural embeddedness are conducive to lowering cost in resource acquisition. Newbert, Tornikoski, and Quigley (2013) further investigate the emergence of entrepreneurship and find that the combination of strong and weak ties contributes to the emergence of new ventures over time. In addition, Xu (2014) finds that the efficacy of the founder's identity on new venture creation is contingent on embeddedness in kinship networks with a curvilinear relationship. Nevertheless, the conditions under which the effects of embeddedness are facilitated or constrained are rarely examined (Xu, 2014). We argue, however, that such an examination is valuable because it addresses the boundary conditions of the embeddedness effects.

There are two motivations for this study. First, it attempts to specify the contexts and reasons for the dark side of embeddedness that hinders entrepreneurial outcomes, which is also a promising field in social capital theory (Kwon & Adler, 2014). Building on the embeddedness arguments, we argue that embedding in kinship networks, including family, relatives, and close friends (Fei, 1947), constrains the channels of information and resource acquisition (Burt, 1992), and thereby deters the emergence of entrepreneurship. Unlike the earlier research conducted in village level (Peng, 2004), our focus is the kinship networks formed by family, relatives, and close friends (Fei, 1947) because this kind of networks is the primary resource on which nascent entrepreneurs rely in transitional economies such as China (Au & Kwon, 2009). As a result, this type of networks will significantly affect new venture creation decision (Newbert, Tornikoski, & Quigley, 2013; Newbert & Tornikoski, 2013; Xu, 2014). Moreover, the potential negative impacts of embedded ties, such as restrictions on individual freedom (Portes & Sensenbrenner, 1993), are expected to be more easily observed in this context because potential entrepreneurs might be under huge pressure from their close kinship networks so as not to start their businesses (Portes, 1998; Portes & Sensenbrenner, 1993). In this light, we contribute to extant embeddedness literature by suggesting that the effectiveness of embeddedness varies depending on the nature of network relations (Granovetter, 1995), which transmits resources but may derail performance in entrepreneurial processes.

Our second motivation is to examine whether the efficacy of embeddedness is contingent on political affiliation. Political affiliation here is defined as whether an individual holds (1) a Communist Party of China (CPC) membership, or (2) cadre status, whose administrative ranking or political position is above Keji title (Nee, 1989, 1991, 1996). These affiliations can facilitate individuals' connections with political elites and thereby extend the existing kinship networks, which is the key to business success (Li, Yao, Sue-Chan, & Xi, 2011; Pearson, 1959). In transitional economies such as China, private entrepreneurship is not widely encouraged politically and culturally (e.g., He, 2014; *The China Youth Daily*, 2008). The formal institutions that support entrepreneurship, such as private property rights and public capital markets, are also insufficient (Li & Zhang, 2007; Peng, Lee, & Wang, 2005; Peng, 2004; Peng & Luo, 2000; Xin & Pearce, 1996; Yiu & Lau, 2008). As such, individuals have to rely heavily on their kinship ties to acquire social and economic resources and to undertake entrepreneurial activities. This implies that embedded ties in kinship network may promote entrepreneurship in China's transitional economy (Peng, 2004). Nevertheless, overembedding in intimate kinship networks may also constrain one's further access to valuable information and resources outside the immediate circle (Adler & Kwon, 2002; Burt, 1992; Granovetter, 1985, 1995; Payne, Moore, Griffis, & Autry, 2011; Uzzi, 1996, 1997), which, however, can be mitigated by ties that transcend the boundary of one's kinship network, such as the hierarchical forces (Adler & Kwon, 2002), or political affiliations that build one's connections to the political elites. In this light, we argue that political affiliation, as a unique form of institutional embeddedness (Li, Yao, Sue-Chan, & Xi, 2011; Peng, Lee, & Wang, 2005; Yiu & Lau, 2008), may mitigate the negative impacts of overembeddedness by extending individuals' political connections to those elites and thereby acquiring necessary information and resources (Li & Zhang, 2007; Peng, 2004; Peng & Luo, 2000; Xin & Pearce, 1996). In sum, the examination of the joint effect of political affiliation and embeddedness on self-employment enhances our understanding in how and when the negative impacts of embeddedness can be overcome.

This study is grounded in a transitional economy—the People's Republic of China. There are two reasons for placing our research in this context. First, China's market transition creates a context in which both socialism and market-oriented economic ideologies prevail (Nee, 1989, 1991, 1996). This makes the context highly relevant to the studies of sociopolitical influences on entrepreneurship. Specifically, large layoffs and asset transfer in the state sector of China present a unique research context for self-employment, in which institutional changes and industrial restructuring coexist. Furthermore, building on the recent finding that ethnic Chinese entrepreneurs tend to rely on nonfamily resources for their businesses (Au & Kwon, 2009), we believe that China serves as an ideal context examining the negative impacts of embeddedness. In particular, we find that embeddedness in kinship networks was negatively associated with the probability of self-employment. However, political affiliation did not exert a significant moderating effect. We discuss the implications for management following our findings.

Theory and Hypotheses Development

Entrepreneurship in the People's Republic of China

After being smothered by planned economy for decades, Chinese entrepreneurs gained an opportunity to thrive in 1978 when the Communist Party of China decided to start the transition toward market economy. Nonetheless, due to the political struggles between conservatives and reformists, entrepreneurs were not officially recognized by the state until Deng Xiaoping managed to reendorse market transition in 1992 (Chen, 2005; Wu, 2006). Entrepreneurs' political status was further promoted in 2001 when they were allowed to join the CPC as representatives of advanced productivity (Bian, 2002). Thanks to the market reform and the official endorsement, the number of registered private businesses grew from 14,000 in 1993 to more than 12 million in 2013 (National Bureau of Statistics of China 2014). However, given the insufficient institutional infrastructures such as the lack of private property protection under the influence of socialism, Chinese entrepreneurs heavily sought protection and support from their kinship networks during the early years of market transitions (Peng, 2004). As the transition toward market-oriented economy progresses, Chinese entrepreneurs have become more profit-driven and realized the potential negative impacts and the limitations of kinship networks (e.g., family interference) (Au & Kwon, 2009). Further, China's economic transition features an ongoing struggle between socialism and market economy. To cope with this institutional ambiguity, Chinese entrepreneurs have to use their political affiliation as a stepping-stone to facilitate entrepreneurship, simultaneously overcoming the disadvantages of traditional kinship networks (Pearson, 1959). China, as a typical research setting for studying transitional economies (e.g., Bian, 2002; Li et al. 2011; Li & Zhang, 2007; Nee, 1989, 1991, 1996; Peng & Luo, 2000; Peng, Lee, & Wang, 2005; Peng, 2004; Szelenyi & Kostello, 1996; Xin & Pearce, 1996; Yiu & Lau, 2008), therefore informs us about entrepreneurship in transitional economies due to its ongoing process of market reform.

Embeddedness in Kinship Networks and Self-employment

Two kinds of embeddedness are generally studied in existing literature. One is relational embeddedness, measured by the trust between and among individuals in dyadic or community level (Granovetter, 1985; Newbert & Tornikoski, 2013; Uzzi, 1999; Putnam, 2000). The other is structural embeddedness, defined as the proportion of direct embedded ties in the overall networks (Newbert, Tornikoski, & Quigley, 2013; Uzzi, 1996, 1997). In this study, we focus only on relational embeddedness, since we are interested in trust in closed kinship networks. Trust in embedded ties is defined as the belief that an exchange actor will not behave in the self-interest at the expense of others' benefits. As such, it is not calculated risk but a heuristic (Uzzi 1997). Specifically, the more trust one holds toward other members in the community, the more frequent interaction and strong ties will form (Xin & Pearce, 1996; Peng, 2004). Extant literature emphasizes the positive effects of embeddedness. For example, Uzzi (1999) finds that the more trustworthy embedded ties an entrepreneur owns with different bank managers, the lower bank loan cost he or she may have. Similar results are also available among nascent entrepreneurs in terms of resource acquisition (Batjargal & Li, 2004; Newbert & Tornikoski, 2013). Further, when formal legal institutions such as private property rights are insufficient, trustworthy embedded ties in kinship networks would significantly promote entrepreneurship (Peng, 2004).

Notwithstanding the numerous studies focusing on the facilitating role of embedded ties in the emergence of entrepreneurship, scholars also acknowledged the dark side of embeddedness (e.g., Portes & Sensenbrenner, 1993; Uzzi, 1996, 1997, 1999). There are three mechanisms that explain the negative impacts of embeddedness (e.g., Putnam, 2000; Portes, 1998; Portes & Sensenbrenner, 1993; Uzzi, 1997). First, institutional changes may rationalize market erosion of the competitive advantage of embedded ties (Adler & Kwon, 2002; Portes, 1998; Portes & Sensenbrenner, 1993). For example, the CPC publicly announced a series of restrictions on the business activities of CPC members and their families since 2008, one of which is to prevent political elites, as well as their families, from entering entrepreneurship. Second, overembedding in a closed network may constrain the inflow of resources and produce redundant information (Burt, 1992), which deters entrepreneurial activities (Granovetter, 1985, 1995; Portes & Sensenbrenner, 1993; Uzzi, 1996, 1997, 1999). It is also important to note that even though embedded ties in kinship can temporarily provide necessary support for self-employment, successful new venture creation requires continuous inflows of capital or information and less internal conflicts (Arregle et al., 2015; Newbert & Tornikoski, & Quigley, 2013; Newbert, Tornikoski, 2013; Xu, 2014). As such, when the capacity of kinship networks in providing support reaches its limit (Arregle et al., 2015; Newbert & Tornikoski, & Quigley, 2013), embedded ties can no longer satisfy the needs for further growth (Arregle et al., 2015; Newbert, Tornikoski, 2013; Portes, 1998; Portes & Sensenbrenner, 1993). As such, social capital supporting entrepreneurship must be sought elsewhere (Putnam, 2000). Third, obligations derived from solidarity within a community may sanction those successful entrepreneurs by trapping them in self-defeating cycles (Portes & Sensenbrenner, 1993; Uzzi, 1997). For example, solidarity in closed kinship networks may require entrepreneurs to reciprocate favors of community members with resources or wealth produced by their new ventures. Individuals, however, may seek opportunities outside existing kinship networks for further growth of new ventures. These contradictory forces may generate tensions between entrepreneurs and their closed kinship networks because the exit of a core member, such as an entrepreneur, may cause substantial losses for kinship networks (Adler & Kwon, 2002; Uzzi, 1997). As a result, members in a kinship network may discourage or even fight against the start-up decisions of these entrepreneurs by taking collective actions (Arregle et al., 2015; Au & Kwon, 2009; Xu, 2014).

Some available evidences also observed the negative impacts of embeddedness in kinship networks. Au and Kwon (2009), for instance, suggest that seeking family financial support might not be regarded as a priority among Chinese entrepreneurs, as these entrepreneurs fear that family interference and high transaction cost would harm their businesses. As a result, managers will extensively cultivate their personal professional networks rather than kinship networks to obtain resources (Xin & Pearce, 1996). A recent cross-country study also demonstrates that entrepreneurs' heavy reliance on family ties for resources and emotional support limits venture growth (Arregle et al., 2015). As such, overreliance on kinship networks may be related to less profit and failure-prone businesses (Bates, 1994). Following these arguments, we hypothesize that

Hypothesis 1: *In a transitional economy, the greater an individual is embedded in his/her kinship networks, the less likely he/she is to be self-employed.*

The Contingent Value of Embeddedness in Kinship Networks

Scholars have reached no consensus regarding when and why embeddedness exerts either positive or negative influence on economic outcomes (Newbert & Tornikoski, & Quigley, 2013; Newbert, Tornikoski, 2013; Uzzi, 1997, 1999; Xu, 2014). We argue that this divergence may be due to the contexts in which scholars conduct research. As such, an investigation of the effect of embeddedness may be grounded in a contingent framework considering both institutional and cultural environments (Granovetter, 1995).

In this study, we limit our scope condition to transitional economies. In particular, we argue that political affiliation can mitigate the negative impacts of relational embeddedness on self-employment. First, extant literature in transitional economies supports the argument that managerial political ties positively promote entrepreneurship (Li & Zhang, 2007; Peng, Lee, & Wang, 2005; Peng & Luo, 2000; Xin & Pearce, 1996; Yiu & Lau, 2008). Second, political affiliation, as a form of network-based capital with a hierarchical nature (Yiu & Lau, 2008), mitigates the negative effects of group-level exclusion and insularity associated with strong ties (Adler & Kwon, 2002). We now turn to the discussion of a contingent model of embeddedness.

Political Affiliation, Embeddedness in Kinship Networks, and Self-employment in a Transitional Economy

Formal institutional arrangements in transitional economies (e.g., China) are often weak due to limited legal and government initiatives (Li & Zhang, 2007;

Peng, Lee, & Wang, 2005; Peng, Lee, & Wang, 2005; Peng, 2004; Peng & Luo, 2000; Xin & Pearce, 1996; Yiu & Lau, 2008). As a result, entrepreneurs have to rely on kinship ties to seek benefits and protection (Peng, 2004). However, kinship networks also have their own limits as discussed earlier. To overcome these limitations, managerial ties with political elites may play a vital role in the growth of entrepreneurship in transitional economies for the following reasons. First, individuals can capitalize on their political ties by acquiring market information and key resources that are otherwise unavailable (Li & Zhang, 2007; Peng & Luo, 2000; Uzzi,1999, 1997, 1996; Xin & Pearce, 1996; Yiu & Lau 2008). Second, the bureaucracy, as a legacy of state socialism, still remains influential during market transitions because bureaucratic agents control key resources in most transitional economies. As such, connections to political elites can mitigate potential risks because these connections extend existing network resources (Li, Yao, Sue-Chan, & Xi, 2011; Li & Zhang, 2007; Peng & Luo, 2000; Pearson, 1959; Yiu & Lau, 2008). Third, elite status is backed by a hierarchical force (e.g., administrative or political power), which endows individuals with the ability to transcend the boundaries of kinship networks (Adler & Kwon, 2002; Burt, 1992; Wu, 2006) and thereby facilitates entrepreneurship. For example, entrepreneurs with CPC memberships or cadre positions can use his/her political power to obtain necessary legal documents endorsing their right to acquire valuable resources, which are otherwise unavailable within the kinship networks. Fourth, socialization through political connections nurtures necessary political skills for entrepreneurs in the process of new venture creation and thereby complements what kinship networks may not provide (Fang et al. 2015; Bian, 1997).

In recognizing the strength and weakness of different types of networks, entrepreneurs in transitional economies such as China have learned to skillfully leverage these networks, especially in permeating political circles. For example, China's Private Enterprise Report (2002) documents that a large proportion of Chinese entrepreneurs have worked in government-related enterprises or agencies before they started their own business. In addition, these entrepreneurs also retain close political relations even after they enter entrepreneurship. Statistically, 29.9% of entrepreneurs hold CPC membership; 17.4% of private enterprise owners are deputies to the People's Congress in local and central governments, and 35.1% of them are members of the Committee of the Chinese People's Political Consultative Conference. As such, political affiliation serves to overcome and complement the shortages of kinship networks. On the basis of these arguments, we hypothesize that

Hypothesis 2: *In a transitional economy, political affiliation mitigates the negative impacts of an individual's relational embeddedness in his/her kinship networks on the probability of being self-employed.*

Method

Sample

The data of this study come from the China General Social Survey (CGSS), 2010. The CGSS aims to systematically monitor the changing relationships between social structure and the quality of life in urban and rural China (Bian & Li, 2013). It published annual surveys from 2003 to 2006, but ceased to operate in 2007, and was resumed in 2008 by Renmin University. Starting from 2010 and onward, Renmin University solely oversees the administration of the CGSS (Bian & Li, 2013). During the development of the CGSS, frequent consultations were conducted with scholars around the world. In addition, the data were compared with equivalent surveys, such as the General Social Survey in the United States, to ensure their reliability, quality, and comparability. Also, the CGSS is a random sample as it uses the list of China's fifth population census to randomly select households and respondents.

Moreover, the response rates for the CGSS from 2008 and onward remain around 77%. The reasons why there is such a high response rate are twofold. First, the administrators of the CGSS use a multiple collection strategy. Specifically, the CGSS collected data from sources such as scholarly networks, formal survey teams, and professional survey firms. Second, the Chinese culture encourages cooperation with academia. To the best of our knowledge, CGSS is the most comprehensive national survey in China with relatively complete working and life history records.

Data Collection

In this study, we use only the CGSS 2010 survey data. There are two reasons for this decision. First, Bian (2002) calls for more attention on emerging social classes in rural and urban China today. As such, we focus on the 2010 survey because post-2010 surveys are not available to the public yet. Second, the incomparability of major independent variables in different surveys limits our ability to conduct a longitudinal analysis.

Although all data in CGSS 2010 were collected using the same survey instrument, we believe that common method bias would not distort our analysis. First, at the beginning of the survey, the respondents are guaranteed by the survey designers for their anonymity, which reduces the probability of socially desirable responses (Podsakoff et al., 2003). Second, we investigated common method biases using a Harman's single-factor test (Christmann, 2004; Kirkman & Shapiro, 2001; Newbert & Tornikoski, 2013). The test produces 14 factors, the first 8 factors account for 70.86% of cumulative variance, the proportions of each 8 factors are 17.87%, 12.08%, 8.25%, 7.99%, 6.60%, 6.22%, 6.07%

and 5.78%. Because no single factor emerged to account for a substantial total variance, no artificial response bias seems to exist in the data (Podsakoff & Organ,1985; Newbert & Torrnikoski, 2013).

In CGSS 2010, there are 11,783 observations, 48.17% of which are males. The average age of the sample is 47 years old, 14.62% of which hold college degrees and 0.8% hold a masters or higher-level degree. In addition, respondents who hold cadre position make up 2.34% of the sample (cadre position, *yes* = 1). Cadre refers to the administrative or political position above Keji title. Moreover, 12.40% of the sample are CPC members, and 90% of the sample are Han nationals (i.e., a majority ethnic group in China). The final usable sample, after excluding missing values, retains 8,680 observations in national level and 4,456 observations in urban level.

Dependent Variable

Self-employment. Following the earlier research (Wu 2006), we define self-employed individuals as respondents who report that they are business founders (siyingqiye), individual owners (getihu), self-employed (In Chinese, "ziyouzhiyezhe"), or persons who help out in a family business with pay (*yes* = 1).

Independent Variable

Relational Embeddedness in Kinship Networks. Trust reflects the relational dimension of embeddedness (Granovetter, 1985; Newbert & Tornikoski, 2013; Uzzi, 1999) and social capital (Tsai & Ghoshal, 1998; Nahapiet & Ghoshal, 1998; Putnam, 2000). As such, we measure the degree of embeddedness in kinship networks by calculating the amount of trust. Kinship networks in China include family, relatives, and close friends, since the relationship around an individual represents a rippling effects of kinship relationship—Chaxu geju, that is, kinship orders first follow by family, then relatives, and finally close friends (Fei, 1947). To establish the relationship between the level of trust and reliance on kinship networks, we first conducted an interview with a local entrepreneur in the mainland of China. In particular, the entrepreneur in city Shishi of Fujian province in China informed us, "I will seek advice and help from those whom I trust first, such as my family, relatives, and close friends" (we interpreted). Moreover, Xin and Pearce (1996) argue that entrepreneurs in China sought to build relationship that was deep in trust. As such, the higher the level of trust in kinship networks, the more likely individuals in China tend to rely on kinship networks for support (Fei 1947; Peng 2004; Xin & Pearce, 1996). In this light, the level of trust is a good proxy for the tendency to rely on kinship networks in contexts such as China.

To measure relational embeddedness in kinship networks, we use the following question in the CGSS: "What degree of trust do you hold toward the following choices: Family, Relatives, Friends, Colleagues, Cadre, Businessman, Classmates, Fellows, and People with Faith (totally untrustworthy = 1 to totally trustworthy = 5)". We then summed the scores toward family, relatives, and friends as an index for relational embeddedness in kinship networks.

Moderating Variables

Political Affiliation. We use two variables to represent political affiliation. The first variable "cadre status" is whether or not a respondent reports that he or she is a cadre (holding cadre positions, yes = 1). Cadre refers to an administrative or political position that is above Keji title. We then use the question: "whether a respondent is currently holding a CPC membership" (yes = 1) to measure our second variable "party membership." These two variables are commonly used in the prior literature to measure political affiliation (e.g., Nee, 1989, 1991, 1996; Wu & Treiman, 2007; Wu, 2006).

Control Variables

We use age and age squared to control for the curvilinear effects of age (Wu, 2006). We also control for a set of demographics characteristics, such as gender (male = 1) and education (e.g., senior high school, college, master, or above). To rule out the wealth accumulation effect, we control for GDP of 2009 in the province where a respondent resides during the survey period. Following the earlier research (Wu 2006), we compute household income per capital in 2009 of an individual as the logarithm of household income divided by the number of working members in a family.

Moreover, we also control for demographic characteristics of father (Shane & Khurana, 2003). Specifically, we measure those characteristics as whether the father of an individual was an entrepreneur at his or her age of 14 (yes = 1) (Shane & Khurana, 2003) and father's education level when the respondent was surveyed.

Finally, Wu and Treiman (2007) argue that China's household registration system (Hukou) directly influences social mobility in China, which might cause potential cofounding effects with our independent variables. As such, we control for Hukou status by including an indicator of whether a respondent holds rural hukou. It is worth noting that the Guangdong province adopted a resident hukou system in May, 2010 to eliminate the previous rural–urban hukou divide system, requiring that anyone who lived in the city could obtain a resident hukou. However, this policy just superficially eliminates the difference between rural and urban hukou but still keeps corresponding rights and obligations for those who originally hold rural hukou. As such, we categorize resident hukou of this kind as rural hukou.

Analysis

The central question in this study is to answer how embeddedness in kinship networks affects self-employment, and the contingent value of political affiliation in this relationship. Because self-employment status is a dichotomous variable, logistic regression serves as an appropriate modeling strategy. Moreover, since the CGSS contains large volumes of zeros in the dependent variable, we employ a rare-event logistic regression to correct for overdispersion (King & Zeng, 1999, 2001; Batjargal & Li, 2004; Sorenson & Stuart, 2001). In addition, the maximum VIF in all variables is 1.80. As such, we are confident that multicollinearity would not seriously affect our results. Table 1 lists the descriptive statistics and correlations.

To obtain more robust results, we analyze our data in both national and urban samples to observe the consistent pattern. In addition, we mean-center all independent variables before computing interaction terms to further avoid multicollinearity issue (Aiken & West, 1991). Finally, traditional ways of explaining variance, such as Pseudo- and Chi-Square, are not applicable to the interpretations of the results following logistic regression because it is meaningless to explain the variance of a probability. However, rare event logistic regression does provide a way of checking model fit (King & Zeng, 2001, 1999). Specifically, if a probability of the outcome falls in a 95% confidence interval, it suggests that the model fits the data well. As shown at the bottom of Table 2, all of our models fit the data well.

Results

Hypothesis 1 examines whether embeddedness in kinship networks negatively influences self-employment. Table 2 presents the results with both national and urban samples. In model 1, embeddedness in kinship networks negatively and significantly influences self-employment ($\beta = -.06, p < .01$). In addition, the same pattern appears in urban sample in model 5 ($\beta = -.06, p < .10$). Following Wiersema and Bowen (2009), we calculate the marginal effect of embeddedness in kinship networks and find that the same negatively significant effect exists. Therefore, Hypothesis 1 is strongly supported.

Hypothesis 2 predicts whether the efficacy of embeddedness is contingent on political affiliation. In model 2 of Table 2, the interaction effect between cadre status and embeddedness in kinship networks on self-employment is only marginally significant ($\beta = -.40, p < .1$), and the same pattern appears in model 6 ($\beta = -.47$). Similarly, the coefficients of the interaction between party membership and embeddedness in kinship networks are both negative but insignificant in models 3 and 7 ($\beta = -.14, \beta = -.10$). In sum, Hypothesis 2 receives no support.

Particularly interesting, both cadre status ($\beta = -.91, p < .01$ in model 1; $\beta = -.90$, $p < .05$ in model 5) and party membership ($\beta = -.51, p < .01$ in model 1;

Table 1
Descriptive Statistics and Correlations

Variables	M	SD	1	2	3	4	5
1. Age	47.48	15.30	1.00				
2. Gender	.49	.50	.04**	1.00			
3. Rural hukou	.52	.50	-.05**	-.01	1.00		
4. Household income per capital in 2009	9.37	1.41	-.16**	.01	-.36**	1.00	
5. Provincial GDP in 2009	2202.90	1472.66	-.01	-.00	-.04**	.12**	1.00
6. High school	.20	.40	-.10**	.03**	-.24**	.12**	.04**
7. College	.14	.35	-.22**	.06**	-.36**	.29**	.07**
8. Master or above	.01	.09	-.08**	.01	-.09**	.08**	.02
9. Father self-employed at the age of 14	.05	.21	-.10**	-.00	-.10**	.09**	.05**
10. Cadre status	.02	.15	-.05**	.08**	-.16**	.13**	-.00
11. Party membership	.13	.33	.11**	.18**	-.24**	.16**	.01
12. Embeddedness in kinship	12.83	1.61	.03*	.03*	.01	-.01	-.03*
13. Father's education	1.42	.79	-.33**	-.02	-.26**	.23**	.04**
14. Self-employment	.10	.30	-.15**	.08**	-.00	.10**	.07**

(Continued)

Table 1 (Continued)

Variables	6	7	8	9	10	11	12	13	14
6. High school	1.00								
7. College	-.20**	1.00							
8. Master or above	-.04**	-.03**	1.00						
9. Father self-employed at the age of 14	.05**	.10**	-.01	1.00					
10. Cadre status	-.03*	.28**	.14**	.00	1.00				
11. Party membership	.05**	.29**	.12**	.00	.28**	1.00			
12. Embeddedness in kinship	-.03*	.02*	.01	-.03*	.01	.03**	1.00		
13. Father's education	.10**	.36**	.15**	.10**	.11**	.07**	.00	1.00	
14. Self-employment	.04**	-.02*	-.01	.06**	-.03**	-.06**	-.04**	.03**	1.00

Note: $N = 8,680$. * $p < .05$. ** $p < .01$.

Table 2
Relationship between Relational Embeddedness and Self-employment

	National Sample				Urban Sample			
	Model 1	Model 2	Model 3	Model 4	Model 5	Model 6	Model 7	Model 8
Intercept	-9.98**	-9.88**	-9.75**	-9.72**	-8.58**	-8.46**	-8.40**	-8.35**
Control Variables								
Age	.22**	.22**	.22**	.22**	.25**	.25**	.25**	.25**
Age^2	-.00**	-.00**	-.00**	-.00**	-.00**	-.00**	-.00**	-.00**
Gender	.74**	.74**	.74**	.74**	.85**	.85**	.85**	.85**
Rural hukou	-.11	-.11	-.11	-.11	.53**	.54**	.54**	.54**
Household income per capital in 2009	.39**	.39**	.39**	.39**	.18**	.18**	.18**	.18**
Provincial GDP in 2009	.00**	.00**	.00**	.00**	.00	.00	.00	.00
High school	-.13	-.13	-.13	-.13	-.30*	-.30*	-.30*	-.30*
College	-.89**	-.89**	-.90**	-.89**	-.68**	-.68**	-.69**	-.68**
Master or above	-1.15*	-1.13*	-1.13*	-1.12*	-.61	-.61	-.60	-.60
Father self-employed at the age of 14	.67**	.67**	.67**	.67**	.63**	.64**	.63**	.63**
Father's education	.02	.02	.02	.02	-.04	-.05	-.04	-.05

Independent Variables

Independent Variables								
Cadre status, mean centered	−.91**	4.05	−.91**	3.34	−.90*	5.06	−.90*	4.80
Party membership, mean centered	−.51**	−.51**	1.23	.81	−.71**	−.71**	.57	.13
Embeddedness in kinship, mean centered	−.06**	−.06*	−.05*	−.05*	−.06†	−.05	−.05	−.05
Cadre status × Embeddedness in kinship		−.40†		−.34		−.47		−.45
Party membership × Embeddedness in kinship	−.10		−.14	−.10	−.10		−.10	−.07
Pr (self-employed)	.06	.06	.06	.06	.07	.07	.07	.07
95% C.I.	[.05,.07]	[.05,.07]	[.05,.07]	[.05,.07]	[.06,.08]	[.06,.08]	[.06,.08]	[.06,.08]
N	8,680	8,680	8,680	8,680	4,456	4,456	4,456	4,456

Note: † $p < .10$. * $p < .05$. ** $p < .01$.

$\beta = -.71, p < .01$ in model 5) are negatively and significantly associated with self-employment, suggesting that China's policy restricting political elites' entry into entrepreneurship is effective. In addition, the insignificant moderating effects of political affiliation in models 2, 3, 6 and 7 also indirectly support the above argument.

Discussion

In this study, we find that embeddedness in kinship networks is negatively associated with self-employment, suggesting that embedding in kinship networks deters self-employment in China. For example, Asian entrepreneurs may proactively choose other networks rather than their family for help because they are aware of potential negative impacts of associating with close family, relatives, and friends (Au & Kwon, 2009). Particularly interesting, we find no support for Hypothesis 2, suggesting that political affiliation may mitigate the negative impacts of embeddedness in kinship networks. A possible explanation is that a series of restrictions on CPC members and their families' entry into entrepreneurship (introduced since 1984) has been effectively implemented. Moreover, as we mentioned earlier, obligations, redundant information, and resource reserve out of close kinship networks restrict the realization of individual achievement, managerial political ties may transcend these obstacles. However, in transitional economies such as contemporary China, market-oriented ideology gradually dominates the market. As such, both state policy and market-oriented ideology start to discourage the extensive use of political networks serving business. Following these social and political changes, entrepreneurs begin to become realistic and more profit-driven. Rather than heavily relying on kinship networks and political networks (Peng, 2004; Pearson, 1959), Chinese entrepreneurs may turn to alternatives for further growth, such as employing innovative business models or developing oversea markets. Therefore, political affiliation may not be effective as it was in the past.

Implications for Management

The implications of the study are that China's entrepreneurs may realize the negative impacts of kinship networks (Au & Kwon, 2009). As such, the challenge for China's entrepreneurs is to search alternative means of acquiring resources. One of the feasible strategies is to start businesses in high-tech industry or knowledge-intensive industry. In these industries, high-tech firms are generally started by the talents who understand the technology well. In addition, investors (e.g., venture capitalists) also prefer to invest in those new ventures started by these talents because investors perceive these talents more likely to provide high quality of commercialized technology. As such, entrepreneurs have to recruit technology talents rather than kinship networks because gaining access to venture capital investment also requires these talents' connections with those investors in China (Batjargal & Li, 2004). As such, kinship networks are not important as it used to be in high-tech industry or knowledge-intensive industry. Further, entrepreneurs are also encouraged to develop their skills through continuous self-learning or implementing professionalism in their businesses so that unqualified family members, relatives, and close friends will not be recruited.

Despite the fact that we did not find any support for the moderating effect of political affiliation, this does not necessarily mean that political affiliation is not important any more in contemporary China. Many scholars have emphasized the important role of political ties in business (e.g., Li et al. 2011; Peng & Luo, 2000; Peng Y., 2004; Xin & Pearce, 1996; Pearson, 1959). One of the differences between these research and our study is that whereas existing studies focus on relatively established enterprises, we focus on self-employment activities that are more relevant to new venture creation stage. As such, business size and age seem to be major factors determining whether or not entrepreneurs rely on political networks. In sum, entrepreneurs in transitional economies, such as contemporary China, are still encouraged to develop their connections with political elites.

Limitations

Despite the strength of our findings, there are several limitations to our research. First of all, we limit our measurements of political affiliation to cadre status and party membership. However, political affiliation embodies a wide variety of meanings such as specific ties with powerful contacts (Bian, 1997) and government linkages (Li & Zhang, 2007; Peng & Luo, 2000; Peng, Lee, & Wang, 2005; Yiu & Lau, 2008), while these variables are arguably less observable than the ones used in our analysis. Therefore, we do not have information to account for different forms of political affiliations that may affect the outcomes of interest.

Second, our study uses only the 2010 CGSS survey, which is a cross-sectional data. We are cautious about the causality of our results. One of the major reasons for us to employ cross-sectional data is the incomparability between main independent variables in different waves of the CGSS surveys, which makes a longitudinal design very difficult. Even though we attempt to incorporate other relevant datasets with the 2010 CGSS survey data, data incomparability issue still deters our efforts in constructing a longitudinal design. We acknowledge that the cross-sectional design is one of our key limitations.

Third, a substantial amount of minority data is excluded from the sample due to missing values, and such a procedure may cause selection biases. However, we believe that this procedure may not distort our substantive findings. First, 90% of the people in the CGSS are Han nationals (the majority ethnic group in China). Most minorities lead a rural life rather than commercial activities in China. Therefore, the exclusion of minorities should not cause underestimation issues. Second, we use both national and urban samples to crosscheck whether the exclusion of these minorities would affect our results in terms of geographical distribution because most minorities in China live in rural areas. The results show a consistent pattern, suggesting that the exclusion of minorities may not affect our analysis.

Fourth, it is also possible that the weights for each of the three components in trust index (e.g., family, relatives, and close friends) are different. However, we are not able to assign corresponding weights due to the lack of the literature guiding us to do so. As such, we acknowledge that assuming equal weights for the three components of trust index is one of our limitations and thereby encourage future scholars to explore this weighting issue.

Directions for Future Research

One of the promising avenues for future research is to explore the multilevel effects of embeddedness in kinship networks. We focus on individual-level analysis in this study. However, social capital is a multidimensional concept that requires more understandings for its consequences in different levels (Payne, Moore, Griffis, & Autry, 2011). For example, scholars can examine how embeddedness in family in a founding team may affect firm-level performance. The other promising avenue is to investigate how the value of political capital is contingent on some specific network attributes, such as centrality and informal social ties, and how those interactions may influence entrepreneurial activities. At last, we encourage some replications and longitudinal designs in other contexts examining the boundary conditions of our results.

References

Adler, P., & Kwon, S.-W. (2002). Social capital: Prospects for a new concept. *Academy of Management Review*, *27*, 17–40.

Aiken, L. S., & West, S. G. (1991). Multiple regression: testing and interpreting interactions. Newbury Park, CA: Sage.

Arregle, J- L, Batjargal, B., Hitt, M. A., Webb, J. W., Miller, T., & Tsui, A. S. (2015). Family ties in entrepreneurs' social networks and new venture growth. *Entrepreneurship Theory and Practice*, *39*, 313–344.

Au, K., & Kwon, H.K. (2009). Start-up capital and Chinese entrepreneurs: The role of family. *Entrepreneurship Theory and Practice*, *33*, 889–908.

Bates, T. (1994). Social resources generated by group support networks may not be beneficial to asian immigrant-owned small businesses. *Social Forces*, *72*, 671–689.

Batjargal, B., & Li, M. (2004). Entrepreneurial access to private equity in china: The role of social capital. *Organization Science*, *15*, 159–172.

Bian, Y. (1997). Bringing strong ties back in: Indirect ties, network bridges, and job searches in China. *American Sociological Review*, *62*, 366–385.

Bian, Y. (2002). Chinese Social Stratification and Social Mobility. *Annual Review of Sociology*, *28*, 91–116.

Bian, Y., & Li, L. (2013). The Chinese general social survey (2003-8). *Chinese Sociological Review*, *45*, 70–97.

Burt, R. S. (1992). *Structural holes: The social structure of competition.* Cambridge, MA: Harvard University Press.

Chen, G. (2005). From elite circulation to elite reproduction. *Study and Discovery, 1,* 1–13.

China Private Enterprise Research Group. (2002). *China's private enterprise report.* Beijing, China: United Front Work Department of the Central Committee of the Communist Party of China.

Christmann, P. (2004). Multinational companies and the natural environment: determinants of global environmental policy standardization. *Academy of Management Journal, 47,* 747–760.

Coleman, J. (1988). Social capital in the creation of human capital. *American Journal of Sociology, 94,* 95–120.

Fang, R., Chi, L., Chen, M., & Baron, R. (2015). Bringing political skill into social networks: findings from a field study of entrepreneurs. *Journal of Management Studies, 52,* 175–212.

Fei, H.-T. (1947). *From the soil: The foundation of Chinese society.* Berkeley, CA: University of California Press.

Granovetter, M. (1985). Economic action and social structure: the problem of embeddedness. *American Journal of Sociology, 91,* 481–510.

Granovetter, M. (1995). *Afterword* (2nd ed.). Chicago, IL, USA: University of Chicago Press.

King, G., & Zeng, L. (1999). *Estimating absolute, relative, and attributable risks in case-control studies.* Retrieved from Department of Government, Harvard University: http://GKing.Harvard.Edu

King, G., & Zeng, L. (2001). Logistic regression in rare events data. *Political Analysis, 9,* 137–163.

Kirkman, B., & Shapiro, D. (2001). The impact of cultural values on job satisfaction and organizational commitment in self-managing work teams: The mediating role of employee resistance. *Academy of Management Journal, 44,* 557–569.

Kwon, S.-W., & Adler, P. (2014). Social capital: Maturation of a field of research. *Academy of Management Review, 39* (4), 412–422.

Li, Hanyang, & Zhang, Y. (2007). The role of managers' political networking and functional experience in new venture performance: Evidence from China's transition economy. *Strategic Management Journal, 28,* 791–804.

Li, S., Yao, X., Sue-Chan, C., & Xi, Y. (2011). Where do social ties come from: Institutional framework and governmental tie distribution among Chinese managers. *Management and Organization Review, 7,* 97–124.

Nahapiet, J., & Ghoshal, S. (1998). Social capital, intellectual capital, and the organizational advantage. *Academy of Management Review, 23,* 242–266.

Nee, V. (1989). A theory of market transition: From redistribution to markets in state socialism. *American Sociological Review, 54,* 663–681.

Nee, V. (1991). Social inequalities in reforming state socialism: Between redistribution and markets in China. *American Sociological Review, 56,* 267–282.

Nee, V. (1996). The emergence of a market society: Changing mechanisms of stratification in China. *American Journal of Sociology, 101,* 908–949.

Newbert, S., & Tornikoski, E. (2013). Resource acquisition in the emergence phase: Considering the effects of embeddedness and resource dependence. *Entrepreneurship Theory and Practice, 37,* 249–280.

Newbert, S., Tornikoski, E. & Quigley, N. (2013). Exploring the evolution of supporter networks in the creation of new organizations. *Journal of Business Venturing, 28,* 281–298.

Payne, G., Moore, C., Griffis, S., & Autry, C. (2011). Multilevel challenges and opportunities in social capital research. *Journal of Management, 37,* 491–520.

Pearson, M. (1959). *China's new business elite: the political consequences of economic reform.* Berkeley, CA, University of California Press.

Peng, Y. (2004). Kinship and entrepreneurs in China's transitional economy. *American Journal of Sociology, 109,* 1045–1074.

Peng, M., Lee, S. -H., & Wang, D. (2005). What determines the scope of the firm over time? A focus on institutional relatedness. *Academy of Management Review, 30,* 622–633.

Peng, M., & Luo, Y. (2000). Managerial ties and firm performance in a transition economy: The nature of a micro-macro link. *Academy of Management Journal, 43,* 486–501.

Podsakoff, P., MacKenzie, S., Lee, J., & Podsakoff, N. (2003). Common method biases in behavioral research: a critical review of the literature and recommended remedies. *Journal of Applied Psychology, 88,* 879–903.

Podsakoff, P., & Organ, D. (1986). Self-reports in organizational research: Problems and prospects. *Journal of Management, 12,* 531–544.

Portes, A. (1998). Social capital: Its origins and applications in modern sociology. *Annual Review of Sociology, 24,* 1–24.

Portes, A., & Sensenbrenner, J. (1993). Embeddedness and immigration: Notes on the social determinants of economic action. *American Journal of Sociology, 98,* 1320–1350.

Putnam, R. (2000). *Bowling alone: the collapse and revival of American community.* New York: Touchstone Books.

Shane, S., & Khurana, R. (2003). Bringing individuals back in: The effects of career experience on new firm founding. *Industrial and Corporate Change, 12,* 519–543.

Sorenson, O., & Stuart, T. (2001). Syndication networks and the spatial distribution of venture capital investments. *American Journal of Sociology, 106,* 1546–1588.

Szelenyi, I., & Kostello, E. (1996). The market transition debate: Toward a synthesis? *American Journal of Sociology, 101,* 1082–1096.

The China Youth Daily. (2008, October 2). *The original sins of Chinese private business entrepreneurs: shall we need to punish them?* Beijing: Retrieved from http://news.ifeng.com/opinion/specials/enterpriser/200810/1021_4816_840103.shtml

Tsai, W., & Ghoshal, S. (1998). Social capital and value creation: The role of intrafirm networks. *Academy of Management Journal, 41,* 464–476.

Uzzi, B. (1996). The sources and consequences of embeddedness for the economic performance of organizations: The network effect. *American Sociological Review, 61,* 674–698.

Uzzi, B. (1997). Social structure and competition in interfirm networks: The paradox of embeddedness. *Administrative Science Quarterly, 42,* 35–67.

Uzzi, B. (1999). Embeddedness in the making of financial capital: How social relations and networks benefit firms seeking financing. *American Sociological Review, 64,* 481–505.

Wiersema, M. F., & Bowen, H. P. (2009). The use of limited dependent variable techniques in strategy research: issues and methods. *Strategic Management Journal, 30,* 679–692.

Wu, X. (2006). Communist cadres and market opportunities: Entry into self-employment in China, 1978–1996. *Social Forces, 85,* 389–411.

Wu, X., & Treiman, D. (2007). Inequality and equality under Chinese socialism: The hukou system and intergenerational occupational mobility. *American Journal of Sociology, 113*, 415–445.

Xin, K., & Pearce, J. (1996). Guanxi: Connections as substitutes for formal institutional support. *Academy of Management Journal, 39*, 1641–1658.

Xu, L. (2014). A tale of trinity in founder's identity: The case new venture creation. *Journal of Management Policy and Practice, 15*, 11–31.

Yiu, D., & Lau, C. -M. (2008). Corporate entrepreneurship as resource capital configuration in emerging market firms. *Entrepreneurship Theory and Practice, 32*, 37–57.

Biographical Notes

Lei Xu is a doctoral student in management at the Rawls College of Business at Texas Tech University. His research interests are organization reputation/status in highly uncertain contexts such as IPO market, strategic management, and entrepreneurship. His publications have appeared in the *Journal of Management Policy and Practice,* and the *Report on the Development of Chinese Talents No.2.* (lei.xu@ttu.edu)

Qinglian Lu is a PhD candidate in sociology at Stanford University. Her research interests include social network analysis, organizational behavior, and political sociology. Her dissertation focuses on the relationship between network connections, career trajectories and mobility inside large bureaucratic systems, using data from China and India. (qlu1@stanford.edu)

Accepted after two revisions: December 28, 2015

Current Topics in Management, Vol. 18, 2016, pp. 123–152

PRODUCT-QUALITY FAILURES IN INTERNATIONAL SOURCING: EFFECT OF INSTITUTIONS

Etayankara Muralidharan
MacEwan University, Canada

William Wei
MacEwan University, Canada

Juan Zhang
Shanghai University of International Business and Economics

Hari Bapuji
University of Manitoba, Canada

Increasing globalization has seen the emergence of hybrid products coming from different countries, which are the sourcing bases for multinationals. Such international sourcing decisions of multinational enterprises have been accompanied by concerns on product safety especially underscored by the increasing product failures leading to recalls from global supply chains witnessed in the recent past. While the past research has focussed largely on the consequences of recalls such as damage to the reputation of the firm and stock price erosion, the antecedents of such failures and recalls remain underresearched. We examine international sourcing through a multitheoretic lens to investigate how the unfavorability of institutions of the countries from where products are sourced increases the likelihood of product failures. We propose that international experience of the firm, supplier development initiatives, and the firm's strategic nature of sourcing all moderate the relationship between institutional constraints and product-quality failures.

Keywords: institutions, product-quality failures, knowledge transfer, monitoring

An increase in the presence of defective or hazardous products in the market has severe consequences. In the United States alone, deaths, injuries, and property damage from consumer products cost the economy more than $1 trillion annually (Consumer Product Safety Commission 2015). Globalization of supply chains may be one of the explanations for the rise in defective products entering the market (Bapuji & Beamish, 2007; Kenney, 2008) and leading to these alarming consequences. As multinational enterprises (MNEs) from developed countries source products from developing countries in order to leverage lower manufacturing costs, product recalls have been found to increase across countries and industries (Beamish & Bapuji, 2008; Bates, Holweg, Lewis, & Oliver, 2007; Coleman, 2004).

Quality failures in global sourcing can arise due to a number of reasons, including "miscommunication, betrayal of trust, cross-cultural differences in values, relationships and rules of reciprocal exchanges" among global supply chain partners (Lyles, Flynn, & Frolich, 2008, p. 169). Although quality management has generated substantial interest among scholars (Sousa & Voss, 2002), quality failures have been underresearched from a supply chain perspective (Steven, Dong, & Corsi, 2014). This paper investigates whether product-quality failures are associated with a firm's international sourcing supply base, and what are some of the measures to prevent quality failures. There is a potential to develop theoretical and empirical basis in this area to generate scholarly understanding and actionable insights.

We use perspectives from institutional theory to first develop a framework in order to understand some of the antecedents of product-quality failures in international sourcing (Muralidharan & Laplume, 2014). We argue that institutional contexts preclude effective knowledge transfer to sourcing partners, undermine monitoring of sourcing units, and lead to product-quality failures in international sourcing. Second, we use insights from the resource-based view of the firm, organizational learning, and social capital theory to suggest initiatives that firms can take to reduce product-quality failures in international sourcing (see Figure 1).

We expect this article to make the following contributions to international sourcing literature. We examine product-quality failures in international sourcing through a multitheoretic lens. The institutional environment of the international sourcing bases is investigated for its influence on product-quality failures. Specifically, we examine the extent to which the institutional environment of international sourcing bases is associated with product failures. In examining the potential moderators, we offer possible solutions to practitioners for managing the institutional contexts from which they source products, to help prevent product-quality failures.

The article is organized as follows. We first introduce a conceptual model of sourcing from extant literature and then discuss perspectives from institutional theory in order to investigate the effects of institutional contexts of the

Figure 1
Multitheoretic Model for International Sourcing

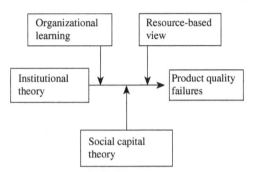

countries from where products are sourced on the operations of firms engaged in international sourcing. Insights from these discussions are drawn to develop propositions to explain the effects of such institutional contexts on product-quality failures. Then, by using insights from organizational learning, social capital theory, and the resource-based view, we discuss various initiatives that organizations can take in order to manage these contexts and help prevent product-quality failures. We conclude the article with an overall discussion on our proposed framework, and suggest some of the avenues for future research.

Sourcing Context

Sourcing of products can take place in different ways. Internal sourcing occurs when the products are sourced from within the corporate system, and external sourcing occurs when they are sourced from independent suppliers (Murray & Kotabe, 1999). Similarly, domestic sourcing occurs when the suppliers are located in the same country as the customer, while international sourcing occurs when the suppliers are located outside the customer's country. International sourcing views the whole world as a potential source for raw materials, components, services, and finished goods (Monczka & Trent, 1991). We use Trent and Monczka (2005) levels of sourcing as a basis for furthering our understanding of international sourcing. The movement of firms from domestic sourcing to the international arena is viewed as a continuum (see Figure 2).

The two stages of international sourcing defined as "international purchasing" and "global sourcing" can be described as follows. International purchasing refers to the process of soliciting, negotiating, and contracting for the supply of goods from different suppliers located worldwide (Chen, Ishikawa, & Yu, 2004; Murray & Kotabe, 1999). These purchases are routine and rarely involve transfer of resources (Chen, Paulraj, & Lado, 2004). They create value

Figure 2
Stages of Sourcing

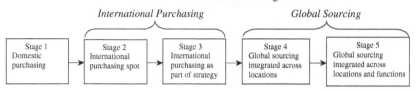

Source: Trent and Monczka (2005).

through cost economics. Global sourcing is an "approach to sourcing and supply management that involves integrating and coordinating common materials, processes, designs, technologies and suppliers across worldwide buying, design and operating locations" (Trent & Monczka, 2005, p. 24). Global sourcing is more strategic when firms rely on intermediate markets or sources located in different countries to provide specialized capabilities that supplement existing capabilities deployed along the firms' value chain, creating value beyond just cost economics (Holcomb & Hitt, 2007). We now examine how international sourcing differs from domestic sourcing.

International Sourcing versus Domestic Sourcing

With globalization, firms have faced increased competition from all around the world. These competitive pressures have forced firms to improve the quality of their products and bring them to the market at lower costs. Such pressures have lead to international sourcing from suppliers who can produce quality products at lower costs (Cho & Kang, 2001). International sourcing may also provide access to specialized technologies, products, economies of scale, and benefits associated with the institutions of the source country. Therefore, the major reasons for international sourcing, as identified by many studies, have been to achieve improvements in the areas of cost reduction, quality, and availability of products (Monczka & Trent, 1991).

Differences in the national contexts from where firms source products, however, matter in international sourcing. The management of international sourcing, when compared to the management of domestic sourcing, risks potential opportunism, and therefore high coordination costs following differences that exist between the countries (Grant 1996; Williamson 1985). These differences can preclude effective transfer of product specifications, product safety requirements, product and process technologies, commercial terms, and other organizational processes and routines to the suppliers or sourcing partners (Bhagat, Kedia, Harveston, & Triandis, 2002; Bartlett & Ghoshal, 1989). Improper management of international sourcing may therefore lead to high operational risks involving slippages in quality, cost, or speed of process execution (Kumar, Kwong, & Misra, 2009). We now examine how national contexts specifically influence product quality.

Institutions and Institutional Contexts

In the previous sections we have discussed the ways that international sourcing differs from domestic sourcing. In order to further understand the influence of countries on international sourcing, we draw insights from institutional theory. One of the basic assumptions of institutional theory is that firms are influenced by common understandings of what is appropriate and meaningful behavior (Zucker, 1983). Institutional environments in which firms are located influence them to conform to practices, policies, and structures that are in line with institutional preferences (Meyer & Rowan, 1977). Institutions are therefore considered to be the rules of the game in a society, or in other words, the constraints that influence and shape human interactions (North, 1990, p. 3). This understanding of institutions is further elaborated by Scott (1995), who defined institutions along regulatory, normative, and cognitive dimensions, giving a three-dimensional structure to the country context.

Regulatory

The regulatory dimension of institutions concerns with the "setting, monitoring and enforcing of rules" (Xu & Shenker, 2002, p. 610). This dimension is basically the "existing laws and rules in a particular national environment that promote certain types of behaviors and restrict others" (Kostova, 1997, p. 180). In other words, the regulatory dimension of institutions "guide[s] organizational action by threat of legal sanctions,"[1] and therefore, this dimension requires firms to comply with rules and regulations in order to avoid penalties for noncompliance (Chao & Kumar, 2010, p. 94). Some examples of such compliance include the maintenance of statutory accounts by organizations in order to meet tax law requirements and the adoption of efficient pollution control mechanisms by organizations in order to comply with environmental regulations (DiMaggio & Powell, 1983).

Normative

The normative dimension of institutions deals with "social norms, values, beliefs, and assumptions about human nature and human behavior that are socially shared and are carried by individuals" (Kostova, 1997, p. 180). This dimension stems from societal norms and beliefs (Xu & Shenkar, 2002). The normative or social aspects of institutions involve taken-for-granted procedures or customs within society. The ability of such procedures or customs to guide action "stems from their social obligation or professionalism," and examples of such customs can be seen in gift-giving and bribery, which are commonly accepted practices in emerging economies like India and China" (Chao & Kumar, 2010, p. 94).

Cognitive

The cognitive dimension of institutions that influences the "schemas, frames, and inferential sets, which people use when selecting and interpreting information," reflects the "cognitive structures and social knowledge shared by people in a given country" (Kostova, 1997, p. 180). Examples of such influences are symbols, words, signs, and gestures as well as the rules and regulations of a cultural framework. Firms follow these rules and regulations without any resistance (Zucker, 1983).

As defined by Eden and Miller (2004, p. 16), these institutions are equivalent to three verb tenses, where the regulatory dimension "defines what organizations and individuals may or may not do," the normative dimension "defines what they should or should not do," and the cognitive dimension "defines what is or is not true and what can or cannot be done." Organizations tend to change their structures in line with the earlier-mentioned institutional dimensions (DiMaggio & Powell, 1983). Understanding the influence of these institutions on international sourcing will therefore require detailed analysis of the environmental contexts from which firms source products and how those contexts influence the particular issue of the quality of the products sourced. Such analysis will entail examining how differences along these institutional dimensions in the source countries affect product quality. In the subsequent sections, we examine how these dimensions affect the quality of internationally sourced products.

Institutional Distance and International Sourcing

When operating in different countries, multinational organizations have to adjust to different institutional contexts in their operations (Dunning & Lundan, 2008; Peng, 2003). The differences between these institutional contexts can be captured by institutional distance. Institutional distance is the difference or the extent of similarity (or dissimilarity) along regulatory, normative, and cognitive institutions between two countries (Kostova, 1999). The greater the distance between the organizations's home environment and source environment, the greater the challenge to adjust to source environment conditions and effectively manage firm operations. This concept of distance is central to scholarly explanations of the variations in strategies and performances of organizations operating across different countries (Tihanyi, Griffith, & Russel, 2005; Kostova & Roth, 2002; Shenker, 2001). Furthermore, the greater the distance, the more difficult it becomes for organizations to bridge the differences between countries in culture, laws, and regulations through its various routines and practices. Hence, an organization must adapt its forms and internal processes to manage these differences, and adaptation becomes more complex when the differences between institutional contexts increase (Kostova & Roth, 2002; Xu & Shenkar, 2002; Johanson & Vahlne, 1977).

We now examine the impact of the differences in institutional contexts on product-quality failures in a firm's international sourcing initiatives. In the case of international purchasing, correct identification of the global supplier and effective contract management and monitoring are key to ensuring quality products. There are two distinct types of transaction costs that arise in such exchanges: those that are associated with the efficiency of the exchange, and those that are associated with monitoring opportunistic behavior by economic agents (Lal, 1999). The former type relates to the costs of finding right suppliers, determining their supply demand offers, communicating appropriately the specifications (both technical and safety standards) of the products sourced; the latter relates to enforcing the execution of promises and agreements of the contracts signed with the suppliers or sourcing partners. These two aspects of transactions will have to be examined in light of the institutional influences of the countries where the firm's suppliers or sourcing partners are located. Differences in institutions between countries lead to ineffective transfer of knowledge in the former case; in the latter case, due to asymmetries in information facing principals and agents, crucial characteristics of the agent relevant for measuring performance can be concealed from the principal (Williamson,1985). These two aspects in international purchasing reveal that an increase in institutional distance will lead to barriers in maintaining quality and safety standards of the sourced products.

Similarly, global sourcing involves increased coordination and integration of a firm's sourcing operations across various foreign locations and functions (Trent & Monczka, 2005). Here, firms entering foreign markets for sourcing operations must find ways to improve coordination and transfer their technology and other internal institutional arrangements that constitute part of their ownership advantages to their global strategic sourcing partners. To achieve improved coordination and successful transfer, it is essential for these firms to overcome their "liability of foreignness," which is a direct outcome of institutional distance (Zaheer, 1995). Specifically, the efficient transfer of product quality and safety standards, product and process technologies, quality management practices, and other organizational routines to the firm's strategic sourcing partners (Kostova & Roth, 2002; Guler, Guillen, & MacPherson, 2002) ensures the quality and safety of the products being sourced.

In summary, when the differences in the institutions between home country and source country increase, a firm's transfer of knowledge and practices, and its monitoring of product quality in the international sourcing process may become less effective (Dunning & Lundan, 2008 ; Xu, Pan, & Beamish, 2004 ; Xu & Shenkar, 2002). We explore the impact of each institutional pillar on the mechanisms of knowledge transfer and monitoring in international sourcing activities. Going by the broadly explicit and tacit nature of regulatory and normative/cognitive pillars, respectively, we conceptualize our propositions around regulatory, normative, and cognitive institutions in developing our framework to predict the impact of the institutional context on product-quality failures. While our central proposition is that unfavorable regulatory, normative, and cognitive source country institutional contexts with respect to product quality and product safety lead to an increase in the likelihood product-quality failures (higher proportion of defective products or those that are noncompliant to technical specifications and safety standards) in international sourcing, we also look at ways in which the likelihood of such failures can be reduced. Increased experience of the firm in international sourcing, supplier development programs, and the strategic nature of sourcing are expected to reduce the likelihood product-quality failures. Our framework that describes our observations is presented in Figure 3. We now examine specifically how regulatory, normative, and cognitive dimensions individually influence product-quality failures in international sourcing operations.

Figure 3
Framework for Managing Institutional Contexts in International Sourcing

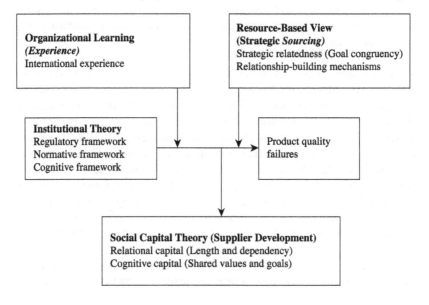

Role of Regulatory Institutional Context

The regulatory institutiona.l environment of the country where the firm sources its products or where it has sourcing operations will play an important role in setting, monitoring, and enforcing the rules of its operations. The determinants of the regulatory dimension are, however, issue-specific (issue of product-quality failures in international sourcing in this study), which is quite in line with extant research (Walsh, 1995; Rosenzweig & Singh, 1991). These determinants play an important role, first in international purchasing, as follows. Legal and regulatory frameworks, which differ across countries, provide regulatory mechanisms by which trade practices for ensuring product quality and safety are effectively monitored, to the benefit of the ultimate consumer. Such mechanisms limit the extent to which defective and hazardous products enter the market. Therefore the extent to which such regulatory practices are developed in a country is one of the main determinants of regulatory institutional strength in a country. For example, the effectiveness of regulatory bodies such as the Consumer Product Safety Commission (CPSC) and the National Highway Traffic Safety Administration (NHTSA) in the United States is an indication of the presence of strong regulatory mechanisms that are already in place to monitor against the entry of defective products into the market.

The legal system, as governed by product liability laws, also differs across countries from where firms source their products and is therefore another key determinant of regulatory institutional strength. Therefore, the extent to which quality standards can be enforced for product quality will be greatly influenced by the regulatory mechanisms that exist in the country where the firm sources its products. Effectiveness of such mechanisms will reduce the burden on firms to improve their monitoring activities in order to ensure defect-free quality of the products that are sourced from their international operations.

In the case of global sourcing, in addition to monitoring for product quality, firms will also need to transfer organizational knowledge to the sourcing units. Unfavorable regulatory contexts in the source country are likely to inhibit the effective transfer of organizational knowledge, such as product technology, process technology, quality management systems, and other organizational routines to the firm's strategic sourcing partners (Kostova & Roth, 2002). Transfer of organizational learning systems, for example, may require an overall change in the organizational structure and design in order to effectively cultivate organizational learning routines (Hong, Easterby-Smith, & Snell, 2006). However, regulatory institutions, such as the local law and labor market regulations, may make it difficult to change existing practices in the organizations of the source country. We therefore argue that the existing regulatory framework in the source country may constrain restructuring, for example, if it involves staff redundancies where stringent labor laws may not allow high rates of downsizing.

Therefore, when the need to introduce new systems (such as new product and process technologies, quality management systems and practices, and foreign organizational routines) collides with the regulatory context governed by formal institutions in the source country, it becomes very difficult to ensure conformance of the quality of products to the required standards of the firm.

We therefore expect the aforementioned challenges for the firm to increase with the extent to which the regulatory framework in the source country is less favorable with respect to product-quality issues. Favorable regulatory frameworks will therefore comprise effective enforcement mechanisms for ensuring quality products to customers and flexibility for organizations to incorporate new routines. Less favorable regulatory frameworks will therefore lead to an increase in the incidence of defective products entering the market. Hence, we propose the influence of the source country's regulatory institutions on product-quality failures experienced by a firm engaged in international sourcing:

Proposition 1: In the context of international sourcing, the likelihood of product-quality failures is positively associated with the unfavorability of the source country's regulatory context.

Role of Normative and Cognitive Institutional Contexts

In addition to the regulatory institutional effects discussed in the earlier section, the impact of normative and cognitive institutions needs to be considered as well. The high level of transaction complexity involved in global sourcing and international purchasing requires effective transfer of product specifications (technical specifications and safety standards), product and process technologies, quality management practices, organizational routines to the sourcing partners, and strict conformance to purchase contracts through adequate monitoring of suppliers in the source country. However, such transfers and monitoring are mainly facilitated through legally enforceable documents that are broadly classified as contracts, and these are "typically written with the enforcement characteristics of exchange in mind" (Dikova, Sahib, & Witteloostuijn, 2010, p. 228). Enforceable characteristics in the case of international sourcing will primarily contain aspects related to quality (technical specifications and safety standards) of the products, technology of the products and processes, and other related parameters of the exchange. However, "because of the costliness of measurement, most contracts will be incomplete; hence informal constraints will play a major role in the actual agreement" (North, 1990, p.61). Such informal constraints, which are outcomes of normative and cognitive institutional pressures on organizational behavior, are broadly accepted standards of conduct, norms, and social conventions. These normative and cognitive constraints, just like regulatory ones, are highly country-specific and stem largely from national culture. Therefore, successfully handling international sourcing initiatives can be a challenge because there is a greater need for sensitivity in resolving incompatibilities stemming from such differences between countries (Morosini, Shane, & Singh, 1998; Weber, Shenkar, & Raveh, 1996).

We again maintain that these normative and cognitive constraints are issue-specific (product quality in international sourcing being the issue in this study), and quite in line with extant research (Rosenzweig & Singh, 1991; Walsh, 1995). The cognitive component stems from the way people notice, characterize, and interpret stimuli from the environment, as represented by national symbols and various stereotypes. In our study, this dimension will comprise the shared social knowledge about what quality is and the way quality has to be managed (Kostova & Roth, 2002). The normative dimension comprises social norms, values, beliefs, and assumptions about human nature that are socially shared among individuals (Kostova, 1997; 1999). In our study, the normative dimension will comprise quality-related norms and values (Kostova & Roth, 2002). As the differences along these dimensions increase, we expect the primary effect of unfamiliarity to increase as well, in terms of the sourcing firm's knowledge of the source country (Eden & Miller, 2004). An increase in unfamiliarity increases the challenges of the sourcing firm to understand the source country's normative and cognitive institutional guidelines (Kostova & Zaheer, 1999). In the case of international purchasing, such unfamiliarity hazards, we argue, may lead to improper contracts being finalized between the sourcing firm and the suppliers because the way suppliers view various specifications and safety requirements of the products will be governed by the normative and cognitive frameworks that exist in their countries. Similarly, in the case of global sourcing, these differences reduce the firm's ability to transfer organizational practices such as product and process technology, quality management practices, and other organizational routines to the sourcing partners, largely because the sourcing partners' view of such practices will be governed by the normative and cognitive frameworks that exist in their countries, which may be different from those prevalent in the home country of the firm. Furthermore such transfers may require changes in the organizational structures of the sourcing partners. Organizational structures are typically part of the firm's administrative heritage and are rooted in the national culture of the country (Calori, Lubatkin, & Very, 1994). Changing these structures in order to facilitate the transfer of organizational practices can be very challenging for the sourcing firm. Similarly, the attention accorded to all the aspects of product quality by the employees of the suppliers or sourcing partners will be influenced largely by the normative institutions (quality-related norms) and cognitive institutions (shared knowledge of what quality is and how it has to be managed) of the country. Unfavorable normative and cognitive institutions will entail increased challenges for the firm in monitoring for adherence of products to quality and safety standards.

Increasing distances in normative and cognitive institutions, caused by unfavorable source country normative and cognitive institutions in international sourcing arrangements of firms, therefore may lead to improper contracts and execution with suppliers because of inefficient transfer of organizational routines to the sourcing partners and inadequate monitoring of operations in the source country. Favorability of the normative and cognitive institutional context in a positive sense will require cognitive structures that help people to understand the essence of product quality and safety, as well as normative structures that provide social norms that enforce a sense of product quality and safety. A lack of these institutions may result in defective or noncompliant (to quality standards or safety standards) products entering the market. Hence, we propose the influence of normative and cognitive institutions on product-quality failures experienced by a firm engaged in international sourcing:

> *Proposition 2a: In the context of international sourcing, the likelihood of product-quality failures is positively associated with the unfavorability of the source country's normative context.*

> *Proposition 2b: In the context of international sourcing, the likelihood of product-quality failures is positively associated with the unfavorability of the source country's cognitive context.*

Regulatory, Normative, and Cognitive Contexts

The fact that institutions matter and that they differ between countries, as discussed in the earlier sections, suggests the importance of a theoretical link between institutional context and firm performance in international sourcing operations. We have used this link to understand the phenomenon of product-quality failures. As we have proposed in the earlier section, favorability of the regulatory, normative, and cognitive contexts of the countries from which firms source products are associated with product-quality failures in global sourcing and international purchasing operations. However, regulatory institutions in source countries are perhaps easier for foreign sourcing firms to study, understand, and correctly interpret, since the existence or nonexistence of such institutions is well codified and formalized in rules, procedures, and common knowledge (Eden & Miller, 2004). On the contrary, normative and cognitive institutions of a country—which broadly comprise societal beliefs and norms (normative), and schemas and inferential sets that people use to interpret information (cognitive)—are tacit and are therefore difficult for outsiders to comprehend and interpret (Kostova & Zaheer, 1999). For these reasons, when it comes to international sourcing issues, we expect that regulatory institutional constraints, which are more explicit, should be easier for firms to overcome compared to normative and cognitive institutional constraints, which are more tacit and opaque. For example, firms can employ consultants or agents in the source country to help understand the regulatory framework of the source country where they have sourcing operations. Therefore, the marginal effect that normative and cognitive institutional source-country constraints have on product quality is expected to be higher than that of regulatory institutional source-country constraints. Hence, we propose a differential effect between the favorability of regulatory institutional context and normative and cognitive institutional contexts on product-quality failures experienced by a firm engaged in international sourcing:

> *Proposition 3: In the context of international sourcing, unfavorable normative and cognitive institutional contexts of the source country are more positively associated with the likelihood of product-quality failures than are the unfavorable regulatory contexts.*

Moderating Effects of International Experience (Organizational Learning View)

We have argued that the product-quality failures of a firm engaged in international sourcing are influenced by the regulatory, normative, and cognitive institutional contexts of the source country from where it sources its products. Organizations have been defined as "purposive entities designed by their creators to maximize wealth, income, or other objectives defined by the opportunities afforded by the institutional structure of the society" (North, 1990, p.73). Also, the institutional contexts in which organizations operate determine the kind of knowledge and skills needed for the "maximizing behavior" (North, 1990). Therefore, studying the institutional context will indicate the kind of knowledge and skills required for organizations to conduct operations efficiently. It is also argued by North that in order to "play a good game," organizations must acquire these skills and knowledge in a learning-by-doing manner, meaning that firms must develop routines and skills that are outcomes of repeated interaction. Organizations benefit from event experience in one country because some of the acquired skills and knowledge can be transferred to operations in other countries. This outcome has frequently appeared in research on cross-border acquisitions, where differences in regulatory, normative, and cognitive institutions do play a significant role in the success of such acquisitions (Barkema & Schijven, 2008; Vermeulen & Barkema, 2001; Hitt, Harrison, Ireland, & Best, 1998; Lubatkin, 1983). International business literature also speaks to the fact that familiarity with an international context can be developed through commercial experience (international purchasing and global sourcing in this study) in a country (Davis, Desai, & and Francis, 2000; Johanson & Vahlne, 1977). Through the process of gaining cultural experience or acculturation (Berry, 1980), firms develop knowledge and familiarity with local country environments in which they operate, which helps to reduce the effects of institutional constraints (Emden, Yaprak, & Cavusgil, 2005; Shenker, 2001). Thus, subsequent transactions are often part of an overall strategy that is implemented in steps and builds on the firm's earlier operations (Meyer & Tran, 2006).

Extending this argument, we expect that the international sourcing experience of a firm in multiple countries will reduce the challenges of sourcing and purchasing from a new country. Through increased experience, we expect firms to develop routines for understanding and adhering to diverse regulatory, normative, and cognitive contextual requirements. In the case of unfavorable regulatory requirements, prior experience will enable firms to develop adequate governance mechanisms to ensure appropriate monitoring for quality, thereby making up for the lack of such mechanisms in the source country. These mechanisms will ensure that suppliers adhere to the product-quality and safety requirements that are the prime requirements in international purchasing. In the case of global sourcing, experience will provide firms with tested mechanisms to coordinate with, integrate, and transform sourcing units from the source country in line with the focal firm, namely, by efficient transfer of knowledge (technical specification, product and process technologies, quality management practices, and other organizational routines). Similarly, we argue that through increased experience, firms can develop routines and skills for managing the sensitivities in handling the differences in the normative and cognitive dimensions in countries. These skills will entail tested mechanisms, by which a common language of quality (cognitive) for employees in the source country can be implemented and a positive attitude toward quality (normative) can be inculcated among the employees of the supplier or the sourcing partner. Hence, in the practice of international sourcing, the accumulation of richer or more diverse experience may moderate the negative effects of institutional contexts on product quality. We propose:

Proposition 4a: Prior experience of the firm in international sourcing moderates the effect of the unfavorability of the source country's regulatory context on the likelihood of product-quality failures; the positive association becomes weaker as experience in international sourcing increases.

Proposition 4b: Prior experience of the firm in international sourcing moderates the effect of the unfavorability of the source country's normative context on the likelihood of product-quality failures; the positive association becomes weaker as experience in international sourcing increases.

Proposition 4c: Prior experience of the firm in international sourcing moderates the effect of the unfavorability of the source country's cognitive context on the likelihood of product-quality failures; the positive association becomes weaker as experience in international sourcing increases.

In the case of overcoming normative institutional constraints, we expect the process of experiential learning to be time-consuming since norms and social conventions are not codified. These norms and conventions are highly tacit and are therefore difficult to comprehend. This expectation is applicable to cognitive institutional constraints as well since their recognition itself is limited by human cognition. Therefore, learning about normative and cognitive institutional constraints in a foreign environment is a long-term process for the firms involved in international sourcing. Over time, these firms may develop capabilities to overcome these constraints and adapt or transfer practices to local organizations (Kostova & Roth, 2002). However, in the case of regulatory institutions, in terms of product quality, most of the regulatory institutions—or lack thereof—are codified and can be understood relatively easily by firms involved in international sourcing. For example, firms may employ consultants, inspection agencies, and legal experts to study the regulatory context and assist in ensuring compliance by suppliers or souring partners of product quality and safety requirements in environments lacking regulatory mechanisms. Therefore, the marginal benefit that international experience can provide toward alleviating normative and cognitive institutional constraints is expected to be greater than it would be toward alleviating regulatory institutional constraints. Hence, we propose differential effects of international sourcing experience in overcoming institutional constraints:

Proposition 5: In terms of likelihood of product-quality failures, prior experience of the firm in international sourcing moderates the effect of unfavorability of the source country's normative and cognitive institutional contexts more so than it moderates the effect of unfavorability of the source country's regulatory context.

Moderating Effects of Supplier Development (Social Capital View)

We have argued that unfavorable institutional contexts in the source countries from where firms source products serve to increase information asymmetries between partners, in turn leading to constraints in monitoring contracts. These constraints result in problems of opportunism by suppliers or sourcing partners. Unfavorable institutional contexts also lead to problems of unfamiliarity between partners, creating obstacles in the transfer of knowledge such as product quality and safety specifications, product and process technologies, quality management practices, and other organizational routines to suppliers or sourcing partners. These obstacles, we expect, will result in noncompliant or defective products entering the markets.

We argue that these negative effects of unfavorable institutional contexts can be reduced through supplier development and by building strong relationships with sourcing partners. The term "supplier development" is used to describe firms' efforts to increase the number of viable suppliers and improve suppliers' performance (Leenders, 1966). More specifically, supplier development has been defined as any effort by a buying firm to improve the performance or capabilities of its suppliers (Krause, Handfield, & Scannell, 1998). The practice of supplier development in Japan and its ensuing global application has been well documented (Turnbull, Oliver, & Wilkinson, 1992), and it stems from extant literature on interorganizational relationships.

Across the various fields associated with organizational research, there is an increasing recognition of the importance of interorganizational relationships as a source of competitive advantage and value creation (Osborn & Hagedoorn, 1997; Smith, Caroll, & Ashfod, 1995). This relationship between value creation and interorganizational relationships has been well explored and well documented using various organizational theories. Some of the theories include resource dependence theory (Pfeffer & Salancik, 1978), transaction cost economics (Williamson, 1985), resource-based theory (Tyler, 2001; Wernfelt, 1995), and social capital theory (Tsai & Ghoshal, 1998; Jones, Hesterly, & Borgatti, 1997). The central argument of each of these theories proposes that when firms invest in relation-specific resources, engage actively in knowledge exchange, and combine various resources through appropriate governance mechanisms, then extra profits can be derived by both parties involved in the exchange. In our study, we extend this understanding by examining how international sourcing relationships between the firm and its partners from various countries can specifically affect product-quality failures. We do so by using insights from social capital theory.

Social capital is a valuable asset that stems from access to resources made available through social relationships (Granovetter, 1992). We use the dimensions of relational and cognitive capital, as proposed by Nahapiet and Ghoshal (1998), to develop the arguments for supplier development. Relational capital refers to the personal relationships that develop through interactions; it is the trust, obligation, and reciprocity that exists between partners (Nahapiet & Ghoshal, 1998). Extant research on relational capital argues that organizational routines and cospecialized assets are established and bilateral dependence increases as interaction between partners increases (Nelson & Winter, 1982; Teece, 1986). This interaction has been found to increase collaboration and stimulate readjustments among partners (Doz, 1996). Furthermore, increased interaction has also shown to increase trust between buyers and suppliers (Sako & Helper, 1998) by reducing their expectations of opportunism and their perceptions of exchange hazards (Parkhe, 1993).

Owing to repeated interactions, partners to an exchange are less likely to act opportunistically for social, psychological, and economic reasons (Granovetter, 1995). Also through repeated interactions, buyers and suppliers develop a common language for discussing product specifications, safety standards, product and process technology issues, quality management practices, and organizational routines connected with sourcing operations (Buckley & Casson, 1976). This ongoing interaction helps firms to overcome problems related to unfamiliarity. Thus, the obstacles of opportunistic behavior of partners and unfamiliarity issues between partners (stemming from unfavorable institutional contexts in international sourcing) can be surmounted by building relational capital. Through supplier development, we argue that relational capital, as represented by the long-term buyer–supplier relationship and the dependency of the buyer and the supplier to the relationship, can alleviate those product-quality problems caused by unfavorable institutional contexts in international sourcing. Hence, we propose:

> *Proposition 6a: Relational capital moderates the effect of unfavorable source country's institutional contexts on the likelihood of product-quality failures; the positive association between unfavorability of the source country's institutional contexts and the likelihood of product-quality failures becomes weaker as the relational capital between firm and sourcing partner increases.*

Cognitive social capital is a resource that gives parties shared interpretations and systems of meaning. Goals are shared when members in a relationship hold similar perceptions in terms of how they should interact and when they have a common understanding and approach to the achievement of tasks and results (Tsai & Ghoshal, 1998). These shared meanings, in the form of common goals and values, are developed by partners through an ongoing and self-reinforcing process of participation in sense-making as they construct a shared understanding (Nahapiet & Ghoshal, 1998; Weick, 1995). In the context of supplier development, this self-reinforcing process of cooperative cognitive sense-making in terms of product quality and safety requirements can be expected to improve sourcing-partner performance (Krause, Handfield, & Tyler, 2007).

If goals and values between buyer and supplier are not congruent where product quality and product safety are concerned (especially due to unfavorable source country institutional contexts), then interactions between the two parties may lead to misinterpretation, resulting in negative effects on productivity and product quality (Inkpen & Tsang, 2005). Therefore, building cognitive capital with suppliers or sourcing partners can alleviate the negative impact of unfavorable source country institutional contexts on the firm's international sourcing operations. When the firm and its partners have similar goals and values with respect to product quality and safety standards, we expect cognitive capital to positively affect product-quality performance. Hence we propose:

> *Proposition 6b: Cognitive capital moderates the effect of unfavorable source country's institutional contexts on the likelihood of product-quality failures; the positive association between unfavorability of the source country's institutional contexts and the likelihood of product-quality failures becomes weaker as cognitive capital between the firm and its sourcing partner increases.*

Moderating Effects of Strategic Sourcing Initiatives (Resource-Based View)

We have argued in the earlier sections that costs associated with managing international sourcing will accrue in response to managing monitoring challenges and transfer of knowledge to the international locations from where products are sourced. Unfavorable source country institutional contexts increase these challenges for international sourcing. We used insights from social capital theory and discussed the fact that long-term relationships and goal congruence between the firm and its sourcing partners can help overcome the challenges associated with international sourcing. We now use insights from the resource-based perspective to explain how strategic sourcing can help manage the challenges that stem from institutional contexts. The resource-based view suggests that competitive advantage can be explained with reference to the firm's idiosyncratic human and capital resources and its capabilities (Barney, 1991). Strategic sourcing is the organizational arrangement that emerges when firms depend on intermediate markets to provide specialized capabilities that supplement the existing capabilities of the firm along the value chain (Holcomb & Hitt, 2007). We use the two dimensions proposed by Holcomb and Hitt (2007)—that is, strategic relatedness and relational capability-building mechanisms—to explain how firms can manage the challenges they face in international sourcing due to unfavorable source country institutional contexts.

Strategic relatedness provides the logic for the sharing of capabilities between firms (Prahalad & Bettis, 1986). It is the congruency of goals and common knowledge platforms between firms that, we argue, will help manage the challenges of unfavorable source-country institutional contexts in international sourcing. Congruency of goals is the extent to which the firm's operational, strategic, and performance goals match with those of its sourcing partners, which helps to resolves potential concerns regarding dissimilar interests (Luo, 2002). Congruency of goals also enables collaborative behavior (Parkhe, 1993). It improves the quality of relationships between the partners and thereby reduces the probability of opportunism (Granovetter, 1985; Uzzi, 1996). Therefore, congruent goals reduce the need for high monitoring, since the threat of opportunism is reduced (Uzzi, 1997; Dyer & Singh, 1998). Similarly, congruency of goals will also reduce the differences in perceptions toward product quality and product safety that stem from institutional differences. We therefore summarize that strategic relatedness between the firm and its suppliers and sourcing partners may help it to manage the challenges of monitoring and of ineffective transfer of knowledge caused by unfavorable source country institutional contexts. This relationship, we argue, will help reduce the quality problems of the products entering the market through international sourcing, and hence, we propose:

Proposition 7a: Strategic relatedness between the firm and its sourcing partner moderates the effect of unfavorable source country's institutional contexts on the likelihood of product-quality failures; the positive association between unfavorability of the source country's institutional contexts and the likelihood of product-quality failures becomes weaker as the strategic relatedness between the firm and its sourcing partner increases.

A firm's managing capabilities represents a dynamic capability that enables it to connect the various productive or sourcing units in its value chain and improve firm performance (Teece, Pisano, & Shuen, 1997; Holcomb & Hitt, 2007), as suggested by the extant research. These capabilities reside within firms as strategic and organizational routines (Helefat & Peteraf, 2003). Relational capability-building mechanisms are such routines that enable firms to leverage specialized or complementary capabilities, such as in international sourcing (Dyer & Singh, 1998).

By building bridges with their overseas sourcing partners, firms can manage the challenges of knowledge transfer and monitoring that are caused by unfavorable source country institutional contexts. As a result, the firm also improves its own ability to integrate and leverage its various sourcing opportunities across a value chain. Such relational capability-building mechanisms represent dedicated resources and processes that support international sourcing activities, enable learning (Fiol & Lyles, 1985), and manage interfirm relationships (Kale, Dyer, & Singh, 2002). Relationship capability resources include managers or departments that are dedicated to developing suppliers, strategic sourcing departments, and foreign coordination offices. These relationship-building mechanisms enable firms to manage the challenges of unfavorable institutional contexts and help reduce the negative effects of such contexts on product quality. Hence we propose:

Proposition 7b: Relationship-building mechanisms moderate the effect of unfavorable source country's institutional contexts on the likelihood of product-quality failures; the positive association between unfavorability of the source country's institutional contexts and the likelihood of product-quality failures becomes weaker as the relationship-building mechanisms of the firm increase.

Discussion

When firms move abroad for their sourcing initiatives, the institutional context in which they operate plays a very important role in their performance (Peng, 2003). Existing literature has not looked in depth the quality consequences of lengthening the supply chain through international sourcing (Steven et al. 2014). Our investigation suggests that the institutional environment of the international sourcing bases influences the likelihood of product-quality failures. Extant research regarding institutional influences on product-quality failures has focused on the role of regulatory agencies in product recalls. The various research articles evaluate the product-recall regulatory framework and offer suggestions for improvement, such as stricter regulations, larger budgets, and stricter import surveillance (Felcher, 2003). Also, from a practitioner's point of view, research suggests that understanding the business culture, legal requirements, and regulatory infrastructure of the supplier's country in order to determine the level of vigilance needed to monitor product quality is primary to managing the risks associated with product-quality failures (Riswadkar & Jewell, 2007).

Drawing insights from institutional theory, social capital theory, organizational learning, and resource-based views, we propose a framework to understand the broader phenomenon of international sourcing in reference to product-quality failures, their challenges, and the various initiatives that organizations can take to overcome these challenges. These perspectives are combined to examine the firm's product-quality failure performance in international sourcing.

Institutional distance and its influences on various phenomena is well known in international business literature specifically in terms of the costs that firms incur in conducting business across international borders. Institutional distance has been used to understand the international entry strategies of multinationals and expatriate strategies (Xu et al. 2004); liability of foreignness and ownership strategies (Eden & Miller, 2004); international diversity/performance relationship (Chao & Kumar, 2010); cross-border acquisition performance (Dikova et al. 2010); and social development (Lal, 1999). By extending the understanding of institutional distance to international sourcing, we attempt to examine its influence on product-quality failures.

We propose a model that provides the basis for investigating some of the causes that lead to product-quality failures in the context of international sourcing. We argue that the institutional contexts of the source countries act as the key drivers of product-quality failures that stem specifically from firms' international sourcing operations. These contexts affect the quality of products through problems that arise due to ineffective transfer of knowledge, such as product specifications, product safety standards, product and process technologies, quality management practices, and other organizational routines directed at the sourcing partners. These contexts also preclude effective monitoring of the suppliers or sourcing partners to ensure that they are adhering to the contracted quality and safety standards; they stand in the way of curbing opportunism among the contracting partners in source countries.

This paper contributes to international sourcing literature in the following manner. We have examined international sourcing and its associated challenges through a multitheoretic lens. Organizational theory has tremendous potential to offer helpful insights in the field of supply chain management (Ketchen, Jr. & Hult, 2007). Using institutional theories to understand aspects of international sourcing, we suggest that institutional unfavorability along regulatory, normative, and cognitive dimensions of the source country increases the likelihood of product-quality failures. Using perspectives from organizational learning, social capital, and resource base view we suggest that increased international experience of the firm, enhanced supplier development initiatives, and improved strategic nature of sourcing by the firm can help overcome institutional constraints and reduce the likelihood of product-quality failures in international sourcing.

Implications for Management

One of the key managerial implications of our paper is that international sourcing may be associated with undesired outcomes such as nonconformance of products with quality standards that may lead to product recalls. This consideration should be taken into account when deciding on cost-saving decisions that result from international sourcing. Specifically, managers deciding to outsource from international locations must be aware that such a strategy entails risks that may lead to expensive product failures. Managers may therefore need to take proactive preventive measures to overcome institutional constraints at international sourcing locations and limit the likelihood of product failures.

While organizational theories have generally been used to explain firm performance, we have used them to specifically understand how organizational initiatives can help to reduce product-quality failures. As outcomes, we have supplier development initiatives, international experience, strategic relatedness, and relationship-building mechanisms with sourcing firms as key factors that can help firms reduce product-quality failures caused by institutional contexts in international sourcing. Specifically, insights from social capital theory and the resource-based view have been used to strengthen our arguments on using interorganizational relationships as a competitive advantage in international sourcing. The outcomes of our arguments focus more on the *processes by which firms source products internationally* rather than on just the achievement of cost economy or value creation. Thus, we provide managers with a richer framework for understanding the benefits of past experience, capabilities, and capability-building mechanisms in reducing product-quality failures within international sourcing operations. Our framework can also inform regulators to ensure regulatory safeguards on the potential risks of products sourced from unfavorable institutional environments.

Limitations of the Study

There are a few limitations to this study. First, the insights from social capital theory and resource-based view need to be integrated further in order to develop the argument on inter-organizational relationships and their influence on international sourcing. In the present study, these two subject areas were conceptualized independently. Strategic relatedness and relationship-building mechanisms (insights from the resource-based view) can be examined as *drivers* to develop long-term relationships and shared values and goals (insights from social capital theory) in future studies. Second, modes of governance structure, based on the country environment, could also affect the likelihood of product-quality failures. Insights from entry mode studies of firms in international business literature can be interfaced with the present discussion to study the effect of the mode of governance on the likelihood product-quality failures. Third, moderating effects of the individual components of cognitive capital and relational capital may interact with the individual dimensions of the institutional context. Our present understanding could be enhanced by an examination individually of the effects of the length of firm-supplier relationship, firm-supplier dependency, shared values, and goals to find out how each of these moderates the relationship between the dimensions of institutional context and product-quality performance in international sourcing. Finally, since knowledge transfer is a key mechanism in international sourcing, insights from knowledge transfer literature may need to be interfaced in the present framework. For example, will the type of knowledge that is transferred in a sourcing exchange have a bearing on the firm's performance in international sourcing? It has been proposed that knowledge transfer is least effective when the type of knowledge is complex, tacit, and systemic and involves dissimilar cultural contexts (Bhagat et al. 2002). It will therefore be beneficial to examine the moderating effects of the type of knowledge transferred on product-quality failures within the context of international sourcing.

Directions for Future Research

A combination of primary and secondary data may be necessary to empirically test our framework. Product recalls serve as a proxy for product-quality failures. Firm-level data can be obtained from Compustat. The archives of the CPSC or Health Canada can yield data on the product recalls of firms involved in international sourcing. Data on regulatory, normative, and cognitive dimensions of institutional contexts can be collected through primary data. Survey items to measure favorability of institutional context that specifically addresses quality can be adapted from the instrument used by Kostova and Roth (2002). Secondary data can also be used to operationalize unfavorability of institutional contexts (Muralidharan, Bapuji, and Laplume 2015). Other data that include inputs on the moderators proposed, such as international experience, strategic sourcing, and supplier development initiatives undertaken by the firms, will also need to be collected through surveys. Appendix 1 shows all the constructs proposed and their potential operationalization.

Appendix 1

Key Constructs and Potential Methods

Propositions	Theory	Key Construct	Reference/ Source	Potential Method
Likelihood of product failure	Dependent Variable	Product Recalls	CPSC/Health Canada	Secondary Data
P1	Institutional Theory	Unfavorable Regulatory Context	Kostova and Roth (2002): Muralidharan et al. (2015)	Survey/ Secondary Data
P2	Institutional Theory	Unfavorable Normative Context	Kostova and Roth (2002): Muralidharan et al. (2015)	Survey/ Secondary Data
P3	Institutional Theory	Unfavorable Cognitive Context	Kostova and Roth (2002): Muralidharan et al. (2015)	Survey/ Secondary Data
P4a,b,c & P5	Organizational Learning	International Experience in Sourcing	Emden, Yaprak, and Cavusgil (2005)	Survey/ Secondary Data
P6a	Social Capital	Relational Capital	Nahapiet and Ghoshal (1998)	Survey
P6b	Social Capital	Cognitive Capital	Nahapiet & Ghoshal (1998)	Survey
P7a	Resource Based View	Strategic Relatedness	Holcomb and Hitt (2007)	Survey
P7b	Resource Based View	Relationship-Building Mechanisms	Holcomb and Hitt (2007)	Survey

References

Bapuji, H., & Beamish, P. (2007). *Toy recalls: Is China really the problem?* Asia Pacific Foundation of Canada: Vancouver, Canada. Available from http://www.asiapacific.ca/analysis/pubs/pdfs/commentary/cac45.pdf

Bapuji, H., & Beamish, P. (2008). Product recalls: Avoid hazardous design flaws. *Harvard Business Review, 86* (3), 23–26.

Barkema, H. G., & Schijven, M. (2008). How much do firms learn to make acquisitions? A review of past research and an agenda for the future. *Journal of Management, 34*, 594–634.

Barney, J. B. (1991). Firm resources and sustained competitive advantage. *Journal of Management, 17*, 99–120.

Bartlett, C., & Ghoshal, S. (1989). *Managing across borders: The transnational solution.* Boston: Harvard Business School Press.

Bates, H., Holweg, M., Lewis, M., & Oliver, N. (2007). Motor vehicles recalls: Trends patterns and emerging issues. *International Journal of Management Sciences, 35*, 202–210.

Berry, J. W. (1980). Social and cultural change. In: H. C. Triandis & R. W. Brislin (Eds.), *Handbook of cross-cultural psychology* (Vol. 5, pp. 211–279). Boston: Allyn & Beacon.

Bhagat, R. S., Kedia, B. L., Harveston, P. D., & Triandis, H. C. (2002). Cultural variations in the cross border transfer of organizational knowledge: An integrative framework. *Academy of Management Review, 27*, 204–221.

Buckley, P., & Casson, M. (1976). *The Future of Multinational Enterprise.* London: Macmillan.

Calori, R., Lubatkin, M. & Very, P. (1994). Control mechanisms in cross-border acquisitions: An international comparison. *Organization Studies, 15*, 361–379.

Chao, M, C-H., & Kumar, V. (2010). The impact of institutional distance on the international diversity–performance relationship. *Journal of World Business, 45* (1), 93–103.

Chen, I. J., & Paulraj, A., Lado, A. A. (2004). Strategic purchasing, supply management, and firm performance. *Journal of Operations Management, 22*, 505–523.

Chen, Y. M., Ishikawa, J. & Yu, Z. H. (2004). Trade liberalization and strategic sourcing. *Journal of International Economics, 63*, 419–436.

Cho, J., & Kang, J. (2001). Benefits and challenges of global sourcing: perceptions of US apparel retail firms. *International Marketing Review, 18*, 542–561.

Coleman, L. (2004). The frequency and cost of corporate crises 1. *Journal of Contingencies and Crisis Management, 12* (1), 2–13.

C.P.S.C. (2015). Consumer Product Safety Commission. http://www.cpsc.gov/en/About-CPSC/ (accessed on 4th October, 2015)

Davis, P. S., Desai, A. B., & Francis, J. D. (2000). Mode of international entry: an isomorphism perspective. *Journal of International Business Studies, 31*, 239–258.

Dikova, D., Sahib, P. R., & Van Witteloostuijn, A. (2010). Cross-border acquisition abandonment and completion: The effect of institutional differences and organizational learning in international business service industry, 1981–2001. *Journal of International Business Studies, 41*, 223–245.

DiMaggio, P., & Powell, W. (1983). The iron cage revisited: Institutional isomorphism and collective rationality on organizational fields. *American Sociological Review, 48*, 147–160.

Doz, Y. L. (1996). The evolution of cooperation in strategic alliances: Initial conditions or learning processes. *Strategic Management Journal, 17*, 55–83.

Dunning, J. H., & Lundan, S. (2008). *Multinational enterprises and the global economy* (2nd ed.). Cheltenham: Elgar.

Dyer, J. H., & Singh, H. (1998). The relational view: Cooperative strategy and sources of inter organizational competitive advantage. *Academy of Management Review, 23*, 660–679.

Eden, L., & Miller, S. R. (2004). Distance matters: Liability of foreignness, institutional distance and ownership strategy. *Advances in International Management, 16*, 187–221.

Emden, Z., Yaprak, A., & Cavusgil, S. T. (2005). Learning from experience in international alliances: Antecedents and firm performance implications. *Journal of Business Research, 58*, 883–892.

Felcher, E. M. (2003). Product recalls: Gaping holes in the nation's product safety net. *Journal of Consumer Affairs, 37*, 170–179.

Fiol, C. M., & Lyles, M. A. (1985). Organizational Learning. *Academy of Management Review, 10*, 803–813.

Granovetter, M. S. (1985). Economic action and social structure: The problem of embeddedness. *American Journal of Sociology, 91*, 481–510.

Granovetter, M. (1992). Problems of explanation in economic sociology. In N. Nohria & R. G. Eccles (Eds). *Networks and organizations* (pp. 25–56). Cambridge, MA: Harvard Business School Press.

Granovetter, M. (1995). Coase revisited: business groups in the modern economy. *Industrial and Corporate Change, 4* (1), 93–130.

Grant, R. M. (1996). Toward a knowledge based theory of the firm. *Strategic Management Journal, 17*, 109–122.

Guler, I., Guillen, M. F., & MacPherson, J. M. (2002). Global competition, institutions, and the diffusion of organizational practices: the international spread of ISO9000 quality certificates. *Administrative Science Quarterly, 47*, 207–232.

Helefat, C. E., & Peteraf, M. A. (2003). The dynamic resource-based view: capability lifecycles. *Strategic Management Journal, 24*, 997–1010.

Hitt, M. A., Harrison, J. S., Ireland, R. D., & Best, A. (1998). Attributes of successful and unsuccessful acquisitions of US firms. *British Journal of Management, 9* (2), 91–114.

Holcomb, T. R., & Hitt, M. A. (2007). Toward a model of strategic outsourcing. *Journal of Operations Management, 25*, 464–481.

Hong, J. F., Easterby-Smith, M., & Snell, R. S. (2006). Transferring organizational learning systems to Japanese subsidiaries in China. *Journal of Management Studies, 43*, 1027–1058.

Inkpen, A. C., & Tsang, E. W. (2005). Social capital, networks, and knowledge transfer. *Academy of Management Review, 30*, 146–165.

Johanson, J., & Vahlne, J. E. (1977). The internationalization process of the firm—A model of knowledge development and foreign market commitment. *Journal of International Business Studies, 8*, 23–32.

Jones, C., Hesterly, W. S., & Borgatti, S. P. (1997). A general theory of network governance: Exchange conditions and social mechanisms. *Academy of Management Review, 22*, 911–945.

Kale, P., Dyer, J. H. & Singh, H. (2002). Alliance capability, stock market response, and long-term alliance success: The role of the alliance function. *Strategic Management Journal, 9*, 159–172.

Kenney, B. (2008, March 7). Whatever happened to quality? *Industry Week,* pp. 42–47.

Ketchen, D. J., & Hult, G. T. M. (2007). Toward greater integration of insights from organization theory and supply chain management. *Journal of Operations Management, 25*, 455–458.

Kostova, T. (1997). Country institutional profile: Concept and measurement. *Best Paper Proceedings of the Academy of Management,* pp. 180–184.

Kostova, T. (1999). Transnational transfer of strategic organizational practices: A contextual perspective. *Academy of Management Review, 24*, 308–324.

Kostova, T., & Roth, K. (2002). Adoption of an organizational practice by subsidiaries of multinational corporations: Institutional and relational effects. *Academy of Management Journal, 45*, 215–233.

Kostova, T., & Zaheer, S. (1999). Organizational legitimacy under conditions of complexity: the case of multinational enterprise. *Academy of Management Review, 24*, 64–81.

Krause, D. R., Hanfield, R. G., & Scannell, T. V. (1998). An empirical investigation of supplier development: Reactive and strategic processes. *Journal of Operations Management, 17*, 39–58.

Krause, D. R., Handfield, R. B., & Tyler, B. B. (2007). The relationships between supplier development, commitment, social capital accumulation and performance improvement. *Journal of Operations Management, 25*, 528–545.

Kumar, S., Kwong, A., & Misra, C. (2009). Risk mitigation in offshoring of business operations. *Journal of Manufacturing Technology Management, 20*, 442–459.

Lal, D. (1999). *Unfinished business*. New Delhi: Oxford University Press.

Leenders, M. R. (1966). Supplier development. *Journal of Purchasing, 24*, 47–62.

Lubatkin, M. (1983). Mergers and the performance of the acquiring firm. *Academy of Management Review, 8*, 218–225.

Luo, Y. D. (2002). Contract, cooperation, and performance in international joint ventures. *Strategic Management Journal, 23*, 903–919.

Lyles, M. A., Flynn, B. B., & Frohlich, M. T., (2008). All supply chains don't flow through: understanding supply chain issues in product recalls. *Management and Organization Review, 4*, 167–182.

Meyer, J. W., & Rowan, B. (1977). Institutionalized organizations: Formal structure as myth and ceremony. *American Journal of Sociology, 83*, 340–363.

Meyer, K. E., & Tran, Y. T. T. (2006). Market Penetration and Acquisition Strategies for Emerging Economies. *Long Range Planning, 39*, 177–197.

Monczka, R. M., & Trent, R. J. (1991). Global sourcing: A development approach. *International Journal of Purchasing and Materials Management, 27* (2), 2–8.

Morosini, P., Shane, S., & Singh, H. (1998). National cultural distance and cross-border acquisition performance. *Journal of International Business Studies, 29*, 137–158.

Muralidharan, E. K., Bapuji, H., & Laplume, A. O. (2015). Influence of institutional profiles on time to recall. *Management Research Review, 38*, 605–626.

Muralidharan, E., & Laplume, A. (2014). The relationship between type of organization, learning, and product failures. *Current Topics in Management, 17*, 67–86.

Murray, J. Y., & Kotabe, M. (1999). Sourcing strategies of US service companies: A modified transaction-cost analysis. *Strategic Management Journal, 20*, 791–809.

Nahapiet, J., & Ghoshal, S. (1998). Social capital, intellectual capital, and the organizational advantage. *Academy of Management Review, 23*, 242–266.

Nelson, R. R., & Winter, S. G. (1982). *An evolutionary theory of economic change.* Cambridge, MA: Belkap Press.

North, D.C. (1990). *Institutions, institutional change and economic performance.* New York: Cambridge University Press.

Osborn, R. N., & Hagedoorn, J. (1997). The institutionalization and evolutionary dynamics of interorganizational alliances and networks. *Academy of Management Journal, 40*, 261–278.

Parkhe, A. (1993). Strategic alliance structuring: A game theoretic and transaction cost examination of interfirm cooperation. *Academy of Management Journal, 36*, 794–829.

Peng, M. W. (2003). Institutional transitions and strategic choices. *Academy of Management Review, 28*, 275–296.

Pfeffer, J., & Salancik, G. R. (1978). *The external control of organizations.* New York: Harper & Row.

Prahalad, C. K., & Bettis, R. A. (1986). The dominant logic: A new linkage between diversity and performance. *Strategic Management Journal, 7,* 485–501.

Riswadkar, A.V., & Jewell, D. (2007). Strategies for managing risks from imported products. *Professional Safety, 52*(11), 44–47.

Rosenzweig, P., & Singh, H. (1991). Organizational environments and the multinational enterprise. *Academy of Management Review, 16,* 340–361.

Sako, M., & Helper, S. (1998). Determinants of trust in supplier relations: Evidence from the automotive industry in Japan and the United States. *Journal of Economic Behavior and Organization, 34,* 387–417.

Scott, A. (1995). *Institutions and organizations.* Thousand Oaks, CA: Sage.

Shenker, O. (2001). Cultural distance revisited: Towards a more rigorous conceptualization and measurement of cultural difference. *Journal of International Business Studies, 32,* 519–535.

Smith, K. G., Carroll, S. J., & Ashford, S. J. (1995). Intra- and inter-organizational cooperation: toward a research agenda. *Academy of Management Journal, 38,* 7–23.

Sousa, R., & Voss, C. A. (2002). Quality management revisited: a reflective review and agenda for future research. *Journal of Operations Management, 20,* 91–109.

Steven, A. B., Dong, Y., & Corsi, T. (2014). Global sourcing and quality recalls: an empirical study of outsourcing-supplier concentration-product recalls linkages. *Journal of Operations Management, 32,* 241–253.

Teece, D. J. (1986). Profiting from technological innovation: implications for integration, collaboration, licensing and public policy. *Research Policy, 15*(6), 285–305.

Teece, D. J., Pisano, G., & Shuen, A. (1997). Dynamic capabilities and strategic management. *Strategic Management Journal, 18,* 509–533.

Tihanyi, L., Griffith, D. A., & Russel, C. J. (2005). The effect of cultural distance on entry mode choice, international diversification, and MNE performance: A meta-analysis. *Journal of International Business Studies, 36,* 270–283.

Trent, R. J., & Monczka, R. M. (2005). Achieving excellence in global sourcing. *Sloan Management Review, 47* (1), 24–32.

Tsai, W., & Ghoshal, S. (1998). Social capital and value creation: The role of inter firm networks. *Academy of Management Journal, 41,* 464–476.

Turnbull, P., Oliver, N. & Wilkinson, B. (1992). Buyer-supplier relations in the UK automotive industry: Strategic implications of the Japanese manufacturing model. *Strategic Management Journal, 13,* 159–168.

Tyler, B. B. (2001). The complementarity of cooperative and technological competencies: A resource-based perspective. *Journal of Engineering and Technology Management, 18* (1), 1–27.

Uzzi, B. (1996). The sources and consequences of embeddedness for the economic performance of organizations: The network effect. *American Sociological Review, 61,* 674–698.

Uzzi, B. (1997). Social structure and competition in interfirm networks: The paradox of embeddedness. *Administrative Science Quarterly, 42* (1), 35–67.

Vermeulen, F., & Barkema, H. (2001). Learning through acquisitions. *Academy of Management Journal, 44,* 457–476.

Walsh, J. (1995). Managerial and organizational cognition: notes from a trip down memory lane. *Organization Science, 6,* 280–321.

Weber, Y., Shenker, O., & Raveh, A. (1996). National and Corporate Cultural Fit in Mergers/Acquisitions: An Exploratory Study. *Management Science, 42,* 1215–1228.

Weick, K. E. (1995). *Sensemaking in Organizations.* London: Sage.

Wernfelt, B. (1995). The resource-based view of the firm: Ten years after. *Strategic Management Journal, 16*, 171–175.

Williamson, O. E. (1985).*The economic institutions of capitalism*. New York: Free Press.

Xu, D., & Shenker, O. (2002). Institutional distance and the multinational enterprise. *Academy of Management Review, 27*, 608–618.

Xu, D., Pan, Y., & Beamish, P. W. (2004). The effect of regulative and normative distances on MNE ownership and expatriate strategies. *Management International Review, 44*, 285–307.

Zaheer, S. (1995). Overcoming the liability of foreignness. *Academy of Management Journal, 38*, 341–363.

Zucker, L. (1983). Organizations as institutions. *Research in the Sociology of Organizations, 2*(1), 1–47.

Biographical Notes

Etayankara Muralidharan is an assistant professor of management at MacEwan University, Canada. He received his PhD from the University of Manitoba in Canada. His research interests are in organizational crisis management, emerging market multinationals, and international entrepreneurship. His research has been recently published in *Journal Business Ethics, Management Research Review, International Journal of Innovation & Technology Management, Current Topics in Management* and has been presented at and appeared in the proceedings of the *Academy of Management, Academy of International Business, Babson Entrepreneurship Conference (BCERC) and the Administrative Sciences Association of Canada.* (muralidharane@macewan.ca)

William Wei is an associate professor, Institute of Asia Pacific Studies of the School of Business at MacEwan University Business School. William is PhD cosupervisor at China University of Petroleum, a founding member of the International Association for Chinese Management Research and editor-in-chief of Asia Pacific and Globalization Review. He has over 100 publications ranging from journal articles, books, book chapters, Ivey Business Cases, and conference proceedings. His research has been published in *Sustainability, Intereconomics, Project Management Journal, and International Journal of Business and Emerging Markets.* William is awarded as distinguished scholar by the Academy for Global Business Advancement in 2012. (weix@macewan.ca)

Juan Zhang is an associate professor of international business in the Institute of International Business at Shanghai University of International Business and Economics (SUIBE) and visiting professor at University of Alberta. She received a BE in international trade in industry from Tianjin Institute of Light Industry, an MEc in industrial economics from Nankai University, and a PhD in world economics from Fudan University, PRC. Her current research interests include the internationalization of Chinese firms, risk management in host countries, and cross-cultural management. Her works have been published in *Project Management Journal, Journal of African Business*, and many Chinese Social Sciences Citation Index (CSSCI) source journals. (madeline.zhang@hotmail.com)

Hari Bapuji is an associate professor at the Asper School of Business, University of Manitoba. He has a PhD from the Richard Ivey School of Business, University of Western Ontario. Dr. Bapuji researches organizational problems that have an effect on society and vice versa. In particular, his research covers how firms can prevent, manage, and learn from crises that affect both organizations and societies. Dr. Bapuji published numerous scholarly articles that appeared in leading management journals, including *Harvard Business Review, Journal* *of Operations Management, Journal of Management Studies, Management and Organization Review, Management Learning, Organization,* and *Journal of Engineering and Technology Management.* In addition, he published a book *Not Just China: The Rise of Recalls in the Age of Global Business,* which has been recognized as an outstanding academic title by CHOICE Magazine. Dr. Bapuji's research on product recalls has been instrumental in shaping public discourse on global product safety and has been widely cited by hundreds of print and electronic media outlets, including *New York Times, Huffington Post, Financial Times, Business Week, Wall Street Journal, Forbes, CNN, Washington Post, China Daily, USA Today, Sydney Morning Herald, People's Daily, CBC, The Globe and Mail,* and *Straits Times.* (hari.bapuji@umanitoba.ca)

Accepted after two revisions: October 10, 2015

Current Topics in Management, Vol. 18, 2016, pp. 153–182

EMPLOYER'S USE OF SOCIAL MEDIA IN EMPLOYMENT DECISIONS: RISK OF DISCRIMINATION LAWSUITS

Roger W. Reinsch
University of Minnesota, Duluth

William H. Ross
University of Wisconsin, La Crosse

Amy B. Hietapelto
University of Minnesota, Duluth

This paper explores several legal issues that apply when employers use social media for employment decisions. In addition to risks based on widely considered federal US nondiscrimination laws such as the 1964 Civil Rights Act and the Americans with Disabilities Act, other federal laws, including the Genetic Information Nondiscrimination Act and the Fair Credit Reporting Act, can also impact the use of social media when hiring. We also note developing EEOC policy in this area, and briefly address the issue of negligent hiring. The paper provides an extensive picture of the risks to those using social media for employment decisions. Finally, we provide recommendations to business people who want to use social media as a valuable information source during their hiring process, but want to reduce the accompanying legal risks.

Keywords: social media, personnel/human resource selection, employment law

Over the past ten years, the use of social media has grown exponentially (Nayak, 2014). Therefore, this paper looks at the use of social media sites at the very beginning of the screening process when the position has been advertised and the employer has received applications for the posting. The employer may have received a hundred applications, and now must screen those to see who is qualified, and whom they wish to keep for the next phase of the process. At this stage the employer is simply eliminating applicants they do not want to pursue further, and may look at social media sites as part of the screening process. During this process, the employer may legitimately eliminate those applicants who are not qualified for the position. However, the employer may also erroneously use social media sites to eliminate others who are qualified. The applicants in that latter category may pose legal problems for employers, and it is that group we are considering here. Our purpose is to provide a comprehensive picture of the legal issues involved and recommendations for employers who want to use a social media search, but want to greatly reduce the risk of an employment discrimination claim.

Many individuals maintain multiple social media profiles on sites such as Facebook, LinkedIn, Twitter, Instagram, Tumblr, and Vine. These multiple online profiles can provide quite a comprehensive picture of one's personal and professional life. Therefore, there may be a legitimate business reason for looking at social media sites in order to discover information about a potential employee that goes beyond the traditional resume.

Facebook, the largest Social Networking Website (SNW) in the United States, has over 1.2 billion users (Adams, 2014). People use SNWs to record many types of life events, offer opinions, and voluntarily provide demographic information. Much of this information is also readily available to anyone searching someone's name. An employer conducting systematic background checks of applicants might use it, or a manager may do an ad hoc search in an unofficial capacity. The results of any of these types of searches could potentially harm an applicant's chance of being hired for legitimate reasons. However, such a search may also inadvertently discover information that should not be asked of a potential employee due to employment discrimination laws.

Prevalence of Social Media Searches

Surveys show that many US employers are either currently using social media or planning on using social media in their applicant screening process, although estimates of the prevalence of this practice vary widely. A 2012 survey of 2,303 hiring managers by CareerBuilder revealed that 37% of companies reported using SNWs to research job candidates and another 11% planned to do so. By 2015, that usage increased to 52%; further, 35% of 2,175 hiring managers reported that they were less likely to hire an applicant if they were unable to discover information about that applicant online (CareerBuilder, 2015). The same survey revealed that approximately one-third of employers who screen via social networks have requested access (e.g., "be a friend") to candidates' private SNW accounts. Of that group, 80 percent say they've been granted permission by applicants.

When do companies typically search SNW sites? Reppler Co. (2011) conducted a survey of 300 professionals who are involved in the hiring process at their companies to understand when they use social networks for screening job applicants. In that survey, 91% reported using social media in the preemployment process. Of these, nearly half screened as early as "[soon] after receiving an application," 27% used it "after the initial conversation with the applicant," 15% used it after an interview, and 4% searched SNWs just before making a job offer. Of those who used social media, 69% said they rejected a candidate based on what they found. Some of those rejections were based on legitimate reasons, such as posting negative comments about a current/previous employer (11%), sharing an employer's confidential information (7%), or lying about their qualifications (13%). However, some rejections were based on such things as drinking habits (9%) or drug use (10%). As we shall see later the use of this kind of information could create potential employment discrimination liability for the employer.

A survey of 67 employers conducted by business faculty members in an upper Midwestern US city of about 100,000 residents shows that, although most employers realize that there are possible legal risks involved in using SNWs for hiring decisions (38 out of 67 know there are risks), most are not aware of any legislation that may restrict use (only 10 out of 67 are aware of restrictive laws). The vast majority of employers in this survey had no policy in regard to the use of social media (only 3 out of the 67 have a policy), and most have never contacted an attorney for legal advice on this matter (only 2 out of 67). Yet, these employers may base their hiring decisions on information that is found, some of which could be legally problematic, as we shall see later in the chapter (R. Reinsch, personal communication, September 10, 2014).

In addition, personal interviews were conducted with several high-ranking human resource professionals from large organizations within a range of industries (e.g., heath care, energy, and retailing). Not surprisingly, practice and policy varied widely. Although all interviewed professionals were aware of general risks in using social media in employment decisions, some organizations banned the practice, while others utilized social media. Some had very specific policies prohibiting usage, while others did not. Of those permitting social media usage, a general policy might be in place; however, ad hoc and/or inconsistent practices in a decentralized environment and/or field locations were potentially problematic. One of the executives stated that, as a government contractor, the organization had a very strict policy regarding the use of social media during preemployment searches. On the basis of these interviews, as well as the survey discussed earlier, it is likely that many organizations utilizing social media in employment decisions could benefit from a more nuanced understanding of all of the legal pitfalls, and the development and consistent implementation of appropriate policy.

These results are somewhat similar to a 2013 Society for Human Resource Management (SHRM) survey of 651 US-based Human Resource managers.

While 77% of organizations report using social networking websites to *recruit* potential job candidates, only 21% report using SNWs to *screen* applicants. The majority of firms (57%) do not have any policy regarding the use of social networking websites to screen job candidates; among those that do have such a policy, it is nearly evenly divided (21%) between those that permit it and those that prohibit such screening. Among firms that do *not* use social media for screening applicants, 74% expressed legal concerns about legal risks of discovering information about protected characteristics (Mulvey, 2013).

The ease and speed with which social media provide supplemental applicant information makes its use tempting. However, by perusing an applicant's various social media accounts, the employer might violate Title VII of the 1964 Civil Rights Act and other US legal mandates, which prohibit the employer from inquiring about race, gender, religion, national origin, disability, and age. The trend of using social media—as well as search engines (which 51% of hiring managers say they use)—when making employment decisions is likely to become even more prevalent (Rosen, 2012; Perkins, 2015). Therefore, it is imperative to use this tool in a manner that will not expose employers to discrimination lawsuits.

Employers know that during the resume review phase of the employment process they may not ask about certain legally protected traits. However, the problem for many employers is that they don't realize, or don't consider, that the use of social media in preemployment decisions may disclose the same type of information they could not specifically ask about, effectively defeating the exposure control of protected traits (Whitehill, 2012). This practice, therefore, creates risks under various US state and federal laws, which will be discussed in the next section.

There have not yet been many cases that address the issue of preemployment social media screening. However, this only means this area of the law is still unsettled. As with any emerging area of law, the possibility exists that prospective employees and their attorneys will find creative ways to apply all of these statutes to sue prospective employers because lawyers are trained to look to the law to solve social problems (Zitrin 2003). In a common law country like the United States, the law moves forward as lawyers discover ways to include new factors such as technology into legal arguments. For example, "[a] trial attorney with the Equal Employment Opportunity Commission's Washington, D.C., field office recently advanced an interesting argument that there could be disparate impact claims brought due to the use of social media in recruiting ... [and] pointed out that companies need to think about potential practices that could give rise to such claims" (Kasarjian, 2013, p. 20). For example, while Hispanic adults' use of LinkedIn has grown from only 2% in 2010 to 18% in 2014, this is much less than the 28% usage rate by blacks and 29% usage rate by whites in 2014. Thus, one could argue that only selecting from among candidates who use this particular SNW may result in adverse impact against

Hispanics (Hazelton & Terhorst, 2015; Duggan, Ellison, Lampe, Lenhart, & Madden, 2015). A 61-year-old plaintiff in *Reese v. Department of the Interior* alleged age discrimination in recruiting because the agency recruited using Facebook, which was used less frequently by older adults than younger adults. The plaintiff lost because she did not prove sufficient disparate impact existed (Miaskoff, 2014); as of 2014, 63% of those age 50–65 use Facebook, whereas 87% of those age 18–30 use this SNW (Duggan, et al., 2015). This is in conjunction with what other authors (e.g., Walters, 2011) have observed, namely, that social media remain an unsettled area in the courts of law.

The Prima Facie Standard for Discrimination Lawsuit

Because existing US discrimination laws have been enforced for decades, many employers have strict rules in regard to their employment policies during the hiring process. These policies are designed to prevent employers from seeking to learn and/or basing hiring decisions upon potentially discriminatory demographic information about prospective employees. However, as social media are relatively new to many, some employers either do not have policies in place for the use of social media in employment decision making, or the policies they have may not be comprehensive enough. There is a risk that some employers don't consider the discrimination risks when viewing SNWs, even though they can discover a good amount of potentially discriminatory information about candidates. For these reasons, "cybervetting" potential employees, without understanding the risks and having a stated policy in place for preemployment social media use, is treading on potentially dangerous legal grounds.

Guidance from the US Supreme Court

In order to understand the legal risks during the initial preemployment screening process it will be helpful to look at what the courts have said is the standard for a plaintiff to bring a discrimination lawsuit. The standard for a plaintiff bringing a Title VII employment discrimination suit, and not being subject to a defendant's motion to dismiss, will be based on the evidentiary framework defined in *McDonnell Douglas Corp v. Green* (1971). The plaintiff must first establish a prima facie case that he was within a protected class. This simply means the plaintiff states that he/she is a member of one of the groups that is protected under any of the antidiscriminatory laws. Next, the plaintiff must assert that he/she was qualified for the position and met the employer's advertised performance expectations, and that similarly situated applicants, not in the plaintiff's protected class, were treated more favorably, and by not being hired the plaintiff was adversely affected. Once those elements are stated, it gives rise to an inference of unlawful discrimination. The plaintiff has then done enough to "shift the burden of proof" to the employer.

The employer must then rebut the presumption of discrimination by producing a legitimate, nondiscriminatory reason for the action. If the defendant is able to produce evidence of a legitimate, nondiscriminatory reason for the action, the burden shifts back to the plaintiff who must then show that the employer's stated reason for the action was only a pretext for illegal discrimination. This back-and-forth process can be time consuming and expensive for the employer. Even if the employer ultimately wins the lawsuit, the employer will still have the legal expenses of refuting the discrimination claim of a plaintiff. For that reason it is best to avoid even exposure to certain types of potentially discriminatory information that may be found on social media sites.

As stated, all the plaintiff is required to demonstrate is that the facts show an "inference of unlawful discrimination"; this is based on *Desert Palace, Inc. v. Costa* (2003). In that case, the US Supreme Court determined that a plaintiff does not have to provide direct evidence of discrimination, because the statutory language found in Section 107(m) of the Civil Rights Act of 1991 states that "an unlawful employment practice is established when the complaining party demonstrates that race, color, religion, sex, or national origin was a motivating factor for any employment practice, even though other factors also motivated the practice." In *Desert Palace* the Court held that circumstantial evidence can be used in order to obtain what is known as a "mixed-motive instruction" (mixed motive means that one of the factors could have been due to the person being a member of a protected group, even though other factors may also have motivated the decision). Knowledge that the applicant is a member of a protected group creates the problem for the employer because the applicant may then claim that the protected-group status was a motivating factor in the hiring decision, and that may be proved by circumstantial evidence "comprised of numerous evidentiary facts and reasonable inferences that, as a whole, establish the existence of the elements of preponderance of the evidence" (Whitehill, 2012, p. 243). Consequently, it is possible for a plaintiff to force a potential employer into a discrimination lawsuit when the defendant had information about the plaintiff's protected status, even though other factors may have been part of the decision-making process. The fact that the social media search revealed information about the plaintiff's protected class status will be the circumstantial evidence that the defendant employer, who knew that information, could have used it. Such evidence will be sufficient to support an allegation by the plaintiff; the burden of proof will then shift to the employer to show either that it was not used or that the employer had business-related reasons for denying the applicant employment and that the protected status had no bearing upon the decision. Therefore, doing a social media search creates the problem because the standard makes knowledge dangerous for the employer. It is very difficult to show that one did not use something that was known to that person or that it carried no weight in a hiring decision. For example, if the employer looked at Facebook and the profile picture shows that the applicant is African

American, the employer now knows the applicant's race, and would have to prove that this information was not used to eliminate the otherwise qualified applicant from the employment pool. That is very difficult to prove; therefore, not knowing is the best defense.

A related point is that the plaintiff does not have to show who the other applicants for the position were. The plaintiff only needs to provide three facts. First, the plaintiff must show that he/she was qualified for the position. Second, the plaintiff must show that he/she is a member of a protected group. Finally, the plaintiff has to show that the person who was actually hired is not in the same protected category.

"Discovery" and "e-Discovery"

An employer might think that it is difficult for a plaintiff to know whether or not a social media search has been conducted on someone's social media sites. However, there is the legal "discovery" process, where each side's lawyer requests evidentiary information from the other prior to the hearing, This can be done by requesting written answers to specific questions, requesting documents, and requesting written depositions. Discovery can be obtained from nonparties using subpoenas. Further, if, say, an employer does not cooperate, the plaintiff may file a motion in court to compel discovery. Increasingly, "e-discovery" is used that permits the examination of computer hardware and searches for both documents and websites visited via a computer's Internet history. "Predictive coding" may also be used; this is the process of developing a coding procedure using a small set of manually reviewed and coded documents. This procedure can then build a complex, computer-generated mathematical model to predict the coding of a larger set of documents. These tools can aid plaintiffs in deciding what documents to seek and what patterns to examine; US Federal Rules of Procedure have also been adapted to reflect e-discovery developments (Bordena & Baronaa, 2014). Also, when a court during discovery issues a subpoena, third party information hosts, such as Facebook, usually provide the requested information (Schulz & Zwerdling, 2013). There is a digital history of who visited a website and that can be discovered during the legal process. In addition, there are apps available that a person can install on their computer that tracks who visits their website. Therefore, if an applicant installs such an application on their personal website they will have their own record of visitors (Visitortrack, 2015). While not many applicants will have such software installed, it illustrates that those who wish to "test" whether prospective employers visit their websites can easily do so—and can use such information as evidence against the nonhiring firm.

An employer might be tempted to use some subterfuge such as a fake e-mail address or an avatar to conduct a search, thinking that this would be hard to find and link back to the employer. For example, suppose an employee creates a false social media account from a public computer at a library and attempts to "friend" a candidate in order to search for information. However, we believe that such a scenario is rare. Even in this scenario, e-discovery can employ forensic evidence to determine which computer was used and when the person attempted to access the candidate's website. It may be difficult to definitively trace such activity back to the hiring firm in a large city. However, if the computer came from a public library in a small-to-medium-sized town, and the only connection between the applicant and that community is the fact that the person applied for a job with one firm in that community, then it raises suspicion that someone from the organization was involved in the "friend" request. As stated above, once there is a legal claim filed there will be discovery. During that discovery process the plaintiff's lawyers will ask for forensic evidence on the employer's computers, and perhaps the privately owned computers of employees in the relevant departments. There will also be depositions of the people involved. One of the questions during the deposition will be something such as, "Have you or anyone in your organization used a fake e-mail, avatar, or anything like that to disguise your identity?" Lying to this question will open one up to a "contempt of court" claim; therefore there is motivation to answer this correctly. The penalties for noncompliance in e-discovery investigations can be significant (Kane 2012).

Applicable Employment Discrimination Laws

In order to more fully understand the risks of social media use, it is important to have a brief overview of relevant federal laws, state laws, and EEOC regulations that could apply to preemployment situations. We limit our discussion to US law due to the diversity among foreign jurisdictions. Some countries have restrictions, and others have no restrictions.

The laws covered include the following: Title VII of the Civil Rights Act of 1964 (Title VII), which prohibits employment discrimination based on race, color, religion, sex, or national origin; the Pregnancy Discrimination Act of 1978, which forbids discrimination based on pregnancy when it comes to any aspect of employment, including hiring, firing, pay, job assignments, promotions, layoff, training, fringe benefits, such as leave and health insurance, and any other term or condition of employment; the Age Discrimination in Employment Act of 1967 (ADEA), which protects individuals who are 40 years of age or older; Title I and Title V of the Americans with Disabilities Act of 1990, as amended (ADA), which prohibit employment discrimination against qualified individuals with disabilities in the private sector, and in state and local governments; the Civil Rights Act of 1991, which, among other things, provides monetary damages in cases of intentional employment discrimination; the Genetic Information Nondiscrimination Act (GINA); and the Fair Credit Reporting Act of 1970. In addition, one needs to consider

the "lifestyle" statutes that have been passed by many states and other state
and local statutes that relate to discrimination, such as sexual orientation or
family responsibilities (caregiver) statutes. For a list of relevant US federal
regulations see Table 1.

Table 1
Applicable Federal Nondiscrimination Statutes

Federal Statutes	Covered Employers
Civil Rights Act of 1964 (Title VII), prohibiting employment discrimination based on race, color, sex, based on race, color, sex, religion, or national origin.	All private employers, state and local governments, and education institutions that employ 15 or more individuals. Also covered: labor organizations, private and public employment agencies, and joint labor-management committees controlling apprenticeship and training.
Age Discrimination in Employment Act of 1967 (ADEA), which protects individuals who are 40 years of age or older.	All private employers with 20 or more employees, state and local governments (including school districts), employment agencies and labor organizations.
The Pregnancy Discrimination Act of 1978, prohibiting discrimination based on pregnancy.	All private employers, state and local governments, and education institutions that employ 15 or more individuals. Also covered: labor organizations, private and public employment agencies, and joint labor-management committees controlling apprenticeship and training.
Title I and Title V of the Americans with Disabilities Act of 1990 (ADA), as amended, prohibiting employment discrimination against otherwise qualified individuals with disabilities.	All private employers, state and local governments, and education institutions that employ 15 or more individuals. Also covered: labor organizations, private and public employment agencies, and joint labor-management committees controlling apprenticeship and training.
Genetic Information Nondiscrimination Act of 2008 (GINA), which prohibits discrimination based on an applicant's genetic information.	All private employers, state and local governments, and education institutions that employ 15 or more individuals. Also covered: labor organizations, private and public employment agencies, and joint labor-management committees controlling apprenticeship and training.
Fair Credit Reporting Act of 1970, which applies when third parties are investigating an applicant's credit status or credit history.	Covers all organizations and individuals who use third parties to conduct an investigation into an applicant's financial or credit status or history.

"Lifestyle statutes is the commonly accepted name of state statutes and lo-cal ordinances that cover choices in regard to how to live made by individuals; they cover a range of activities from smoking to hang gliding" (Lipps 2011). All of these laws generally make it illegal to discriminate in any aspect of em-ployment, including job advertisements; recruitment; testing; use of company facilities; hiring; compensation and granting of related benefits; assignment or classification of employees; training and apprenticeship programs; transfer, promotion, layoff, firing, or recall; granting of disability-related leave; or other terms and conditions of employment. However, in this particular paper, we are concerned only with the hiring process under these laws and not the other areas. Having said that, we will briefly discuss the issue of negligent hiring and the balancing act an employer must be aware of in regard to this cause of action and discrimination. Also, some employers select candidates for lengthy training or apprenticeship programs, which must be successfully completed in order to work in a specific job; many of the observations made in this paper apply to those programs, as well.

Discriminatory practices in the hiring process include making employment decisions based on stereotypes or assumptions about the abilities, traits, or performance of individuals of a certain sex, race, age, religion, ethnic group, or individuals with disabilities or those who are pregnant/may consider becom-ing pregnant. Intentional discrimination, also known as *disparate treatment* discrimination, is the purposeful exclusion of protected class members from jobs. In addition to deliberately excluding a candidate because, say, a recent photograph shows that they are pregnant, hiring managers must also consider unintentional discrimination, known as *disparate impact (adverse impact)* discrimination. Adverse impact exists when employment policies, regardless of neutral intent, adversely affect protected groups more than others, and cannot be adequately justified on the basis of something like a bona fide occupational qualification. Federal nondiscrimination laws prohibit not only disparate treat-ment but also adverse impact against individuals because of their race, color, national origin, religion, sex, and so on. To purposely conduct an SNW search with the goal of discovering each applicant's race, and hiring only, say, white applicants, demonstrates disparate treatment. To conduct an SNW search that was neutral in its *intent* (e.g., to the goal of excluding those not qualified) but that had the *effect* of excluding most people of color and keeping most white applicants in the pool demonstrates disparate impact.

Here are some brief examples and brief discussion of the problems that could be created by a social media search under the various laws.

Analysis of Potential Risks under the Specific Laws/Regulations

For this section we first look at what kinds of information can be discovered on social media that create the potential for a discrimination claim.

The Civil Rights Act of 1964 and the Civil Rights Act of 1991

As indicated earlier, this legislation prevents discrimination based on race, color, religion, sex, or national origin; it is possible to find out all, or much of this information, by looking at potential employee's social media entries. The social media user will probably have his/her picture posted somewhere on the site, which will likely disclose one's gender and race. Besides the specific demographic information that could be discovered (gender, race, age, etc.), there is information in regard to one's likes and posts (e.g., preferences) that might also include information that should not be known at this stage of the hiring process, such as one's religious beliefs, and/or the person's national origin. Either, or both, could give rise to a claim that that information was allegedly used to make a hiring decision.

The fact is that the use of social media provides recruiters with personal information about applicants at the very beginning of the resume review stage, which would probably be inaccessible otherwise. The 1964 Civil Rights Act prohibits discrimination in hiring based on some types of applicant demographic characteristics. Therefore, the risk of a discrimination lawsuit is present, because once the employer has the prohibited demographic information, the candidate can easily allege that it was used against the candidate in the hiring decision. As we shall see an employer could have a difficult time proving otherwise.

Pregnancy Discrimination Act of 1978

An employer cannot refuse to hire a pregnant woman because of her pregnancy, because of a pregnancy-related condition, or because of the prejudices of coworkers, clients, or customers toward pregnant women. In spite of this law, discrimination against pregnant women continues to exist. One experiment showcased that hiring managers demonstrated significantly higher levels of discrimination toward pregnant applicants in job interviews (Morgan, Walker, Hebl, & King, 2013). The use of social media could easily disclose that a female candidate is pregnant, through either photos or posts made on the site. If the employer knows this information, and if the candidate is qualified but not hired, she has a potential claim for pregnancy discrimination.

Age Discrimination in Employment Act (ADEA) of 1967

By using social media, a hiring manager can see pictures and other references that provide information about the candidate's age. A post, such as "I just became a grandfather for the first time," could easily indicate that the person is over 40 years old. Posts by the person about his/her social habits might also be used against the potential employee based on a bias against older people behaving in such a manner. A large amount of age-related information is available that could be used against a candidate. Innocuous posts, such as, "I just attended my 25th (or 40th) high school reunion and had a great time" has the potential of giving rise to a lawsuit under the ADEA. It should be noted that the ADEA allows for jury trials and "double-damages" awards for willful discrimination, where an employer has shown blatant disregard of the ADEA.

The Americans with Disabilities Act (ADA) of 1990, as Amended by the ADA Amendments Act of 2008

This legislation has some nuances that may pose problems for employers. As defined by the ADA, an individual with a disability is a person who has a physical or mental impairment that substantially limits one or more major life activities; has a record of such impairment; or is regarded as having such impairment. Clearly, one can learn about another person's disability from a social media site through pictures, posts, likes, and other information. While the physical or mental disability may be fairly easy to discern, the less obvious issue is that Title I of the Americans with Disabilities Act specifically permits employers to ensure that the workplace is free from the illegal use of drugs and alcohol and to comply with other US federal laws and regulations regarding drug and alcohol use.

Therefore, employees and applicants who are currently engaging in the illegal use of drugs are not protected by the ADA when an employer acts on the basis of such use. According to the US Department of Justice, Civil Rights Division, any employee or job applicant who is "currently engaging" in the illegal use of drugs is not a "qualified individual with a disability." However, the ADA does provide limited protection from discrimination for recovering drug abusers and alcoholics. An employer may not discriminate against a person who has a history of drug addiction, but who is not currently using drugs, and who has been rehabilitated. "Qualified individuals" under the ADA includes individuals who have been successfully rehabilitated and who are no longer engaged in the illegal use of drugs or those who are currently participating in a rehabilitation program and are no longer engaging in the illegal use of drugs. Also, a former drug addict may be protected under the ADA because the addiction may be considered a substantially limiting impairment. However, according to the EEOC Technical Assistance Manual on the ADA, a former *casual* drug user is not protected under the ADA (United States Commission on Civil Rights 2000).

The problem with information on an SNW that has pictures and comments about drug and alcohol use is that the employer doesn't know whether the applicant is (1) a current user who is not protected; (2) a former casual user who is not protected; or (3) a former user who was addicted, has been rehabilitated, is no longer using drugs/alcohol, and is protected. If rejected, the last type of candidate could have a claim that he/she was discriminated against. It is difficult to know whether a person is covered by the ADA from just viewing statements about drug or alcohol use on an SNW, or by viewing pictures or comments about various related organizations or activities (e.g., volunteering at or donating to a rehabilitation center for teenage addicts).

Genetic Information Nondiscrimination Act of 2008

The Genetic Information Nondiscrimination Act (GINA) applies to employers with 15 or more employees, and provides federal protection from genetic discrimination in health insurance and employment (Foster, 2010). Several states have similar—and in some instances—more expansive legislation. For example, in Delaware these prohibitions apply to employers with four or more employees (Delaware, 1999, 2003, 2005).

Title II of GINA makes it illegal, as of November 2009, for employers to use a person's genetic information when making decisions about hiring, and promotion. The purpose of GINA is to prevent any employers from acquiring an employee's and/or an employee's family "genetic information." Just like most antidiscrimination laws, there is no need to know that the employer had any specific intent to acquire that genetic information; simply possessing the information is a violation. As shown, GINA prohibits two different actions—the use of genetic information in employment decisions and the act of acquiring genetic information.

In 2010, the Equal Employment Opportunity Commission (EEOC) issued regulations to implement GINA. These provide that, subject to specific exceptions, an employer may not "request, require, or purchase genetic information of an individual or family member of the individual." It then goes on to specifically address the Internet: "Request" includes conducting an Internet search on an individual in a way that is "likely to result in a covered entity obtaining genetic information" (Equal Employment Opportunity Commission, 2010b, p. 1).

Because the discovery on the Internet could be inadvertent, there is an exception—if, through *authorized access* on a social networking site, a supervisor or manager learns of an employee's genetic information, the employer does not violate GINA. If, however, the supervisor then probes the individual further, asking questions and eliciting genetic information, the exception no longer applies (Genetic Information Nondiscrimination Act, 2015). Therefore, when such information is inadvertently learned, the employer must be very cautious not to probe further. In addition, an exception applies to genetic information obtained via commercially and publicly available information, such as that found through a Google Search. Therefore, the exception would apply if the employer did a general Internet search of the applicant and found out specific information on a site that is publically available—no password required. The exception would not apply to any site that requires a password for access.

The nondiscrimination provisions of GINA are similar to those in Title VII of the Civil Rights Act of 1964, prohibiting discrimination at all stages of the employment process (Rush, 2009). GINA prohibits employers from the following: "(1) to fail or refuse to hire, or to discharge, any employee, or otherwise to discriminate against any employee with respect to the compensation, terms, conditions, or privileges of employment of the employee, because of genetic information with respect to the employee; or (2) to limit, segregate, or classify the employees of the employer in any way that would deprive or tend to deprive any employee of employment opportunities or otherwise adversely affect the status of the employee as an employee, because of genetic information with respect to the employee" (Equal Employment Opportunity Commission, 2008, p. 5).

After exploring the legal implications of employers obtaining genetic information via the Internet, Davik (2013) reported the following: "Therefore under the Act...if an employer conducted a preemployment background check and [inadvertently] obtained genetic information from a data aggregation service provider, or alternatively by performing his or her own Internet search, this would not run afoul of GINA so long as there was no evidence that the specific goal of such an inquiry was to acquire genetic information. While in the past the likelihood that an employer would even be able to obtain materials that could possibly shed light on a current or potential employee's genetic status was quite low, today such a risk is far from merely theoretical" (Davik, 2013, p. 46).

Using a third party to screen SNWs may not completely avoid liability under GINA for a client employer. Even though the third party has screened out specific genetic information such as candidate A is BRCA1 positive (a breast cancer genetic marker), they might not screen out genetically relevant information such as: Candidate A mentions that she has searched online for information related to BRCA testing, or has "liked" the Facing Our Risk of Cancer Empowered (FORCE, a nonprofit organization dedicated to improving the lives of individuals affected by hereditary breast and ovarian cancer), or has participated in fundraising events for hereditary breast cancer research. "Such data may provide a potential employer with substantial clues as to the fact that this individual has probably tested positive for a known genetic mutation or is at a much higher than normal risk for carrying a genetic mutation due to family medical history" (Davik, 2013, pp. 48–49).

The EEOC has acted on GINA in two different cases. The first federal court case, *EEOC v. Fabricut,* was initiated on May 7, 2013. Fabricut had withdrawn an offer of permanent employment as a clerk to Rhonda Jones, who had performed satisfactorily as a temporary memo clerk. The EEOC alleged that the company believed she was predisposed to develop carpel tunnel syndrome (CTS) on the basis of a postoffer medical examination that required disclosure of family medical history to a third party medical laboratory. According to the EEOC, the family history profile led to additional medical testing. Even though the laboratory concluded that the applicant was unlikely to acquire CTS, Fabricut rescinded its employment offer. Ultimately, the firm paid $50,000 to settle the claim (Equal Employment Opportunity Commission, 2013). In *EEOC v. Founders Pavilion* (2013), the EEOC filed its first class action lawsuit under GINA. The EEOC sued Founders Pavilion, a nursing home and rehabilitation facility in Corning, NY. The EEOC alleged that founders requested family medical history as part of its preemployment hiring procedures; it also allegedly requested such information as part of its annual staff medical examinations. As part of a consent decree, the firm agreed to pay $370,000 (Equal Employment Opportunity Commission 2014).

The conclusion for Human Resource (HR) managers is that, even if genetic-related information is acquired legally, the use of such information can create legal problems for a potential employer. Further, once the information is acquired by the employer, it will be difficult to prove that it was not used. For that reason, the safest approach is not to discover genetic information via any social media search.

Fair Credit Reporting Act (FCRA) of 1970

Since some employers use the option of hiring third parties to do their cyber-vetting so that the hiring agent only receives screened information, those employers need to be familiar with the Fair Credit Reporting Act of 1970 (FCRA). The Fair Credit Reporting Act is a federal law that was designed to ensure that the information provided by third parties to employers or creditors is accurate, and that consumers are informed of any adverse decisions that are made about them, based on such information. The FRCA covers information gathered by third parties (typically, consumer-reporting agencies) on individuals to evaluate a variety of qualifications, including employment. FRCA does not apply to background checks conducted in-house. Compliance includes informing the applicant of the investigation, giving the applicant an opportunity to consent, and notifying the applicant if the report is used to make an adverse decision.

Turning to private data-collection firms is a viable option to avoid possible discrimination claims or problems. These private firms can collect data and "scrub" it (e.g., by removing someone's race) before sending other relevant information to the employer. Until recently the question as to whether companies that compile social media data are subject to the FCRA was unclear, but in 2012 the Federal Trade Commission (FTC) imposed an $800,000 fine against one of these social media data companies, Spokeo, for its failure to adhere to the FCRA when collecting social media data and passing it on to prospective employers (Federal Trade Commission, 2012b).

Spokeo collects personal information from many sources on millions of individuals. This information is then merged to create comprehensive personal profiles. The FTC claimed that these profiles were marketed to HR professionals to use as applicant screening tools. In addition, the FTC claimed that Spokeo didn't use reasonable procedures to assure accuracy and that they didn't tell employers about their obligation to meet FCRA requirements.

In a separate investigation, FTC has considered the legality of new, expanded forms of background screening by third party information providers in light of the FCRA. The FTC investigated Social Intelligence Corporation's Internet and social media screening reports; the company provided the FTC with samples of actual reports provided to employers. In May 2011, the FTC determined that no further action was warranted. The above two investigations and resulting settlements indicate that the FTC is monitoring the use of such information.

To summarize, private data-collection firms should not disclose information like race, gender, national origin, pregnancy, and so on to client employers because that might allow applicants to raise claims of discrimination. However, there is another aspect of the FCRA that is also problematic: when using a third party for such a search that might discover credit or other financial information, there is a duty to disclose that fact and get the applicant's permission. This is problematic because most employers (and some third parties) are probably unaware of this provision. Here is a summary of the most relevant requirements under the FCRA.

First, the prospective employer must notify the applicant that they will use credit information for decisions related to their employment. The notice may not be in the employment application, but must be in writing and stand alone. Second, before obtaining a consumer report and using it, the employer must get the applicant's permission in writing (Federal Trade Commission 2012a). Also, because at least ten states now restrict the use of consumer reports for employment purposes, the employer should check with relevant state laws (National Conference of State Legislatures, 2013).

The employer must also know that even if it obtains a "scrubbed" report, using it still carries legal responsibilities. After receiving a consumer report, the employer, prior to taking adverse action, must give the applicant an oral, written, or electronic notice including a copy of the report that was used to reject the applicant, and a copy of "A Summary of Your Rights under the Fair Credit Reporting Act." The purpose of the notice is to allow the applicant to correct inaccurate information. Failure to do this may result in the violation of an FTC rule, which enforces the FCRA. If the FCRA is violated, applicants may seek damages in state or federal court from (1) a consumer-reporting agency (or other third party hired to provide information); (2) a user of consumer reports (i.e., the employer who hires the reporting agency); or (3) a furnisher of information to a consumer-reporting agency. Finally, after an adverse decision is made, the employer should notify the applicant, telling them where they obtained the credit report, that the company that supplied the report did not make the unfavorable employment decision, and give the contact information of the credit agency so that the applicant can contact them to correct or dispute information. States may enforce the FCRA, and many states have their own consumer-reporting laws. In some cases, applicants may have more rights under state law. As one can see, careful compliance is necessary in order to avoid potential fines, and/ or lawsuits for damages.

Clearly, the law applies to third party data aggregation and reporting agencies such as Spokeo. But what about the SNWs that host the source information? Because the FCRA predates the Internet, the law does not specifically identify general search engines (such as Google) or SNW hosts (such as Facebook) as third party information providers. Nor does it exempt them. Thus, whether search engines or SNW hosts are potentially liable under the law has remained a murky legal area, and hiring managers will be advised to remain abreast of new developments. However, one court decision provided a limited exemption to "professional" job search SNWs from liability under the FCRA. As summarized by Attorney Jeff Starling,

> Interestingly, a federal court in California recently … dismiss[ed] a claim that LinkedIn Corp. violated the Fair Credit Reporting Act by providing employers with an online feature that allows businesses to check prospective employees' references without the applicants' knowledge. The court found that the reference searches could not be considered "consumer reports" under the law and that LinkedIn was not a "consumer reporting agency" because the plaintiffs had voluntarily provided their information for the express purpose of being published online. (Welkowitz, 2015, p. 1)

Legal Restrictions Addressing Social Media Use

Statutory Restrictions

There is also a strong movement by both states and the federal government to protect potential employees from employers gathering information from social media pages. Many states have enacted "password protection" statutes protecting information that is not publicly available. "Since April 2012, a growing number of states have enacted social media privacy laws regulating the use of social media by employers... The various laws, in varying degrees, prohibit employers and/or higher education institutions from requesting or requiring employees, prospective employees, students, or applicants to provide access to their social media accounts… whether through username/password disclosure, opening the accounts in a boss's presence, adding an employer representative to a contact list [e.g., 'friending' them], or altering the account's privacy settings" (Milligan & Hart, 2015, p. 2). A detailed discussion of those statutes and related privacy issues are beyond the scope of the purpose of this paper; however, an employer should check with the regulations in his/her state.

Relevant Case Law

In addition to the statutes, there are also some case laws that are applicable. An excellent illustration is *Gaskell v. Univ. of Kentucky* (2010), which involved the potential employment of Professor Gaskell as a scientist. An employee at the university looked at Professor Gaskell's personal website and found remarks that were favorable toward Intelligent Design theories. That employee circulated information about Professor Gaskell's "creationist" religious beliefs. Gaskell was not hired, and he filed a lawsuit claiming discrimination under Title VII. The university filed a motion for summary judgment, which the court denied, saying there was a triable issue of fact in regard to whether his religious beliefs were a motivating factor in the decision not to hire him. "The Gaskel case serves as a cautionary tale: Even if the impermissible information is not used in making the employment decision, the mere fact that the employer accessed the information may infer improper motive" (Morgan & Davis, 2013, p. 3). The case was eventually settled out of court for $125,000 (Lovan, 2011).

EEOC Policy

Even though the EEOC has not published specific guidelines in regard to the use of social media in preemployment screening, it has published guidelines in regard to background checks, which would include preemployment screening (Equal Employment Opportunity Commission 2010a). In addition, an EEOC lawyer has said that use of social media in an employment context has "been on the radar screen of the commission for several years now. ... Although it might not be obvious," he said, "navigating issues that arise from social media use in the workplace involves EEOC-related topics and 'can create an absolute legal mine field for employers'" (Larson, 2012, p. 1). On July 17, 2013, the EEOC also held a workshop on Employment Screening Procedures on Recruitment and Hiring, where they explored various cutting-edge topics, such as "social media searches and other new background checks." These warnings give a strong indication that an EEOC policy statement will be created in the near future in regard to cybervetting potential employees.

Negligent Hiring

Even though the purpose of this paper, as stated above, is to cover the risks associated with the use of social media in preemployment decision making at the very early screening process, it is also important to recognize that some employers use social media to conduct criminal background checks. Indeed, some argue that if they do not, such employers may be guilty of negligent hiring.

Negligent hiring is a common law tort claim where an injured party (e.g., a customer) files a claim against an employer for an injury caused by that employer's employee. In a negligent hiring suit, the victim usually claims that the employer knew (or should have known) that the employee could pose a risk of injury to third parties. "To sustain an action for negligent hiring or retention, the plaintiff must show that the employer hired an individual whom 'the employer knew or should have known posed a risk of harm to others where it [was] reasonably foreseeable from the employee's tendencies or propensities that the employee could cause the type of harm sustained by the plaintiff'" (Haas, Clifton, Martin, & Morris, 2013, pp. 205–206). Therefore, what is "reasonably foreseeable" by an employer within the exact wording of the state's tort laws becomes a key issue (Kittling 2010).

For example, in *Connes v. Molalla Transport System, Inc.* (1991), the court found that Molalla was not liable for negligent hiring when it hired a truck driver who had a criminal history but during the interview denied any criminal record. Molalla did conduct a check of truck driver's driving record and received good reports from his prior employer. However, it did not do an independent criminal records check. A few months after he was hired, the truck driver was driving for Molalla and had checked into a motel, where he sexually assaulted the clerk (Connes). Molalla's employment policy states that truckers are to sleep in their truck except in unusual circumstances. Connes sued Molalla on the basis of negligent hiring, claiming that the trucking company knew or should have known the driver would come into contact with the public, and, therefore, they should have checked his criminal record. The trial court granted Molalla's motion for summary judgment (no cause of action), which was appealed.

> Connes contested to the court of appeals on the basis that Molalla had a legal duty to members of the public to use reasonable care in hiring its truck drivers and that its duty included conducting an independent investigation of a potential driver's non-vehicular criminal record. In resolving the duty question, the court of appeals weighed such factors as the risk and foreseeability of harm to members of the public from Molalla's failure to investigate Taylor's criminal background, the burden placed on Molalla to guard against such harm, and the practical consequences of placing that burden on Molalla. After weighing these factors, the court of appeals concluded that Molalla had no legal duty to Connes to investigate [the driver's] non-vehicular criminal record and, accordingly, upheld the summary judgment. (*Connes v. Molalla Transport System, Inc.*, 1992)

She appealed that decision, and the Supreme Court of Colorado said, "A duty of reasonable care arises when there is a foreseeable risk of injury to others from a defendant's failure to take protective action to prevent the injury. While foreseeability is a prime factor in the duty calculus, a court also must weigh other factors, including the social utility of the defendant's conduct, the magnitude of the burden of guarding against the harm caused to the plaintiff, the practical consequences of placing such a burden on the defendant, and any additional elements disclosed by the particular circumstances of the case [e.g., whether the employee has frequent contact with other persons]. No one factor is controlling, and the question of whether a duty should be imposed in a particular case is essentially one of fairness under contemporary standards—whether reasonable persons would recognize a duty and agree that it exists." The Colorado Supreme Court agreed that Molalla had no independent duty to investigate his criminal record in these circumstances and affirmed the judgment to dismiss the case. However, in the *Johnson v. USA Truck, Inc.* case (2007) if the negligent hiring claim would have been based on something that an employer could have reasonably foreseen, then the employer would be liable. Even though both of these are Colorado cases, the Molalla case has been cited and followed in several other jurisdictions. The best practice for an employer is to be familiar with their particular state's decisions in regard to negligent hiring.

How are such cases relevant to social media? The employer has to figure out what might be reasonably foreseeable when one is hiring a particular employee, and then it is allowed to search for that type of information—including searching SNWs. The problem is that this search might disclose other information that may not legally be used in the employment decision process. For example, assume that an employer is looking to hire a person to work as a cashier in a retail store. A criminal search to determine whether this potential employee has been charged with any crime relating to dishonesty (theft embezzlement, etc.) is legitimate. During such a search, the employer may also discover that the person has been convicted of criminal assault. The issue for the employer is whether or not that is relevant to this particular position. How likely is it that a clerk would assault someone while working? There are no clear guidelines; the court decides what is "reasonably foreseeable" after a particular case comes to court. In the course of uncovering such information, it is also possible that the employer may discover demographic information, such as the applicant's race or religion that should not be used in hiring. Therefore, the employer is required to "walk a tightrope" between compliance with discrimination laws and simultaneously avoiding negligent hiring.

The best policy may be to have the criminal search conducted by someone who is not part of the hiring process, and who is trained to screen out the inappropriate information. This policy should be followed, whether the search is done in-house or by a third party provider. Even then, gray areas exist, so the employer needs to be aware of the risk and balance a possible claim of negligent hiring by an injured third party versus a claim of discrimination by the potential employee.

Discussion

Implications for Management

Management should understand that even though there are risks to using social media as a preemployment screening tool, there might also be benefits to the employer, such as not hiring someone who publicly libels his/her employer, coworkers, or customers. If an employer decides that the benefits outweigh the risks, several things should be considered. The critical aspect that needs to be considered is exposure control. This means that the policy should state that the person making the employment decision does not do the social media check. As Whitehill (2012) states, "Exposure control eliminates the presence of implicit bias by depriving the decision maker of information regarding the applicant's protected trait and therefore precluding implicit bias from driving the decision" (p. 257). That would protect the employer from someone alleging bias since the employer could show that the decision making was not exposed to any potentially discriminatory information. In addition, there should be a written policy for preemployment search of social media. It is important to ensure that a written policy exists that is specifically tailored to each employer's needs and meets the guidelines discussed here.

When using preemployment testing or social media screening for competencies, the employer must follow these guidelines:

1. Identify and list specific competencies required for the specific position that is being filled.
2. Of the required competencies, the employer should determine which skills can be assessed through the evaluation of an applicant's social networking profile and which would be better assessed through a preemployment test, an interview, or other means. The employer should draft directive guidelines for hiring managers and staff to follow.
4. The skills looked for or tested must directly relate to the relevant job competencies for that specific position.
5. The employer must implement a uniform policy regarding the use of social media sites. For example, the same SNWs should be searched for each applicant for a given vacancy. The same is true for preemployment testing—uniform questions should be administered to all applicants for that position.
6. Finally, the organization should require that the person evaluating the social networking profiles and/or administering the test keep a detailed record of what was looked at for every candidate.

The policy of keeping a detailed record may be used to show consistency, relevance, and adherence to the policy in case of a discrimination claim. This, in part, is based on a Tenth Circuit decision. In *Turner v. Public Service Co. of Colorado* (2009), the court delineated parameters for subjective criteria in employment decision making. The court particularly emphasized the need for consistency in the hiring process across candidates, the relevance of the evaluation criteria to the job in question, and the adherence of the interviewers to guidelines provided by the company.

The written policy at a minimum should contain the following components:

1. It must state when in the selection process social media will be used.
2. It must state which social media venues will be used.
3. It must emphasize that the social media search will occur at the same point for each applicant, and that the same social media venues will be searched for each applicant.

4. It should state that records, including such things as screen shots, must be made and kept, and that those records will be the same for each applicant.
5. The reviewer must be knowledgeable of all applicable federal and state rules and regulations.
6. It should state whether the social media search would be carried out in-house or by a hired third party. If in-house, it must be clear that the person who does the social media search is not the person who makes the hiring decisions.
7. Whether in-house or by a hired third party the policy must state what information will not be shared with the person making the hiring decision.

Once the policy is established, it must be consistently followed.

If the decision is to conduct an in-house social media review then we also recommend the following steps:

1. Designate one or more specific employees who will do the screening for every candidate.
2. Make sure that employee is totally insulated from other aspects of the hiring process.
3. Thoroughly train that employee in regard to what information is legal to use and what information may not be legal to use. That employee must scrub all information that may be illegal to use and provide only a sanitized report to the hiring agent.
4. Be consistent and maintain the same records for each search.
5. Others who may be involved in the search process must be clearly told to refrain from social media searches of job candidates. This means that no one other than those designated and trained to do a social media search may conduct such a search, even on their own computers or personal devices (e.g., iPhones).
6. The policy should include consequences for anyone who conducts a "lone wolf" search of social media.

If the decision is to use a third party social media venue reviewer, then we recommend the following steps:

1. Engage in a thorough vetting process of prospective third parties to ensure that they understand the legal issues, stay current of the changing legal landscape, and engage in searches that are consistent for each applicant.
2. Understand that compliance with the Fair Credit Reporting Act and its requirements will most likely need to occur.
3. Use the information the third party provides in a consistent manner with each applicant.

Whichever method a manager, hiring agent, or search committee uses, detailed, accurate, written records of the entire decision-making process must be maintained. This should include justifications for each candidate hired and each rejected applicant. This information can be critically important if a firm is sued for employment discrimination. Even in the case of a capricious lawsuit with no basis in fact, the information will be needed to document the decision-making process and refute claims of discrimination. Finally, be consistent for all applicants for a particular decision.

Implications for Research

While voluminous research has been conducted on employment discrimination issues, almost no studies have investigated the intersection of social media and personnel selection issues within the context of employment law. Most research on social media has been done in the laboratory and has not explicitly dealt with discrimination. For example, Kluemper and Rosen (2009) report that individuals often make reasonably accurate personality inferences based on information gleaned from a person's SNW, and Back et al. (2010) show that most people post profile information that is fairly accurate, rather than an idealized profile. However, managers should exercise caution when assessing personality traits via SNWs and using those assessments for making hiring decisions: not only are such judgments often poor predictors of job performance (even well-designed personality tests have only modest predictive validities), some behaviors and inferred personality traits (e.g., narcissism, depression) may touch on mental health status or other issues that implicate the Americans with Disabilities Act. Consider that Bohnert and Ross (2010) report that people are less interested in interviewing applicants who emphasized excessive drinking on their SNWs. Also, Ballweg, Ross, and Secchi (2013) report that people make little distinction whether excessive drinking information is from five years ago or only a few weeks ago; it receives similar, negative weight. These two studies provide interesting findings in light of protection that the Americans with Disabilities Act affords to recovered alcoholics. It would be interesting to extend their findings to various conditions where applicants are clearly protected (and not protected) under the ADA to see if hiring managers consider—or ignore—such legal distinctions.

Race-based discrimination is illegal according to the 1964 Civil Rights Act. However, psychological research suggests that reading a descriptive profile of a minority male who strongly identifies with his minority ethnic group elicits discrimination against him among white readers (Kaiser & Pratt-Hyatt, 2009). It seems likely that similar findings would emerge when whites examine minority applicants' SNW profiles, group memberships, and activities. Investigators may wish to consider which SNW components play a significant weight in eliciting such discrimination, and under what situational conditions.

In one field experiment that did examine discrimination using social media, Acquisti and Fong (2015) created fake SNWs for fictitious job candidates and systematically varied selected background characteristics (religion and sexual orientation). They then sent resumes to employers and tracked how many were invited to job interviews. The authors reported that "about one-third of the employers ... likely searched online for the candidates' information" (p. 5). These authors found distinct patterns of religious employment discrimination that covaried with the dominant political party of the county in which the company was located; they found no such pattern of discrimination against homosexuals. In future studies, field researchers may extend this research to other characteristics and even identify which employers visit such SNWs (and when) using website tracking software.

Rosenblat, Wikelius, Boyd, Gangadharan, and Yu (2014) observe that large companies are increasingly turning to sophisticated algorithms to screen prospective hires. While some screening criteria are obviously job-related, other criteria are not. Algorithms have been developed to identify who is likely to file a Worker's Compensation claim, pose a credit risk, or likely to regularly take their prescription medicines. Certain web-browsing habits can be traced (and predicted); individuals who have posted material to social media—only to have it removed by a moderator as "hateful" or sexually explicit—are identifiable. Those who have had unproven criminal allegations (not convictions) made against them may also be identified, even though blacks are more likely to have data entered into such criminal databases than whites. These authors warn that to the extent that such hiring algorithms utilize information from SNWs, they may perpetuate adverse impact against minority group applicants. They also warn employers that using algorithms instead of human judgment will not necessarily alleviate discrimination; it may merely continue it. Future research should investigate this emerging area.

Finally, researchers should investigate methods of promoting equal opportunity in hiring. If SNWs play a role in hiring, what specific procedures seem to be most effective for reducing adverse impact or disparate treatment? At what point in the hiring process should they be used? What types of training methods for hiring managers and their staff work well for insuring compliance with nondiscrimination laws? These are questions for future research.

Limitations

This paper has focused on federal legislation. One limitation of this paper is that consideration of state and local laws is beyond its scope. This was intentional: State and local laws are more numerous, vary considerably, apply to fewer managers, and are usually subordinate to federal legislation; instead we have focused on federal laws that apply to managers throughout the United States. A second limitation is that the paper has reviewed laws, court cases, and EEOC guidance in interpreting these laws only as they pertain to gathering social network information concerning job applicants. The paper does not examine other aspects of the employment relationship such as training, compensation issues, or employee relations (e.g., we did not examine National Labor Relations Board cases involving discipline for "insubordination" posted to social media—"insubordination" that may involve "protected, concerted activity" under the Labor-Management Relations Act). Nor did the present paper address broader concerns of employee (and employer) information privacy and security (see Ross, Meyer, Chen, & Keaton, 2009). Finally, the paper does not gather empirical data on firm practices or policies; nor does it report surveys or experimental data gathered from plaintiffs, lawyers, or judges regarding typical practices or responses to systematically varied hypothetical cases. For example, do people react differently when managers use social media screening systematically versus occasionally (with cause) versus randomly? Such research must await future studies. This paper's contribution lies in reviewing the legal landscape, informing managers of potential legal hazards from screening applicants via social media and providing researchers with an adequate legal context as they explore variations in social media procedures and practices.

Conclusion

Our study focuses on the areas of law that can create problems for employers who use social media for potential employee screening. Using social media to evaluate job applicants carries substantial and sometimes nonobvious legal risks. Employers must understand these risks and balance them against the benefits they might receive from searching social media.

What this paper adds to this discussion is a review of the preemployment screening risks in regard to employment discrimination claims based on numerous federal and state laws. We intend the information, and especially the recommendations, to help employers to reduce the risk of legal exposure to a discrimination claim. With greater awareness of probable risks, the business person may make an informed decision as to whether or not to use social media—and if so, how.

Using these recommendations may not eliminate all claims arising out of preemployment screening, but it will have the effect of greatly reducing the likelihood of those claims prevailing in court.

Finally, for researchers, this is a newly emerging area of study. We expect interest in this topic to only increase, commensurate with the increased use of social media in all its many forms in society.

References

Acquisti, A., & Fong, C. M. (2015, July 17). *An experiment in hiring discrimination via online social networks.* Retrieved November 17, 2015 from http://ssrn.com/abstract=2031979

Adams, S. (2014, Feb. 6). Four ways to use Facebook to find a job [electronic version], *Forbes.* Retrieved from http://www.forbes.com/sites/susanadams/2014/02/06/4-ways-to-use-facebook-to-find-a-job/

Back, M. D., Stopfer, J. M., Vazire, S., Gaddis, S., Schmukle, S. C., Egloff, B., & Gosling, S. D. (2010). Facebook profiles reflect actual personality, not self-idealization. *Psychological Science, 21* (3), 372–374.

Ballweg, C., Ross, W. H., & Secchi, D. (2013, August 9–13*). How job applicants evaluate prospective supervisors based on their social networking websites.* Paper presented at the National Academy of Management convention, Orlando, Florida.

Bohnert, D. & Ross, W. H. (2010). The influence of social networking websites on the evaluation of job candidates. *Cyberpsychology, Behavior, & Social Networking, 13,* (3), 341–347.

Bordena, B. B., & Baronaa, J. R. (2014). Finding the signal in the noise: Information governance, analytics, and the future of legal practice [electronic version]. *Richmond Journal of Law and Technology, 20* (2), 1–32. Retrieved from http://jolt.richmond.edu/v20i2/article7.pdf

CareerBuilder (2012, Apr. 18). *Thirty-seven percent of companies use social networks to research potential job candidates, according to new CareerBuilder survey.* Retrieved September 10, 2014 from http://www.careerbuilder.com/share/aboutus/pressreleasesdetail.aspx?id=pr691&sd=4%2F18%2F2012&ed=4%2F18%2F2099

CareerBuilder (2015, May 14). *Thirty-five percent of employers less likely to interview applicants they can't find online.* Retrieved November 17, 2015 from http://www.careerbuilder.com/share/aboutus/pressreleasesdetail.aspx?sd=5%2F14%2F2015&id=pr893&ed=12%2F31%2F2015

Civil Rights Act of 1991, Pub. L. 102–166, Section 107(m) (1991).

Connes v. Molalla Transport System, Inc., 90CA0675 (Colorado Court of Appeals, Div. 4., March 28, 1991).

Connes v. Molalla Transport System, Inc., 91SC358 (Supreme Court of Colorado, En Banc, June 29, 1992).

Davik, C. S. (2013). We know who you are and what you are made of: The illusion of internet anonymity and its impact on protection from genetic discrimination. *Case Western Reserve Law Review, 64* (1), 17–59.

Delaware Code Ann. tit. 16, §§ 1220–1227 (2003).

Delaware Code Ann. tit. 18, § 2317 (1999).

Delaware Code Ann. tit. 19, §§ 710–718 (2005).

Desert Place Inc. v. Costa, 539 U.S. 90 (2003).

Duggan, M., Ellison, N. B., Lampe, C., Lenhart, A., & Madden, M. (2015, Jan. 9). Social media update, 2014: Demographics of key social networking platforms. *Pew Research Center: Internet, Science, and Tech Report.* Retrieved November 17, 2015 from http://www.pewinternet.org/2015/01/09/demographics-of-key-social-networking-platforms-2/

EEOC v. Fabricut, 13-CV-248-CVE-PJC (U.S. District Court for the Northern District of Oklahoma , May 7, 2013).

EEOC v. Founders Pavilion, Inc., 6:13-cv-06250 (W.D.N.Y., May 16, 2013).

Equal Employment Opportunity Commission (2008, May 21). *The genetic nondiscrimination act of 2008.* Retrieved November 20, 2015 from http://www.eeoc.gov/laws/statutes/gina.cfm

Equal Employment Opportunity Commission (2010a). *Background checks: what employers need to know.* Retrieved November 21, 2015 from http://www.eeoc.gov/eeoc/publications/background_checks_employers.cfm

Equal Employment Opportunity Commission (2010b, Nov. 9). *Questions and answers for small businesses: EEOC final rule on Title II of the Genetic Information Nondiscrimination Act of 2008.* Retrieved November 20, 2015 from http://www.eeoc.gov/laws/regulations/gina_qanda_smallbus.cfm

Equal Employment Opportunity Commission (2013, May 7). *Fabricut to Pay $50,000 to Settle EEOC Disability and Genetic Information Discrimination Lawsuit.* Retrieved November 20, 2015 from http://www.eeoc.gov/eeoc/newsroom/release/5-7-13b.cfm

Equal Employment Opportunity Commission (2014, Jan. 13). *Founders pavilion will pay $370,000 to settle EEOC genetic information discrimination lawsuit.* Retrieved November 20, 2015 from http://www.eeoc.gov/eeoc/newsroom/release/1-13-14.cfm

Federal Trade Commission (2012a, January). *Using consumer reports: What employers need to know.* Retrieved November 20, 2015 from https://www.ftc.gov/tips-advice/business-center/guidance/using-consumer-reports-what-employers-need-know

Federal Trade Commission (2012b, June 12). *Press release: Spokeo to pay $800,000 to settle FTC charges company allegedly marketed information to employers and recruiters in violation of FCRA.* Retrieved June 1, 2015 from https://www.ftc.gov/news-events/press-releases/2012/06/spokeo-pay-800000-settle-ftc-charges-company-allegedly-marketed

Foster, A. (2010). Critical dilemmas in genetic testing: Why regulations to protect the confidentiality of genetic information should be expanded [electronic version]. *Baylor Law Review, 62* (2), 537–572. Retrieved from http://www.baylor.edu/content/services/document.php/117439.pdf

Gaskell v. University of Kentucky, Civil Action No. 09-244-KSF, (United States District Court, E.D. Kentucky, November 23, 2010).

Genetic Information Nondiscrimination Act, 29 C.F.R. § 1635 (2015). *Electronic code of federal regulations.* Retrieved November 20, 2015 from http://www.ecfr.gov/cgi-bin/text-idx?tpl=/ecfrbrowse/Title29/29cfr1635_main_02.tpl

Haas III, M., Clifton, W. M., Martin, Jr. W. J., & Morris, A. P. (2013). Labor and employment law. *Mercer Law Review 63* (1), 197–263.

Hazelton, A. S., & Terhorst, A. (2015). Legal and ethical considerations for social media hiring practices in the workplace [electronic version]. *The [Western Michigan University] Hilltop Review, 7* (2), Article 7, 53–59. Retrieved from http://scholarworks.wmich.edu/cgi/viewcontent.cgi?article=1093&context=hilltopreview

Johnson v. USA Truck, Inc. 06-cv-00227 (US Colorado District , August 27, 2007).

Kaiser, C. R., & Pratt-Hyatt, J. S. (2009). Distributing prejudice unequally: Do whites direct their prejudice toward strongly identified minorities? *Journal of Personality and Social Psychology, 96* (2), 432–445.

Kane, S. A. (2012, Jan.). Breaking into e-discovery. *Law Practice Today,* 1–4. Retrieved November 20, 2015 from http://www.americanbar.org/content/dam/aba/publications/law_practice_today/breaking-into-e-discovery.authcheckdam.pdf

Kasarjian, A. (2013, Mar.). The social media checklist for companies: What your clients should do, know, and learn. *Arizona Attorney, 49* (3), 16–21.

Kittling, N. M. (2010, November 6). *Statutory claims: everything old is new again, negligent hiring and negligent retention: a state by state analysis.* Paper presented at the American Bar Association 4th Annual Section of Labor and Employment Law Conference, November 6, 2010, Chicago, Illinois. Retrieved November 21, 2015 at http://www.americanbar.org/content/dam/aba/administrative/labor_law/meetings/2010/annualconference/087.authcheckdam.pdf

Kluemper, D. H., & Rosen, P. A. (2009). Future employment selection methods: Evaluating social networking web sites. *Journal of Managerial Psychology, 24* (6), 567–580.

Larson, C. R. (2012, September 4). EEOC Lawyer Advises Careful Navigation of Issues in the Workplace. *Bloomberg BNA News*. Retrieved November 21, 2015 from http://www.bna.com/eeoc-lawyer-advises-n17179869380/

Lipps, J. (2011). State lifestyle statutes and the blogosphere: Autonomy for private employees in the internet age. *Ohio State Law Journal, 72*, 645–685.

Lovan, D. (2011, January 18). University of Kentucky settles suit with astronomer Martin Gaskell [electronic version]. *The Huffington Post*, Retrieved from http://www.huffingtonpost.com/2011/01/18/university-of-kentucky-se_n_810540.html

McDonnell Douglas Corp. v. Green, 411 U.S. 792 (May 14, 1973).

Miaskoff, C. (2014, Mar. 12). Testimony before the Equal Employment Opportunity Commission. *Social media in the workplace: Examining opportunities for equal employment law* [Transcript]. Retrieved November 18, 2015 from http://www1.eeoc.gov//eeoc/meetings/3-12-14/transcript.cfm?renderforprint=1

Milligan, R. B., & Hart, D. P. (2015). *Social media privacy legislation desktop reference: What employers need to know, 2015–2016 edition*. Los Angeles: Seyfarth & Shaw. Retrieved November 21, 2015 from http://www.seyfarth.com/uploads/siteFiles/practices/131317SocialMediaSurveyM13.pdf

Morgan, H. A., & Davis, F. A. (2013). *Social media and employment law: Summary of key cases and legal issues*. Los Angeles: Paul Hastings. Retrieved November 21, 2015 from http://www.americanbar.org/content/dam/aba/events/labor_law/2013/04/aba_national_symposiumontechnologyinlaboremploymentlaw/10_socialmedia.authcheckdam.pdf

Morgan, W., Walker, S., Hebl, M. R., & King, E. B. (2013). A field experiment: Reducing interpersonal discrimination toward pregnant job applicants. *Journal of Applied Psychology, 98* (5), 799–809.

Mulvey, T. (2013, April 11). *SHRM survey findings: Social networking websites and recruiting/selection*. Washington D.C.: Society for Human Resource Management. Retrieved November 26, 2015 from http://www.slideshare.net/shrm/social-networkingwebsitesrecruitingselectingjobcandidatesshrm2013final

National Conference of State Legislatures (2013). *The use of credit information in employment*. Retrieved November 20, 2015 from http://www.ncsl.org/research/financial-services-and-commerce/use-of-credit-info-in-employ-2013-legis.aspx

Nayak, V. (2014, Jan. 30). Google+ reaches 1 billion users mark: +1 button is viewed 5 million times a day. *Dazeinfo*. Retrieved November 17, 2015 from http://dazeinfo.com/2014/01/30/google-plus-users-2014-statistics-social-media/

Perkins, O. (2015, May 14). More than half of employers now use social media to screen job candidates, poll says; even send friend requests [electronic version]. *[Cleveland, OH] Plain Dealer.* Retrieved from http://www.cleveland.com/business/index.ssf/2015/05/more_than_half_of_employers_no_1.html

Reppler Co. (2011). How employers use social media to screen applicants. *Undercover recruiter.* Retrieved November 17, 2015 from http://theundercoverrecruiter.com/infographic-how-recruiters-use-social-media-screen-applicants/

Rosen, L (2012, Jan. 5). Social media background screening checks of job applicants becoming more prevalent and more controversial. *Employment Screening Resources* [weblog], Retrieved November 18, 2015 from http://www.esrcheck.com/wordpress/2012/01/05/social-media-background-screening-checks-of-job-applicants-becoming-more-prevalent-and-more-controversial

Rosenblat, A., Wikelius, K., Boyd, D., Gangadharan, S. P., & Yu, C. (2014, October 30). *Data & civil rights: employment primer*. Data & Civil Rights Conference. Retrieved November 21 from http://ssrn.com/abstract=2541512

Ross, W. H., Meyer, C. J., Chen, J. V., & Keaton, P. (2009). The role of human resource management in protecting information at telecommunications firms. *The Journal of Information Privacy and Security, 5,* (1), 49–77.

Rush, M. B. (2009, Oct.). Genetic information non-discrimination act (GINA). *Potter, Anderson, & Carroon Newsletter,* 1–2. Retrieved November 20, 2015 from http://www.potteranderson.com/media/publication/125_Genetic_20Information_20Non_20Discrimination_20Act_20MBR_2010_2030_20090.pdf

Schulz, G. W., & Zwerdling, D. (2013, Sept. 30). Easily obtained subpoenas turn your personal information against you. *Center for Investigative Reporting Reports.* Retrieved November 19, 2015 from http://cironline.org/reports/easily-obtained-subpoenas-turn-your-personal-information-against-you-5104

Turner v. Public Service Co. of Colorado, 563 F.3d 1136, 1145–1146 (10th Cir. 2009).

United States Commission on Civil Rights (2000, Oct.). Substance abuse and the ADA. In *Sharing the dream: Is the ADA accommodating all?* (Ch. 4). Retrieved September 5, 2014 from http://www.usccr.gov/pubs/ada/ross-final/ross-final.htm

VisitorTrack (2015). VisitorTrack: Caller ID for your website. http://netfactor.com/visitortrack/

Walters, E. (2011, Apr. 15). Social media discrimination. *Fastcase* [Weblog], Retrieved November 19, 2015 from http://www.fastcase.com/social-media-discrimination/

Welkowitz, W. (2015, Apr. 17). Job applicant screening: Is social media fair game? *BNA Labor and Employment Blog.* Retrieved November 18, 2015 from http://www.bna.com/job-applicant-screening-b17179925375/

Whitehill, M. (2012). Better safe than subjective: the problematic intersection of prehire social networking checks and Title VII employment discrimination. *Temple Law Review, 85* (1), 229–267.

Zitrin, R. (2003). Five who got it right. *Widner Law Journal, 13,* 209–232.

Biographical Notes

Roger W. Reinsch (JD, the University of Missouri—Columbia), is a professor of business law at the University of Minnesota, Duluth. He writes about Equal Employment Opportunity issues. He has won numerous research awards. His recent articles have appeared in *Northwestern Journal of Law & Social Policy, Journal of Legal Studies in Business, Texas Journal of Women and the Law,* and *Ohio Northern University Law Review.* (rreinsch@d.umn.edu)

William H. Ross (PhD, Psychology, University of Illinois) is human resource management professor at the University of Wisconsin, La Crosse. He writes about technology and HRM as well as dispute resolution procedures. His articles appear in *Personnel Psychology, Cyberpsychology Behavior & Social Networking, Info, International Journal of Organizational Analysis, Journal of Applied Psychology, Labor Law Journal,* and *Academy of Management Review.* (wross@uwlax.edu)

Amy B. Hietapelto (PhD, Organizational Studies, University of Minnesota, Twin Cities) is Dean and Professor of Management, Labovitz School of Business and Economics, University of Minnesota, Duluth. She writes about diversity, management education, and organizational change management. She has published articles in *Journal of Diversity Management, Journal of Legal Studies in Business, Change,* and *Journal of Management Education.* (ahietape@d.umn.edu)

Accepted after two revisions: December 23, 2015

Current Topics in Management, Vol. 18, 2016, pp. 183–200

CASE STUDY

FROM SOCIAL ENTREPRENEUR TO SOCIAL ENTERPRISE: ORGANIZATIONAL CHANGE AT THE WORLD TOILET ORGANIZATION

Imran Chowdhury
Pace University

This case study examines how social entrepreneurs might restructure their businesses to meet the demands of growth as they move beyond an initial, founder-centric business model. The World Toilet Organization (WTO), an innovative, Singapore-based social enterprise focusing on sanitation-related issues, provides a compelling context for exploring the challenges faced by social entrepreneurs as they manage the issues of business model innovation and organizational design. Results from this study relate how early-stage social enterprises might start to develop greater structure and a more-focused strategy in order to multiply their social impact.

Keywords: business model innovation, organizational design, scaling social impact, social entrepreneurship, Southeast Asia

Note: I would like to thank Jack Sim and his team at the World Toilet Organization in Singapore for participating in this research. I would also like to thank Thierry Sibieude of ESSEC Business School's Institute for Social Innovation and Entrepreneurship for encouraging me to work on this project. Mohammed S. Ghani and Matthew Spanarkel provided invaluable research assistance.

Jack Sim, an operator of several small businesses in Singapore, got into the "business of toilets" in the late 1990s. At the time, building a social enterprise had been a rewarding diversion into community development, and a contrast to Jack's day-to-day life in the business world. His efforts paid off: after more than a decade of steadily working as a social entrepreneur, Jack's organization, the

World Toilet Organization (WTO), was globally recognized as a leader in the world of sanitation-focused social enterprises. But despite the success he had found in his new line of work, the problem that led Jack to focus on toilets as a vocation still remained as compelling as ever: clean, safe toilets for everyone is a dream for countless citizens of (mostly poor) countries around the globe, and as of 2010 more than 1.1 billion people, or one-sixth of the world's population, had no access to sanitation facilities (WHO/UNICEF, 2010). WTO had to be scaled up to impact greater numbers of people, and this change in organizational structure presented a unique set of challenges.

To better understand the barriers and constraints surrounding the growth and development of a social enterprise, I present a case study of the WTO and its attempts to reorganize itself in order to create greater social impact. WTO is an ideal organization for studying the challenges associated with the growth and development of a social enterprise, as it is an early-stage organization that is trying to mature from a founder-focused operational style to one that relies on the coordinated efforts of a larger group of individuals to achieve its goals. I developed my insights into WTO based on fieldwork with the organization at its headquarters in Singapore, as well as through in-depth interviews with Jack Sim, two key WTO managers, and five members of stakeholder organizations associated with the broader social entrepreneurship environment in Singapore.

This study adds to the research on social enterprises and organizations more broadly by relating the actions of social entrepreneurs to the organizations they create. While these organizations often start as individual endeavors, for the social enterprise sector as a whole to be successful there has to be a greater understanding and awareness of the challenges social entrepreneurs face as they attempt to build organizations that will outlive them, organizations that will contribute to the greater social good for years to come. Although this case study of the WTO and its operations in the greater Southeast Asia region may not necessarily be generalizable to the entire field of social enterprises, sharing the growth challenges of the organization may provide an opportunity for other social enterprises to learn about and thereby avoid pitfalls on the path to scaling social impact (Pache & Santos, 2013; Battilana & Dorado, 2010; Chowdhury & Santos, 2010).

Literature Review

In recent years, the emergence of social entrepreneurship as a burgeoning field of business practice has led to a reconsideration of the ways in which a wide range of companies organize themselves and manage their operations. For instance, research on "hybrid" organizations (Pache & Santos, 2010) has started to examine how the embededdness of organizations in organizational environments with multiple, distinct guiding values and cultural understand-ings, or different institutional logics (Friedland & Alford, 1991; Thornton &

Ocasio, 1999), influences the development of organizational business models and human resource practices (Battilana & Dorado, 2010). This body of literature thereby situates hybrid organizations on a continuum between traditional commercial firms and not-for-profit organizations: while firms are commercial organizations, embedded in commercial institutional spheres and shaped by a commercial logic, not-for-profit organizations are guided by a social welfare logic and concerned with social value creation, delivering services to communities, and with achieving a broader state of well-being for target populations (Pache & Santos, 2010).

As organizations combing aspects of the commercial logic and the social welfare logic, hybrids pose a unique set of challenges and require the development of new theory to address these challenges, particularly with respect to the development of hybrids' organizational practices (Pache & Santos, 2013). In this sense, the literature on institutional logics, or "socially constructed, historical patterns of material practices, assumptions, values, beliefs, and rules by which individuals produce and reproduce their material subsistence, organize time and space, and provide meaning to their social reality" (Thornton & Ocasio 1999: 804), has given scholars a powerful lens for studying hybrid organizations such as social enterprises, and has further allowed the examination of distinct areas of organizational behavior in situations of "institutional complexity" wherein different institutional logics prescribe different and potentially contradictory set of actions for actors (Greenwood, Raynard, Kodeih, Micelotta, & Lounsbury, 2011).

With respect to the field of social entrepreneurship in particular, scholars who have theorized about social entrepreneurship have argued that organizations with a social value creation focus go about their work in a manner that is quite distinct from what we observe in traditional commercial firms (Santos, 2012; Chowdhury & Santos, 2010; Mair & Martí, 2006). The interaction of the social entrepreneur's motivations with the problems of day-to-day operations and long-term organizational strategy gives rise to a distinct set of practices and activities for the social enterprises that they create (He, 2008; Stewart & Roth, 2007). These practices and activities can serve as both assets and liabilities for social enterprises: while their deep commitment to a social mission facilities work with disadvantaged communities and individuals, the organizational structures that are created to serve these populations are often not developed to most efficiently serve them. Frequently, these structures emerge after the success of one "heroic" social entrepreneur and his or her actions, but they are not well-suited for continuing and expanding social impact when the efforts of one individual are insufficient to serve a burgeoning set of social needs (Bornstein, 2007; Mair & Martí, 2006; Tracey & Jarvis, 2007).

To highlight this gap between the needs of social enterprises and potential shortcomings in their practical operation, it is necessary to look to the literature on business models and business model innovation (Zott & Amit, 2007; Teece, 2010). Scholars in these research traditions have noted that organizational redesign emerges from a range of different factors, including a need for greater efficiency of operations (Khandwalla, 1973), an opportunity to achieve greater "fit" with the external environment (Dunbar & Starbuck, 2006), and the desire to produce human resources policies that better integrate employees as a strategic resource for the organization (Lakatos, Soucy, & Bukowy, 2011). With respect to social enterprises, social entrepreneurs might, in an ideal case, develop business models that allow social goals to be balanced against profit goals in their pursuit of delivering value to society. In practice this often doesn't happen, and frequently the failure to develop business models that balance social and economic demands is tied to an inability of certain founding social entrepreneurs to change their organizations' structures to comport with changing needs as their organizations grow. By examining WTO's attempted transition from a model that focuses solely on social value creation to one with the hybrid foci of social value and economic value, I illustrate one such change process, including the pitfalls and opportunities contained therein.

Method

In order to gain better insight into the growth and development of early-stage social enterprises, I conducted a single case study of the WTO in Singapore. By engaging with the organization using the methods of qualitative research, I was able to get involved with the organization's day-to-day operations and thereby gain a stronger understanding of some of its internal processes. Following the standard for inductive studies, I formed no testable hypotheses prior to data collection (Glaser & Strauss, 1967).

There were three primary sources of data for this research: (1) interviews; (2) fieldwork; and (3) archival data and secondary material. The main source of data was the set of interviews, eight of which were conducted in total during the course of 2010. Three interviews were with staff at the WTO: founder Jack Sim and two senior managers at the organization. In addition, I spoke with five members of stakeholder organizations that constitute part of the broader social entrepreneurship environment in Singapore. These interviews helped flesh out the study and provide a view of the WTO beyond the members of the organization. Most of these interviews were taped and then transcribed, though at the request of the interviewees two of the interviews were not recorded; in these instances I relied on hand-written notes to provide a record of the interviews. The interview process was semistructured, and follow-up questions were used to gain greater insight into issues as the conversations developed. In the course of my conversations, I was most interested in understanding the processes involved in the development of the WTO as an early-stage social enterprise and its planning processes with respect to its future planned growth and development. Speaking with a wide range of stakeholders allowed me to develop a broad perspective on these processes.

I also conducted fieldwork at the offices of the WTO in Singapore for two days in April and May 2010, and during this period I was able to observe the operations of the organization and sit in on several meetings held by staff members; this gave me further insight into the organization's day-to-day activities. Beyond the interviews and fieldwork, the collected documents and archival data served as important triangulation and supplementary sources for understanding key events and developing further perspective on the WTO and its operations (Miles & Huberman, 1984); these documents were available at the WTO's archives in Singapore. In addition, I examined supplementary information, including newspaper articles, reports, and publically available information from social entrepreneurship foundations such as Ashoka and the Schwab Foundation, to provide a more comprehensive view of the organization.

Focusing on the emergence and growth of WTO as a social enterprise, the interview transcripts, field notes, and archival materials were examined for common themes and with reference to the literature on founding entrepreneurs as well as the literatures on hybrid organizations, social enterprises, and organizational business models. Using this approach allowed me to develop a narrative of the organization that was grounded in empirical realities and that provided an analytical framework for examining social enterprises that may have relevance outside the setting of the WTO. I present these findings and my emerging framework in the next section.

Findings

As I explored the data from my case study of the WTO, three distinct categories began to emerge with regard to the process of WTO's growth and development as a social enterprise: (1) the development of the organization from its origins in the personal interests of founder Jack Sim; (2) the changing needs of the organization as it began to outgrow Mr. Sim's personal charisma and interests; and (3) the need to develop a sustainable business model that would allow the organization to outlive its founder and thereby emerge as a more independent entity not tied to any one individual for its survival. While I found that the commercial and social welfare logics (Pache & Santos, 2010; Pache & Chowdhury, 2012) were indeed present within the WTO, it seemed that the organization's strong linkage with its founder's motivations and actions (Stewart & Roth, 2007) greatly influenced its ability to emerge as an independent entity. This interplay between the commercial logic, social welfare logic, and the founder's motivations and actions led to tensions at the organization, and it was clear that organization members were influenced by and worked to resolve these tensions. In the following sections, I discuss these tensions and the ways in which organization members attempted to resolve them as the WTO sought to develop from an early-stage social enterprise with unclear survival chances to one that was more mature and sustainable.

From Individual Interest to Social Enterprise

Up to the age of 40, Jack Sim had worked as an entrepreneur in Singapore. Having started his career in 1979 at age 18 as a building-supply salesman, he founded his first company with his brother 6 years later. By the year 2000 they had created 16 separate businesses working in different areas such as textiles, manufacturing, building materials, and information technology. In addition to entrepreneurial and commercial experience, Jack gained important international exposure through the numerous cross-border operations that his companies were involved in. However, with the emergence of the financial crisis in 1997, economic growth slowed and commerce suffered (Nanto, 1998). The downturn hit Jack's businesses hard, and he began to wonder whether he might start working on other projects.

Jack had always been interested in social issues, and he started to consider applying some of his business expertise to dealing with the social problems in Singapore. One area that he had always felt needed more attention was the idea of sanitation, particularly in the public realm. After a period of research and deliberation, Jack set up his first socially oriented company, the Restroom Association of Singapore (RAS) in December 1998. From dealing with business owners while operating his own companies Jack understood that they viewed toilets as cost centers, as necessary but not essential to their sales. Thus, toilets weren't something to spend much money on. He wanted to persuade business owners that there was economic gain in providing good toilets, and used RAS to push forward this message. For instance, Jack discovered from some basic field research that many shoppers didn't linger in Singapore's shopping malls due to the poor quality of public restroom facilities. Instead, they came in, got what they wanted, and left. Pointing to the principles that the McDonald's fast food chain had developed decades before in the United States, Jack convinced shopping mall operators that having clean toilets would actually retain shoppers: better bathroom facilities would make the shopping experience more comfortable and enjoyable. In turn, this would cause customers to stay longer, buy more, as well as to eat and drink in the mall. Indeed, as a large number of purchases are actually caused by impulse buying, the longer people they stay in a shopping area, the more likely they are to make purchases. Following this logic, having better toilet facilities can actually contribute positively to business profits.

Spurred by the initial success of the RAS, which was decidedly a side venture from his main business activities, Jack created a second socially oriented company, the WTO, in 2001. The organization's abbreviation "WTO" was a tongue-in-cheek reference to the World Trade Organization, the Washington, DC,-based multilateral institution charged with setting the rules of international trade. Jack believed that a name such as WTO would attract great media interest to the toilet and sanitation agenda. Although RAS had been very much a Singapore-oriented organization, with WTO he sought to create a broader, global platform for dealing with sanitation issues.

And the problem of sanitation was certainly one with global dimensions. According to the WHO, more than 2.5 billion people worldwide lack access to basic sanitation. Of these 2.5 billion, 1.1 billion, or approximately one out of six people worldwide (over 16% of the world's population), have no sanitation facilities at all (WHO/UNICEF 2010). These individuals are forced to defecate in the open, often in fields or waterways in rural areas, as well as in roadside sewers and open drains in urban locales. In addition, World Bank figures note that over 1.2 billion people have to defecate in the open, and only about 800 million people have access to very primitive latrines. Both these groups are inevitably potential carriers of disease as they are unlikely to have piped water to wash their hands with or to drink. Beyond this, the largest single cause of child deaths is diarrhea or other waterborne diseases (World Bank Group, 2009).

In sum, a wide range of factors is responsible for the poor sanitation environment in developing countries. As Jack moved from operating the RAS, a Singapore-focused organization looking at local issues, to a broader focus with WTO, he had to take this broad spectrum of factors into account. Having understood the sanitation situation globally, Jack oriented WTO as an advocacy organization to increase awareness of the huge gap between industrialized and emerging economies in this area. Choosing to operate an advocacy organization was also practical: in 2001, when the organization was founded, Jack lacked funds and staff, and he found that he could do most of his advocacy work working alone and at relatively low cost. The goal was to broadcast the message of WTO—clean toilets for all—by working at multiple levels of society and by targeting different "customer groups," including the general public, workers, and officials associated with the sanitation sphere, and high-level individuals in the public and private domains.

Jack's efforts paid off. In the first few years of its existence, WTO met with a number of important successes. For instance, through its work with workers and officials in the sanitation sector, WTO was able to mobile workers by launching a drive to "professionalize" sanitation-related work, resulting in higher salaries for rank-and-file workers and a greater status overall for the sector in Singapore. Developing this kind of "win–win" partnership increased WTO's profile as an important voice in the sanitation sphere in Singapore, and helped the organization to develop important contacts with government officials, union leaders, and business people in the city-state. Beyond this, organization's global reach was expanded with the organization of a "World Toilet Summit," held annually in November starting with the first such event in Singapore on November 19, 2001. The summit's objective is to highlight the problems of clean water and sanitation, focusing in particular on an audience of key decision makers and concerned citizens. The resulting media exposure brought WTO much-needed legitimacy in its early existence, and the organization—and

Jack Sim in particular—became well known in the public health and social enterprise communities.

Events such as the World Toilet Summit increased the WTO's partnerships with organizations working in the sanitation field, and these collaborations led to national and international recognition for Jack Sim and the organization at large. Jack found himself going to even more speaking platforms like the World Economic Forum, the Clinton Global Initiative, and numerous UN-sponsored events as the years went by. At these venues, a ready-made audience for sanitation-related initiatives, combined with the presence of print and broadcast media, helped WTO increase its base of support. Also, success at international events increased WTO's profile in Singapore as well.

Changing Organizational Needs

However, despite WTO's considerable and fairly rapid success, the principal problem that the organization faced, and which has consistently been voiced as a criticism since the WTO's emergence as a leading social enterprise in the sanitation sphere, is that it is too focused on Jack Sim himself. Some of this is an outgrowth of the advocacy model itself: as with RAS, in the early stages of its history, WTO was a charismatic-founder-centered organization and Jack was the main driving force of all aspects of the company. His strengths in promotion and marketing led him to conclude that promoting the organization would have to mean promoting himself. Although there was a constant churn of supporting organizational members over the years, Jack remained the reliable "face" of WTO. In this sense, WTO's history reflects a consistent finding of research in entrepreneurship: for numerous early-stage entrepreneurial ventures, it is difficult to separate the founder from the organization itself (He, 2008; Stewart & Roth, 2007).

In order to move the organization forward from its initial "heroic entrepreneur" phase to a more mature organization with improved systems and processes, Jack understood that more focus had to be put on WTO the social enterprise and less on Jack Sim the social entrepreneur. But this was a shift that was easy to discuss but very difficult to implement in practice. For many of the stakeholders around WTO in Singapore, from employees at social enterprises to government officials, Jack Sim and the World Toilet Organization were synonymous. He was present at all of the organization's events, and indeed had a hand in running every aspect of the organization.

Clearly, this was a situation that could not last, and there were many forces both inside and outside the organization pushing for the organization to evolve. To this end, WTO has tried to undertake a number of changes to its organizational structure in recent years, a process that has yielded mixed results. Part of this attempted shift has entailed the redesign of the organization's operating procedures, recruiting function, and day-to-day management. For instance, in the first seven or eight years of the organization's existence, Jack and at most a few other staff members had managed all of WTO's activities in a relatively ad hoc manner. In many instances, the organization's focus on Jack and the lack of structure at the organization's headquarters meant that staff didn't stay long: employee tenure at the organization was short. Following years of such unstructured change, in 2010, Jack hired a new Chief Operating Officer (COO) in order to e-design the WTO's organizational structure. Together, they developed separate divisions to segregate the organization's activities: Administration and Finance; External Relations and Business Development; Advocacy and Communications; Project Management; and Training.

The idea of this redesign was simple: to move the organization away from the advocacy-focused activities of WTO's first decade of operation into the next phase of the organization's life. For instance, the administration and finance function, if better managed, could help the organization to increase its social impact. Streamlined financial reporting held the potential to increase the trust of the organization's various individual supporters, as well as program and grant managers in government organizations and foundations. Also, by hiring a COO the organization strengthened internal functioning and designated a key senior manager focused on the organization's day-to-day activities (Khandwalla, 1973). In theory, this would free Jack up to spend time engaging in the relationship-building and partnership development activities he has excelled at throughout the life of the organization.

Developing WTO's Next Business Model

Despite these changes, however, by 2010 the organization had only about ten staff members counting Jack Sim, and was struggling to grow. Although it had added some activities beyond advocacy and was starting to operate on the ground internationally by working with local nongovernmental organizations (NGOs) in Cambodia and Indonesia, its internal structure was limited by the business model it had developed. Relying almost exclusively on grants from the government or foundations and support from individual donors, program-matic initiatives were often subordinated to the needs of raising funds to keep the organization going. In this environment, considering a redesign of the organization's business model had to accompany the changes it was making internally (Zott & Amit, 2007; Teece, 2010).

WTO started as a not-for-profit organization, and its origins in this sphere, despite Jack's business background, have for the most part guided its approach to raising revenues. Up to 2010, nearly all of the organization's revenue came from outside sources, primarily grants from within and outside Singapore and a few scattered contributions from individual donors (see Appendix A for more information on WTO's financial status). With the different management team in place, Jack and the new COO began to consider in early 2010 how the organization might move to a "hybrid" model of social enterprise that combines the legal structure and goals of a not-for-profit organization with at least some degree of earned revenue and cost recovery (Pache & Santos, 2013).

Creating a franchise-oriented hybrid business model (Tracey & Jarvis, 2007) that focuses on the sanitation needs of underserved populations in developing nations is one path that the WTO has considered as it moves to its next stage of development as an organization. This requires tackling both the demand and supply sides of the sanitation equation to develop an approach that will not only help underserved populations, but also allow WTO to create some capacity to recoup its costs beyond donations and government support. The success of a franchise approach depends on the organization's on-the-ground efforts in developing nations, thereby working to implement sanitation solutions directly in addition to advocacy efforts. Thus, WTO, instead of donating toilets, which governments and numerous sanitation and clean-water-focused NGOs have traditionally done, would sell toilets to the end-user, often a villager living in the rural areas of developing countries, and help to create a "business ecosystem" around the idea of sanitation itself. According to Jack Sim,

> We have to create a training model of how the local poor can start a business to manufacture, promote, maintain, finance and reach out to customer. This is a franchise training program! (Personal communication, April 30, 2010)

A franchise-oriented approach to sanitation requires demand- and supply-side efforts. On the demand side, WTO would work to create toilets and associated sanitation products as "aspirational" items for villagers in developing nations. By partnering with NGOs and local community leaders to generate both aware-ness and demand for toilets, the organization could thus develop its own desired brand in the sanitation product space. The supply side of the equation would similarly work to engage local stakeholders and involve them in the process of improving sanitation conditions in underserved areas, perhaps by helping them to develop businesses that address these needs. As noted by Jack Sim in a recent article (2014),

> On the supply side, we need to create convenient accessibility at affordable prices. The World Toilet Organization's SaniShop social franchise trains local populations to start small $2,000 factories that produce very affordable latrines and shelters, and sell them to the local community. These local entrepreneurs take loans, create jobs and earn profits. Their sales associates—mostly women—earn commissions for every toilet sold and this extra income creates gender equality at home too. The training is donated free and the model is self-sustaining once the associates become proficient at promoting and selling. Driving demand and supply at the BoP [Base of the Pyra-mid] is done with much empathy, and if done with love, it can be very successful.

More broadly, the so-called SaniShop social franchise system being developed by WTO signals the organization's involvement in "sanitation marketing" efforts.

WTO works with local entrepreneurs in areas where improved sanitation can be implemented to develop their ability to sell sanitation-related products. This approach builds on the assumption that individuals with poor access to sanitation may aspire to changed behaviors and improved facilities through heightened awareness of perceived need or aspiration. People can thus be convinced to "buy into" new and better sanitation practices with the right messages and by investing some financial resources as they make the transition from older, more harmful practices. The philosophy underlying sanitation marketing is the following: when a toilet is given without requirement payment, oftentimes commitment to its use is not simultaneously obtained. Instead of using the toilet for its intended purpose, many villages use the toilet area as a store room, or leave it unclean and ill-maintained. Behaviors are thus not changed. Indeed, some villages disregard the sanitation function of the toilet space and may use it as a living space (Chowdhury & Santos, 2010). As noted by one of the managers at WTO working directly with the organization's sanitation program in countries outside of Singapore,

> When you give people toilet without educating them there is no mindset change. You may have a toilet but you don't believe in a toilet, if you don't believe in a toilet you don't maintain the toilet, you don't use the toilet. (Personal communication, April 30, 2010)

By utilizing sanitation marketing, WTO would work to upend some of these traditional, harmful, sanitation practices by trying to create mindset change among beneficiaries. Villagers paying their own money for a toilet and sanitation products would be likely to be committed to using it for its intended purpose. At the same time, the entrepreneurial capabilities of some villagers are used to support the purpose of improved access to sanitation. In this sense WTO's business development activities can be coupled with the traditional communications, advocacy, and training activities that WTO has gained great competence in throughout its young history.

Discussion

This case study offers an opportunity to examine the development of an early-stage social enterprise as it develops from a deeply founder-oriented organization (He, 2008) to one that relies more explicitly on the coordinated efforts of a team of individuals. By examining these issues at the WTO, the case study attempts to tie these changes in organizational structure (Khandwalla, 1973) to the unique challenges of business model innovation within the social entrepreneurship context, where commercial and social welfare logics coexist (Pache & Santos, 2010) and result in an organizational hybridity that requires explicit attention to both social and commercial value creation. I find that by adopting commercial practices (e.g., the SaniShop social franchise system) that are adapted to the social demands of both the organization and the context in which it is operating, early-stage social enterprises can begin to overcome the challenges that founder-centric organizing can pose.

As the WTO has developed from an initial "heroic entrepreneur" phase to a more mature organization with improved systems and processes, it has had to redesign its operating procedures, recruiting function, and day-to-day management focus as well. However, despite these changes, WTO remains a not-for-profit organization with emerging commercial business practices: in other words, a not-for-profit entity with a commercial bent. This crucial distinction helps us to understand why, despite the fact that the organization has historically received all its income from outside sources, it has been very tentative about integrating these business-oriented practices into its structure, a difficulty that may be related to the organization's limited capacity to operate with a dominant commercial logic driving its operations (Pache & Santos, 2013; Pache & Chowdhury, 2012).

As a result, despite the changes that the organization has undertaken over the past few years, WTO has been accumulating financial losses in recent years (see Appendix A for further details), mostly as a result of increased expenses due to the organization's internationalization. For instance, WTO piloted its SaniShop franchise in Cambodia in seven different provinces with the help of 600 agents between 2010 and 2012. However, due to the increasing costs of supporting this program, expansion in Cambodia was terminated in early 2013; the organization narrowed its focus into a single province, Kampong Chhnang, in order to gain efficiencies in production (World Toilet Organization, 2014). This focused approach in the organization's redesign of its operations in Southeast Asia following an initial period of difficulty is consistent with prior work on business model innovation (Zott & Amit, 2007) and work on change at organizations with a hybrid organizational structure (Battilana & Dorado, 2010).

Despite these operational challenges, the organization has continued its traditional work in advocacy, with Jack Sim continuing to lead the charge. In 2014, the organization launched "Urgent Run for World Toilet Day," a globally coordinated enterprise with 22 global events in 13 countries. The result: thousands of individuals around the world were engaged with the issue of sanitation at the same time, a growing critical mass of awareness. As WTO seeks to grow in the next phase of its existence, it must consider whether the "hybrid" social franchise model (Tracey & Jarvis, 2007) it has adopted, which combines the legal structure and goals of a not-for-profit organization with at least some degree of cost recovery by relying on the sale of goods and services to outside entities, is one that it can sustain without overrelying on Jack as the organization has for the first decade or so of its existence (Stewart & Roth, 2007). Answering this question will be key to the organization's future.

Implications for Management

Studying the WTO's efforts at moving beyond its initial, founder-centric business model offers important lessons for managers. The problems encountered by the WTO during its early existence largely reflect the problems faced by other early-stage organizations and those organizations that have retained a founder's imprint on their structures and strategies (He, 2008; Bornstein, 2007). Moving beyond this stage requires careful examination of the founder's motivations and their relationship to the organizational structure that has been created. Often, these motivations result in a structure that is not optimal for the organization as it matures and evolves beyond the actions of any one individual. The key in developing a more mature organization is to recognize that social enterprises are particularly susceptible to the influence of a charismatic founder, as the social mission and good intentions are seen as sufficient driving forces for legitimating a wide range of actions, leaving in subordinate position questions of commercial viability and organizational sustainability.

In addition, by examining the changes in organizational structure that can take place within the context of an early-stage social enterprise, students and executives can gain a better understanding of the dynamics of organizational redesign policies in situations where organizations have to balance the commercial and social welfare logics. WTO offers one way to go about this: by partnering with NGOs or other nonprofit organizations to manage on-the-ground operations and social advocacy efforts, social enterprises can focus on building viable, revenue-generating business models that can support these social activities. When these business models become profitable or reach a break-even point—a process that may take some time to develop, as the experience of WTO over the past few years shows—both the focal social enterprise and its partner organizations can benefit from this division of labor.

Directions for Future Research

Although this study has contributed to better understanding the dynamics of change and organizational redesign in early-stage social enterprises, particularly as these relate to moving from a founder-centered organization to one that has greater structure, further research is needed to clarify change processes within the realm of social entrepreneurship. Indeed, there are surprisingly few studies examining how social enterprises shift from a purely nonprofit model to one that explicitly relies on earned revenue. In these situations, how-to organizations manage to keep their "social" identities? Beyond this, the relationship between a social entrepreneur's founding motivations and the organizational structure of the social enterprise he or she creates is not yet well defined. It would be useful to examine how sectoral and contextual differences impact this relationship, and whether there are cultural factors at play that have not been examined.

Limitations of This Study

This case study helps us to comprehend some of the challenges faced by early-stage social enterprises. Examining the WTO helps us to better understand how early-stage social enterprises might manage their growth and development, but the case and findings contained in this study need to be expanded with further work in this area. In this sense, these findings should not be generalized or extrapolated, but rather used as a base for further inquiry into the management and growth challenges of social enterprises and other hybrid organizational forms.

Appendix A

Table 1
World Toilet Organization: Financial Statements

Income and Expenses Statement	(Monetary Figures Calculated in US Dollars)					
Year	2005	2006	2007	2008	2009	2010
Revenue	190,183	265,619	178,698	985,243	622,836	799,032
Cost of sales	69,770	131,746	58,655	837,901	172,259	169,837
Gross profit	120,413	133,873	120,043	147,342	450,577	629,195
Expenses	26,833	112,647	153,954	207,800	248,306	463,020
Surplus/(Deficit) after taxes	93,580	22,215	(33,911)	(60,458)	202,271	166,175

References

Battilana, J., & Dorado, S. (2010). Building sustainable hybrid organizations: the case of commercial microfinance organizations. *Academy of Management Journal, 53,* 1419–1440.

Bornstein, D. (2007). *How to change the world: Social entrepreneurs and the power of new ideas.* New York: Oxford University Press.

Chowdhury, I., & Santos, S. (2010). Scaling social innovations: The case of Gram Vikas. In P. Bloom & E. Skloot (Eds.), *Scaling social impact: New thinking* (pp. 147–168). New York: Palgrave Macmillan.

Dunbar, R., & Starbuck, W. (2006). Learning to design organizations and learning from designing them. *Organization Science, 17,* 171–178.

Friedland, R., & Alford, R. R. (1991). Bringing society back in: Symbols, practices and institutional contradictions. In W. Powell & P. D. Maggio (Eds.), *The new institutionalism in organizational analysis* (pp. 232–266). Chicago: University of Chicago Press.

Glaser, B., & Strauss, A. (1967). *The discovery of grounded theory: Strategies for qualitative research.* Chicago: Aldine.

Greenwood, R., Raynard, M., Kodeih, F., Micelotta, E. R., & Lounsbury, M. (2011). Institutional complexity and organizational responses. *Academy of Management Annals, 5,* 317–371.

He, L. (2008). Do founders matter? A study of executive compensation, governance structure and firm performance. *Journal of Business Venturing, 23,* 257–279.

Khandwalla, P. (1973). Viable and effective organizational designs of firms. *Academy of Management Journal, 16,* 481–495.

Lakatos, J., Soucy, D., & Bukowy, S. (2011). BSL printing company: A case study. *Current Topics in Management, 15,* 175–186.

Mair, J., & Martí, I. (2006). Social entrepreneurship research: A source of explanation, prediction and delight. *Journal of World Business, 41* (1), 36–44.

Miles, M., & Huberman, A. (1984). *Qualitative data analysis.* Beverly Hills, CA: Sage.

Nanto, D. K. (1998). *Congressional Research Service report on the 1997–98 Asian financial crisis.* Washington, DC: Congressional Research Service.

Pache, A., & Chowdhury, I. (2012). Social entrepreneurs as institutionally embedded entrepreneurs: toward a new model of social entrepreneurship education. *Academy of Management Learning & Education, 11,* 494–510.

Pache, A., & Santos, F. (2010). When worlds collide: The internal dynamics of organizational responses to conflicting institutional demands. *Academy of Management Review, 35,* 455–476.

Pache, A., & Santos, F. (2013). Inside the hybrid organization: Selective coupling as a response to competing institutional logics. *Academy of Management Journal, 56,* 972–1001.

Santos, F. (2012). A positive theory of social entrepreneurship. *Journal of Business Ethics, 111,* 335–351.

Sim, J. (2014). World toilet organization founder on turning poop culture into pop culture. *The Guardian,* August 22, 2014 (accessed online: 10 March 2015).

Stewart, W., & Roth, P. (2007). A meta-analysis of achievement motivation differences between entrepreneurs and managers. *Journal of Small Business Management, 45,* 401–421.

Teece, D. (2010). Business models, business strategy and innovation. *Long Range Planning, 43,* 172–194.

Thornton, P., & Ocasio, W. (1999). Institutional logics and the historical contingency of power in organizations: Executive succession in the higher education publishing industry, 1958–1990. *American Journal of Sociology, 105*, 801–843.

Tracey, P., & Jarvis, O. (2007). Toward a theory of social venturing franchising. *Entrepreneurship Theory & Practice, 31*, 667–685.

WHO/UNICEF Joint Monitoring Programme for Water Supply and Sanitation. (2010). *Progress on sanitation and drinking-water: 2010 update.* Geneva: World Health Organization.

World Bank Group. (2009). *The State of the world's communities.* Washington, DC: World Bank Group.

World Toilet Organization. (2014). *WTO 2014 annual report.* Singapore: World Toilet Organization.

Zott, C., & Amit, R. (2007). Business model design and the performance of entrepreneurial firms. *Organization Science, 18*, 181–199.

Biographical Note

Imran Chowdhury is an assistant professor of management at the Lubin School of Business, Pace University. His current research focuses on social entrepreneurship, social responsibility, and communities and organizational action. His articles have been published in *Academy of Management Learning and Education, Social Networks, Academy of Management Best Papers Proceedings*, and in several edited volumes. He received his PhD from ESSEC Business School, an MSc from INSEAD, and a BA in Anthropology and Geography from Hunter College (CUNY). (ichowdhury@pace.edu)

Accepted after two revisions: September 28, 2015

Current Topics in Management, Vol. 18, 2016, pp. 201–212

Research Note

REDUCING JOB BURNOUT THROUGH EFFECTIVE CONFLICT MANAGEMENT STRATEGY

M. Afzalur Rahim
Western Kentucky University

The objective of the study was to investigate the relationships of effective conflict management strategy (i.e., higher uses of the integrating and obliging styles and lower uses of the dominating and avoiding conflict-handling styles) and less effective conflict management strategy (i.e., higher uses of the dominating and avoiding styles and lower uses of the integrating and obliging conflict-handling styles) to the three components of job burnout (emotional exhaustion, depersonalization, and lack of personal accomplishment). Data for the study were collected from a collegiate sample of 869 employed MBA and undergraduate students. A MANCOVA analysis showed that respondents who used effective conflict management strategy reported lower job burnout than those who used less effective strategy. Implications for management, limitations, and directions for future research were discussed.

Keywords: conflict-handling styles, effective conflict-management strategies, job burnout

Conflict is inevitable in organizations. It is a natural outcome of human interaction that begins when two or more employees come in contact with one another in attaining their objectives. Relationships among such entities may become incompatible or inconsistent when two or more of them desire a similar resource that is in short supply; when they have partially exclusive behavioral preferences regarding their joint action; or when they have different attitudes, values, beliefs, and skills (Rahim, 2011).

Conflict among employees can have both functional and dysfunctional consequences (de Wit, Greer, & Jehn, 2012; Jehn, Jonsen, & Rispens, 2014; Pelled, Eisenhardt, & Xin, 1999). Constructive management of organizational conflict, such as the conflict between employees and their supervisors that is the focus of this study, requires that its negative consequences be minimized and its positive consequences maximized. The value-added contribution of the present study is that it is designed to show how a mixture of certain conflict-handling styles can lead to reduction in job burnout of employees.

The Dual Concern Model of Conflict Management Styles

One factor that has an important impact on the effective management of organizational conflict is the style employees use to handle conflicts they are involved in. The styles of handling interpersonal conflict in organizations were first conceptualized in 1926 by Mary P. Follett (1940). She discussed three main ways of handling organizational conflict—domination, compromise, and integration—as well as other, secondary ways of handling conflict, such as avoidance and suppression. Blake and Mouton (1964) first presented a conceptual scheme for classifying the modes for handling interpersonal conflicts into five types: forcing, withdrawing, smoothing, compromising, and problem solving. They described the five modes of handling conflict on the basis of the attitudes of the manager: concern for production and for people. Their scheme was reinterpreted by Thomas (1976) who considered the intentions of a party (cooperativeness, i.e., attempting to satisfy the other party's concerns; and assertiveness, i.e., attempting to satisfy one's own concerns) in classifying the modes of handling conflict into five types.

Rahim and Bonoma (1979) and Rahim (1983) differentiated the *styles* of handling interpersonal conflict on two basic dimensions: concern for self and concern for others. The first dimension explains the degree (high or low) to which a person attempts to satisfy his or her own concern. The second dimension explains the degree (high or low) to which a person wants to satisfy the concern of others. It should be pointed out that these dimensions portray the motivational orientations of a given individual during conflict. Studies by Ruble and Thomas (1976) and Van de Vliert and Kabanoff (1990) yielded general support for these dimensions. Combination of the two dimensions results in five specific styles of handling interpersonal conflict, as shown in Figure 1. The five-category nomenclature of the styles of handling interpersonal conflict is described as follows.

1. **Integrating Style.** This style is associated with high concern for self and others. It involves collaboration between the parties (i.e., openness, exchange of information, and examination of differences to reach a solution acceptable to both parties). This style has two distinctive

Figure 1
Problem Solving and Bargaining Strategies for Managing Interpersonal Conflict

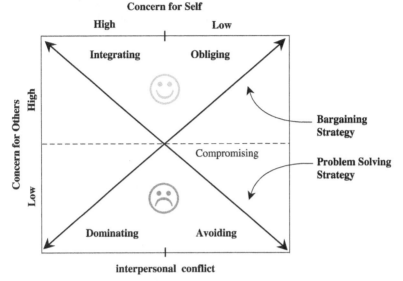

elements: diagnosis of and intervention in conflict. Diagnosis involves open communication, clearing up misunderstanding, and analyzing the underlying causes of conflict. Intervention in conflict involves solution to a right problem identified in the diagnosis phase to provide maximum satisfaction of concerns of both parties.

2. **Obliging Style.** This style indicates low concern for self and high concern for others. This is also known as accommodating and is associated with attempting to play down the differences and emphasizing commonalities to satisfy the concern of the other party. There is an element of self-sacrifice in this style. It may take the form of selfless generosity, charity, or obedience to another party's order. An obliging person neglects his or her own concern to satisfy the concern of the other party.

3. **Dominating Style.** This style indicates high concern for self and low concern for others. This is also known as competing and has been identified with a win–lose orientation or with forcing behavior to win one's position. A dominating or competing person goes all out to win his or her objective and, as a result, often ignores the needs and expectations of the other party. Sometimes a dominating person wants to win at any cost. Dominating supervisors are likely to use their position power to impose their will on the subordinates and command their obedience.

4. **Avoiding Style.** This style indicates low concern for self and others. This is also known as suppression and is associated with withdrawal, buck-passing, sidestepping, or "see no evil, hear no evil, speak no evil" situations. It may take the form of postponing an issue until a better time,

204   Intelligence, Sustainability, and Strategic Issues in Management

or simply withdrawing from a threatening situation. An avoiding person fails to satisfy the concern of self as well as the other party.

5. **Compromising Style.** This style indicates moderate concern for self and others. It involves give-and-take or sharing whereby both parties give up something to make a mutually acceptable decision. It may mean splitting the difference, exchanging concession, or seeking a quick, middle-ground position. The present study did not use this style of handling conflict.

The literature indicates that more cooperative conflict management styles, such as integrating and obliging (in which a meaningful amount of concern is shown for the other party) are likely to produce positive individual and organizational outcomes, while less cooperative styles like dominating and avoiding (in which little concern is shown for the other party) frequently result in the escalation of conflict and negative outcomes (Korbanik, Baril, & Watson, 1993; Rahim, Antonioni, & Psenicka, 2001; Johnson, 1989).

Problem Solving and Bargaining Styles

Follett's (1940) conceptualization is the forerunner of Walton and McKersie's (1965) distinction between integrative and distributive bargaining. It has been suggested by Thomas (1976) that further insights into the five styles of handling interpersonal conflict may be obtained by organizing them according to the integrative and distributive dimensions of labor–management bargaining suggested by Walton and McKersie. These two dimensions have been described as cooperation and competition by Deutsch (1949), the principle of creating value for all and the principle of claiming value for each by Lax and Sebenius (1986), and mutual gains and concession–convergence by Rubin (1994). These two dimensions may be reconceptualized as problem solving and bargaining strategies for managing conflict and are represented by the heavy lines in the diagonals of Figure 1.

The problem solving style (integrating *minus* avoiding) represents the extent (high or low) of satisfaction of concerns received by self *and* others. The bargaining style (dominating *minus* obliging) represents the satisfaction of concerns received by self *or* others. In the problem solving strategy, the integrating style attempts to increase the satisfaction of the concerns of both parties by formulating problems and finding effective solutions for them. The avoiding style leads to the reduction of satisfaction of the concerns of both parties as a result of their failure to confront and solve their problems. In the bargaining style, whereas the dominating style attempts to obtain high satisfaction of concerns for self (and provide low satisfaction of concerns for others), the obliging style attempts to obtain low satisfaction of concerns for self and provide high satisfaction of concerns for others.

The problem solving and bargaining strategies are portrayed in Figure 1. The present investigation wants to find out if greater use of the problem solving strategy plus lower use of the bargaining strategy leads to lower job burnout.

Job Burnout

Job burnout is a syndrome of physical and mental health caused by prolonged exposure to stress involving emotional responses. People who work in human services, such as nursing, emergency and trauma, and police services are susceptible to higher job burnout than others. Some of the symptoms of job burnout are irritability; hopelessness; unexplained headaches, backaches or other physical problems; lack of energy to be productive; and disillusionment about job. Maslach and Jackson (1982) and Maslach, Schaufeli, and Leiter (2001) described job burnout as a tripartite syndrome involving feelings of emotional exhaustion, depersonalization, and lack of personal accomplishment. These three components are factorially independent of each other.

Emotional Exhaustion

This is associated with a syndrome of depletion of physical and mental energy.

Depersonalization

This refers to negative attitudes toward supervisor, subordinates, colleagues, clients, and the other people that one has to work with.

Lack of Personal Accomplishment

This is associated with an employee's feelings of reduced job performance and other contribution to the organization.

Scholars have generally neglected to investigate how interpersonal conflict influences job stress and burnout. There is a study that reported a significant positive relationship between conflict and job burnout (Rahim 1990). There was no published study that investigated how conflict management strategies can influence job burnout. Rahim's (2011) literature review suggests that conflict management (involving greater use of the problem solving style and lower use of bargaining style) should lead to desirable individual outcomes. Conflict management strategy (involving greater use of the bargaining style and lower use of the problem solving style) leads to relatively higher job burnout.

It is expected that a higher score in problem solving strategy and a lower score in bargaining strategy will be associated with lower job burnout.

A higher job burnout will be associated with lower score in problem solving and higher score in bargaining. Therefore, the hypothesis for the present study is as follows:

Hypothesis: *Employees who use higher problem solving strategy plus lower bargaining strategy will report lower job burnout than employees who use higher bargaining strategy plus lower problem solving strategy.*

Method

Sample

Data were collected from a collegiate sample (N = 869) of MBA and undergraduate students who had jobs. The average age and work experience of the respondents were 22.71 (SD = 4.82) and 4.19 (SD = 6.07) years, respectively; 42% of the respondents were female. The respondents reported working in various industries, including manufacturing, service, IT, healthcare, and education.

Measurement

Conflict Management Styles. (Time 1). The four styles of handling conflict with a supervisor (integrating, obliging, dominating, and avoiding) were measured with 24 of the 28 items of the Rahim Organizational Conflict Inventory–II (ROCI–II), Form A (Rahim 1983). The instrument uses 5-point Likert scale (5 = Strongly Agree ... 1 = Strongly Disagree) to rank each item, and the index of each style was computed by averaging responses to its items. A higher score indicates greater use of a style to handle conflict with supervisor. Rahim (1983) and Rahim and Magner (1995) provided evidence of adequate internal consistency and retest reliabilities and convergent and discriminant validities of this instrument in domestic and cross-cultural samples. These and other studies (e.g., Rahim, Antonioni, & Psenicka, 2001; Ting-Toomey et al., 1991) provided evidence of construct validity of the instrument. The instrument was free from social desirably responding. The scales for the problem solving and bargaining styles were computed as follows:

Problem Solving strategy = Integrating – Obliging
Bargaining strategy = Dominating – Obliging

Effective Strategy. This is a higher-level strategy that indicates a positive score on the problem solving strategy and a negative score in the bargaining strategy. Putting it in another way, this strategy involves using more integrating and obliging styles and using less dominating and avoiding styles.

Less Effective Strategy. This is a lower-level strategy that indicates a positive score on the bargaining strategy and a negative score on the problem solving strategy. In other words, this strategy involves using more dominating and avoiding styles and using less integrating and obliging styles

Job Burnout. (Time 2). The three components of job burnout—emotional exhaustion, depersonalization, and lack of personal accomplishment—were measured with the 23 items of the Maslach Burnout Inventory (MBI) (Maslach & Jackson, 1982). The items are ranked on a 7-point Likert scale (7 = Very Much Like Me … 1 = Very Much Unlike Me), and the index of each burnout component was computed by averaging responses to its items—a higher score indicates a greater level of burnout in one of the three components. Maslach and Jackson (1982) and Maslach, Jackson, and Leiter (1996) provided evidence of psychometric properties of the instrument. The instrument was completed at Time 2, which was four weeks from Time 1.

Effective and Less Effective Strategies

Respondents who had a positive sign in the problem solving strategy and a negative sign in the bargaining strategy were put in the effective strategy group. Respondents who had a negative sign in the problem solving strategy and a positive sign in the bargaining strategy were put in the less effective strategy group.

Figure 1 shows a broken line in the middle of the matrix in the dual concern model that separates the effective strategy from less effective strategy. The effective strategy (indicated by a happy face) is located above the broken line. The measure of less effective strategy (indicated by a sad face) is located below the broken line.

Analysis and Results

The relationships of conflict management strategies to the three components of job burnout were tested with Multivariate Analysis of Covariance (MANCOVA). The analysis was done with the effective–less effective strategies as a categorical independent variable, gender and age as covariates, and the three components of job burnout as dependent variables. The analysis shows a significant multivariate relationship between the two strategies—effective and less effective—and the three components of job burnout ($Wilks'$ $\lambda = .70$, F (3, 863) = 1.30, $p < .005$). The effects of control variables—gender and age—on job burnout were not significant. Descriptive statistics and the results from MANCOVA are presented in Table 1.

The three components of burnout were significantly different between effective and less effective strategies. The results show that respondents who were in the effective strategy group reported lower emotional exhaustion,

Table 1

MANCOVA for Effective and Less Effective Conflict-Management Strategies and the Three Components of Job Burnout

Criterion Variables	*Mean*	*SD*	α	*F*
Emotional exhaustion			.83	3.01*
Effective strategy	2.88	1.19		
Less Effective strategy	3.06	1.15		
Depersonalization			.72	8.43***
Effective strategy	2.53	1.05		
Less Effective strategy	2.71	1.01		
Lack of personal accomplishment			.65	4.19**
Effective strategy	3.23	.98		
Less Effective strategy	3.44	.89		

Note: $N = 869$. *Wilks'* $\lambda = .70$, $F (3, 863) = 1.30$, $p < .005$.
* $p < .05$. ** $p < .01$. ** $p < .001$.

depersonalization, and lack of personal accomplishment than respondents who were in the less effective group. This provided full support for the study hypothesis. The Cronbach αs for the three components of job burnout were .83, .72, and .65, respectively, are acceptable.

Discussion

The study contributes to our understanding of the relationships of the conflict management strategies to job burnout. It shows that a mixture of appropriate conflict-handling styles by subordinates can lead to a functional outcome, such as reduced job burnout. It is also expected that the use effective conflict management strategy by employees will lead to other beneficial outcomes for the organization.

Implications for Management

The implication of this study is that supervisors can encourage employees to enhance their problem solving conflict management strategy and reduce their bargaining conflict management strategy through education and training. The challenge for a contemporary organization is to enhance the conflict management skills of their members through appropriate training that will involve case analysis, exercises, survey feedback, and readings (see Rahim

2011). Training should be made available to both management and nonmanagement employees.

Organization members should also be encouraged to enhance their conflict management skills through continuous self-learning. Organizations should provide appropriate reinforcements for learning and improving employees' conflict management skills so that they can handle various situations effectively. To attain this goal, appropriate changes in organization design and culture would be needed (Rahim, 2002). Changes in organization design would require creating flatter, decentralized, and less complex structures. Also, there should be appropriate changes in organizational culture that provides rewards for learning new behaviors. These changes will encourage employees to acquire conflict management competencies needed for reducing job burnout and probably improving their job performance and other desirable outcomes.

Limitations

The limitations of this field study should be noted. The self-report measures of conflict styles and job burnout that were taken from each respondent present the problem of common method variance, that is, the lack of independence between criterion and predictor variables. An attempt was made to overcome the problem of common method variance by separating the measures of conflict styles and the criterion variable by four weeks (Podsakoff and Organ 1986).

It should be noted that a study by Spector (1987) concluded that properly developed instruments are resistant to the method variance problem. In the present study, two well-developed and published measurement instruments were used that probably minimized the effect of common method variance. Data collected from a convenience sample might limit generalizability of the results.

Directions for Further Research

Further research is needed to enhance our understanding of the interrelationships of conflict management styles and job burnout of employees. An important area of future research concerns carefully designing and evaluating the effects of intervention in enhancing effective conflict management strategies. Field experiments are particularly useful in evaluating the effects of training to enhance effective conflict management strategies on individual and organizational outcomes. There is also need for scenario-based studies and laboratory studies that control some of the extraneous variables to better understand the effects of conflict management strategies reported in the present study. Attempts should be made to obtain independent measures of some of the criterion variables.

References

Blake, R. R., & Mouton, J. S. (1964). *The managerial grid.* Houston, TX: Gulf.

De Wit, F. R., Greer, L. L., & Jehn, K. A. (2012). The paradox of intragroup conflict: A meta-analysis. *Journal of Applied Psychology, 97,* 360–390.

Deutsch, M. (1949). A theory of cooperation and competition. *Human Relations, 2,* 129–152.

Follett, M. P. (1940). Constructive conflict. In H. C. Metcalf & L. Urwick (Eds.), *Dynamic administration: The collected papers of Mary Parker Follett* (pp. 30–49). New York: Harper. (Original work pub 1926).

Jehn, K. A., Jonsen, K., & Rispens, S. (2014). Relationships at work: Intragroup conflict and the continuation of task and social relationships in workgroups. *Current Topics in Management, 17,* 1–22.

Johnson, P. E. (1989). *Conflict in school organizations and its relationship in school climate.* Unpublished doctoral dissertation, Auburn University, AL.

Korbanik, K., Baril, G. L., & Watson, C. (1993). Managers' conflict management style and leadership performance: The moderating effects of gender. *Sex Roles, 29,* 405–420.

Lax, D. A., & Sebenius, J. K., (1986). *The manager as negotiator: Bargaining for cooperative and competitive gain.* New York: Free Press.

Maslach, C., & Jackson S. E. (1982). *Maslach burnout inventory.* Palo Alto, CA: Consulting Psychologists Press.

Maslach, C., S. E. Jackson, & M. P. Leiter (1996). *Maslach burnout inventory manual* (3rd ed.). Palo Alto, CA: Consulting Psychologists Press.

Maslach, C., Jackson, S. E., & Leiter, M. P. (2001). Job burnout. *Annual Review of Psychology, 52,* 397–422.

Pelled, L. H., Eisenhardt, K. M., & Xin, K. R. (1999). Exploring the black box: An analysis of work group diversity, conflict, and performance. *Administrative Science Quarterly, 44,* 1–28.

Podsakoff, P. M., & Organ, D. W. (1986). Self-reports in organizational research: Problems and prospects. *Journal of Management, 12,* 531–544.

Prein, H. C. M. (1976). Stijlen van conflicthantering [Styles of handling conflict]. *Nederlands Tijdschrift voor de Psychologie, 31,* 321–346.

Rahim, M. A. (1983). A measure of styles of handling interpersonal conflict. *Academy of Management Journal, 26,* 368–376.

Rahim, M. A. (1990). Moderating effects of hardiness and social support on the relationships of conflict and stress to job burnout and performance. In M. A. Rahim (Ed.), *Theory and research in conflict management* (pp. 4–14). New York: Praeger.

Rahim, M. A. (2002). Toward a theory of managing organizational conflict. *International Journal of Conflict Management, 13,* 206-235.

Rahim, M. A. (2011). *Managing conflict in organizations* (4th ed.). New Brunswick, NJ: Transaction.

Rahim, M. A., Antonioni, D., Psenicka, C. (2001). A structural equations model of leader power, subordinates' styles of handling conflict and job performance. *International Journal of Conflict Management, 12,* 191–211.

Rahim, M. A., & Bonoma, T. V. (1979). Managing organizational conflict: A model for diagnosis and intervention. *Psychological Reports, 44,* 1323–1344.

Rahim, M. A., & Magner, N. R. (1995). Confirmatory factor analysis of the styles of handling interpersonal conflict: First-order factor model and its invariance across groups. *Journal of Applied Psychology, 80,* 122–132.

Rubin, J. Z. (1994). Models of conflict management. *Journal of Social Issues, 50* (1), 33–45.

Ruble, T. L., & Thomas, K. W. (1976). Support for a two-dimensional model for conflict behavior. *Organizational Behavior and Human Performance, 16*, 143–155.

Spector, P. E. (1987). Method variance as an artifact in self-reported affect and perceptions at work: Myth or significant problem? *Journal of Applied Psychology,* 72: 438–443.

Thomas, K. W. (1976). Conflict and conflict management. In M. D. Dunnette (Ed.), *Handbook of industrial and organizational psychology* (pp. 889–935). Chicago: Rand McNally.

Ting-Toomey, S., Gao, G., Trubisky, P., Yang, Z., Kim, H. S., Lin, S. L., & Nishida, T. (1991). Culture, face maintenance, and styles of handling interpersonal conflict: A study in five cultures. *International Journal of Conflict Management, 2*, 275–296.

Van de Vliert, E., & Kabanoff, B. (1990). Toward theory-based measures of conflict management. *Academy of Management Journal, 33*, 199–209.

Walton, R. E., and McKersie, R. B. (1965). *A behavioral theory of labor negotiations: An analysis of a social interaction system.* New York: McGraw-Hill.

Biographical Note

M. Afzalur Rahim (Ph.D., University of Pittsburgh) is a University Distinguished Professor of Management and Hays Watkins Research Fellow, Western Kentucky University. He is also the Founding Editor of *Current Topics in Management* and is the founder of the *International Journal of Organizational Analysis, International Journal of Conflict Management*, International Association for Conflict Management, International Conference on Advances in Management, International Conference on Social Intelligence, and Bangladesh Academy of Business Administration. Dr. Rahim is the author/editor of 23 books; 117 articles, book chapters, case studies, and research instruments; and 96 conference papers. His articles were published, among others, in the *Academy of Management Journal, Intelligence, Journal of Applied Psychology, Journal of Management, and Multivariate Behavioral Research*. His current research interests are in the areas of conflict management, leaders' emotional, cultural, and social intelligence. His citation index is over 7,200 in scholar.google.com. (1988mgmt@gmail.com)

Accepted after two revisions: November 12, 2015

Current Topics in Management, Vol. 18, 2016, pp. 213–226

BOOK REVIEWS

Mackenzie, K. D. (2015). *Group and Organizational Processes*, Volume I: *The Quest to Discover Their Essence.* Deutschland, Germany: LAP Lambert Academic Publishing. ISBN: 978-3-659-76508-7 (softcover)

Reviewed by William H. Money, The Citadel School of Business (willmny@ gmail.com)

Many researchers seek to make a true breakthrough in their field by attacking and solving a great and significant problem or answering an unknown with a new theory (or proof) that can (and will) be recognized as a significant advancement. However, picking the right problem to attack (that other respected researcher agree is important) and developing a breakthrough theory or vital contribution that explains or solves the problem is easier said than done. After the fact, some few researchers who accomplish this explain and illustrate their work as if they always had it figured out and only lacked the critical data, the unique tools, or some insightful examples essential to prove the theory correct. But, in the world of science, no matter how many new ideas you explore and new proofs you encounter, there is always something left out or unclear that the then next big breakthrough or finding will clarify and thus lead to an even more complete or improved understanding. When assessing a theory or proposed contribution and its description we always seem to be left with some elements or phenomena that can't quite be explained and some factors that (if known) might still change our conclusions.

Explaining what processes are, how groups and organizations can be represented with mathematical structures, and how this representation and networks built from the structures can be derived and generalized to many organizations is a very significant undertaking. In it, Mackenzie has tackled an enormous theoretical task (which has taken him on a life-time journey lasting his academic and work career). He has upped the ante by making the work more difficult by ambitiously seeking to develop methods of "deciding among competing process representations, and applying them to organizational; problems that required solutions." The most enjoyable part of his book is that as you read Mackenzie's thoughts, you also learn about his growth as an insightful individual, explore his personality as he becomes a researcher and theoretician, and see the development of the process theory through his life. The life story is intricately woven into the process understandings he acquires, and into this theory he develops. We learn how his early life, schooling, father, and high school contributed to his understanding and representation of group and organizational processes. Mackenzie's life experiences are threaded (with other examples) into the elaborately detailed development of a complex and dynamic group and organization process (GOP) that is explained by sets of steps, stages, and considerations. The book describes well how all are intertwined from their initiation to an outcome, and how the pattern of the linkages can then be viewed as a network that describes the outcomes that occur. This brief and unfortunately incomplete description of the GOP does not do justice to the well-developed and comprehensive reasoning presented in the text, nor provide the detailed examples included in the discussions, but it is included here to give the reader a very brief taste of the whole contribution and benefits of this work.

The GOP constructively addresses the process problems of complexity—analyzing and describing how even the very simple and ordinary processes may become very complex. It grants that routine task processes are difficult to unravel in "messy" organizations that are not well structured, or clearly defined. But, with understandable examples, like the process of answering a phone, the language and representation of the GOP unfolds for the reader (or student and future researcher). The work appreciates that all are born with some understanding of processes and how to use them in life situations (perhaps with affordances, or through cognitive or social learning theories, according to me). However, the book does not seek to address the questions of how or why all seem to have or acquire this process understanding, but focuses on clarifying and elaborating the GOP itself.

After explaining the GOP in chapter 1, the book assesses the state of group and organizational processes as a science. The justification for developing and substantiating this theory is that the science of group and organizational processes will advance far more rapidly when the various communities that theorize develop analysis techniques, produce engineering methods for implementing processes, and end users applying the processes and tools can work more independently of each other. To accomplish this, the book postulates that an agreed definition, with a language of representation, will enable and therefore further enhance the development of the science. One can only concur with the similes the book draws to advancements made in other sciences and areas of study where independent innovations of the development through theory, tools, measurements, and testing of implementations had an enormous magnifying effect on the development of the overall scientific endeavor. Mackenzie notes that there are still many unaddressed issues with the study and theory of GOPs—how to conduct the research, handle time, goals, methods, data collection, and inferences that must still be addressed; and that some researchers are attacking these issue. Finally, there are questions of ethics that have not been addressed. But Mackenzie wins the point, without conceptual agreement, definitions, and language—the process field cannot go far nor can many of these concerns be addressed until there are future standards and policies guided by a professional group that agrees on what it is studying and how to accurately describe the phenomena.

The comprehensive nature of the work is readily apparent, but not over-whelming. The book serves as a very useful reference, in that it describes in detail the concepts and work of other authors who have developed systems seeking to advance our understanding of processes. The three research efforts incorporated into the text include the MIT Center for Coordination Science (Malone), Knowledge Representation Tool (Sowa), and Dynamic Simulation (Melcher). The similarities, strengths, weaknesses, and underlying differences with the GOP framework are identified. Thus, this book provides a valuable overview of both the process theory field and those who are actively advancing it through research and their various approaches. A critical distinction is drawn between the GOP framework and the conceptualizations of these other primary researchers. Notably, the GOP framework derives a mathematical or algebraic approach for the GOP framework that makes it subject (and possible) to test. (Those with a deep understanding of mathematical proofs and equations will find this a beneficial contribution.) But the tests themselves are somewhat dif-ferent from the traditional independent, dependent, and moderator tests applied to variables in many organizational studies. In capturing or at least identifying and explaining the process essence, ranges of GOPs are viewed as producing outcomes that are possible but not unique. The book argues that many paths in the network of possible paths may thus result in the same outcome. It states that the essence is found in the GOPs' focus on *how what is going on indeed works*—to produce the outcomes and results. The GOP is not studying and describing variables, rather models connecting considerations to outcomes according to Mackenzie.

The book notes very early that the program of research began many years ago with an analysis of small groups and processes that differed when group solved inference and routine problems. Structures for stages and responses varied according to different rewards and incentives. Understanding how written communications can be used to explain structural changes and those messages could themselves be coded and analyzed for interactions and patterns were important realizations for Mackenzie. This understanding of messages and communication seems so relevant and insightful in today's world where data analytics are being applied to assess individual responses to marketing programs and to design experiments that it will further elicit individual desired responses. The work has obviously progressed far, for now the massive process interactions documented in communications, various media (e-mail, phone calls, texts, messaging, uses of video, etc.) have been successfully introduced into many fields of organizational studies such as business, education, medicine, international negotiations, sports, and security. The GOP elements appear to be present in these efforts, including sets of steps, stages, and considerations intertwined from their initiation to an outcome. The pattern of the linkages can be viewed as networks that describe the outcomes that occur. The observable outcomes may be processes that deliver new products (again and again), direct marketing campaigns, plan and complete mergers, establish treaties, or even test for, find, or prevent security breaches. Perhaps the work of a future researcher with the new analytical capabilities and massive computation power available today will be able to apply this GOP theory and language to analyze the billions of messages swirling around the world, identify the subprocesses and process, patterns and networks embedded in those messages, and thus deduce or predict the purpose of the process analyzed and its eventual outcome.

Early in the book, Mackenzie describes this work as his lifetime quest to answer a number of key questions. The last, which seemed to be more rhetorical, was "Does it help?" It refers to the GOP and essence (I assume). It also deserves an answer—well, you bet it does.

Edmondson, A. C. (2012). *Teaming: How Organizations Learn, Innovate, and Compete in the Knowledge Economy.* San Francisco, CA: Jossey-Bass. ISBN: 978-0787970932. (hardcover)

Reviewed by Paul C. Gratton, George Fox University (pgratton11@georgefox.edu)

Teaming: How Organizations Learn, Innovate, and Compete in the Knowledge Economy by Harvard professor Amy C. Edmondson explores how leaders can reshape work practices through the power of teaming and organizational learning. This book shares Edmondson's 20 plus years of research on teaming and organizational learning in a variety of industries including manufacturing, financial services, product design, telecommunications, government, and construction.

"Teaming" provides an excellent introduction to organizational learning and systems thinking. For readers new to these concepts, Teaming is filled with practical and applicable knowledge. The theories presented are made clear through Edmondson's straightforward writing style, and major concepts are highlighted through the use of case studies and examples. In addition, scholars familiar with the work of other leading organizational thinkers such as Peter Senge, Edgar Schein, and Chris Argyris will find Teaming an enjoyable compilation of research findings from the past few decades related to learning, organization, and culture—making this book an excellent reference for the management reader.

Early in the book Edmondson defines teaming as a verb, recognizing that teams are not static; rather they are dynamic workgroups that employ a number of practices and structures in order to achieve goals. Teaming attempts to take advantage of all the abilities of an organization's membership, rejecting the mechanistic mindset and command-and-control hierarchies that emerged from classical management theory and the industrial revolution.

In the second section of the book the concept of teaming is tied directly to developing a culture of organizational learning. Edmondson masterfully pulls from research in the area of organizational psychology and organizational behavior, providing clarity on the values and practices that are required for teaming to succeed. Foundational to the success of teaming are four key organizational behaviors: speaking up, collaboration, experimentation, and reflection. These behaviors are further elaborated throughout the book, as each section builds on previous sections in a way that keeps the reader interested and engaged.

One of the constructs that I found most useful from the book is the Process Knowledge Spectrum: a thoughtful way of recognizing and addressing the uncertainty that exists in a given process. In well-defined, routinized processes uncertainty tends to be low. In these situations tools such as Six Sigma and Total Quality Management (TQM) are used to improve efficiency and reduce variation. In fast-paced, complex environments where process uncertainty is high, a different mindset is required. In these settings leaders must expect broad variation in outcomes, employing teaming to adapt to the variation and using identified failures as learning opportunities.

Each process type identified by the Process Knowledge Spectrum (routine, complex, and innovation) has a different focus and goal from the others; however, in each process type, execution-as-learning can be employed through teaming. Execution-as-learning empowers small teams that are close to the front lines of operations to engage in problem identification and problem solving as part of their work process—allowing organizational learning to occur on an ongoing basis.

The final section of Teaming reviews the major themes of the book through a trio of real-life examples. Case studies based on mattress-maker Simmons Bedding Company, Children's Hospital and Clinics of Minneapolis, Minnesota, and innovative design firm IDEO are reviewed to relate the Process Knowledge Spectrum to actual situations. In this part of the book Edmondson's teaching experience is evident as she skillfully blends storytelling with research findings in a way that is both entertaining and enlightening.

Teaming is an easy read and is full of insights that can be immediately applied. It provides straightforward, hands-on advice for management practitioners, and well-founded, scholarly research for discerning academics. Overall, it is a valuable book for anyone involved in organizational leadership, and I highly recommended it to the readers of *Current Topics in Management*.

Grenny, J., Patterson, K., Maxfield, D., McMillan, R. & Switzler, A. (2013). *Influencer: The New Science of Leading Change* (2nd ed.). New York: McGraw Hill Education. ISBN: 978-0-07-180886-6. (hardcover)

Reviewed by S. Brook Henderson, American Public University System, sheila .henderson5@mycampus.apus.edu.

The purpose of writing this book is for the authors to propagate the results of leadership research they have done over many years. The authors write from their own perspective, telling one story after another to illustrate their points. This book is about how to effect quick, profound, and lasting change, regardless of the type of environment. It is not a textbook—rather, it is a business "self-help" book. Written for those who want to create change and make it work, it is in a clear, conversational style that suits the audience. One of the aspects of the book I particularly like is that it is based on research.

It is somewhat embarrassing that, as a research scientist, the book reminded me of the importance of measurement. In describing the "Three Keys to Influence," Key One is Focus and Measure. It talks about clear goals, as well as about the criticality of measuring the effectiveness of the changes. The authors list three pitfalls that change agents fall into. They are (1) fuzzy, uncompelling goals; (2) infrequent or no measures; and (3) bad measures. The fact that they have two measurement pitfalls to one goal setting pitfall is an indication of how seriously they take the measurement of progress.

Key Two is Find Vital Behaviors. If large-scale change is desired, the change agent must identify which critical behaviors need to change to act as a fulcrum for rapid change. The authors spend a good deal of time recounting examples of how leaders have identified vital behaviors. One of those examples is about lifeguards and the statistics on drowning in public pools. It was discovered that lifeguards were spending time with tasks other than scanning the pool for people in trouble. When they returned to scanning, the rate of drowning dropped dramatically. Studying a situation to discover vital behaviors reinforced my training in research.

Key Three is Engage All Six Sources of Influence. Naturally, the reader now wants to know what those six sources are. I will leave it to you to find out by reading the book. Suffice it to say that I suspect none of the sources of influence will come as a great surprise to anyone. It is the measurement and identification of vital behaviors that has impressed me.

These writers support their thesis with extensive descriptions of specific examples that illustrate every point they make in support of that thesis. The book is very persuasive, with many positive conclusions drawn from the research they have done and the many interviews they conducted.

The book also has a good Index and a Works Cited section that will help you find specific topics as well as look more deeply into the subject matter. Although many of the entries in the Works Cited section are citations of personal interviews, there is written material that can be found and studied. For a "self-help" business book, it is nice to have these sections.

Influencer: The New Science of Leading Change is written in two parts. The first part is about the three keys to influence and how to use them. The second part is about using the six sources of influence. It develops each of the six extensively and comprises most of the book. The final chapter is first a summary of the book and then a call to action. After recapping what an influencer should do, the authors invite their readers to join a community—not to work alone. They assert that working with others increases the power of the influence that can be brought to bear on the problem.

I would certainly recommend this book to anyone who is interested in change and how to effect it. People in business, social scientists, leaders, or just plain folks who want something to be different will enjoy this book. It is not a text and it is not written for an elite audience. It can easily be read and understood. The authors are credible because of the extensive research they have done, and they impart that research in a warm and friendly style without "talking down" to the reader.

Deresiewicz, W. (2014). *Excellent Sheep: The Miseducation of the American Elite & the Way to a Meaningful Life.* New York: Free Press. ISBN: 978-1-4767-0271-1. (hardcover)

Reviewed by S. Brook Henderson, American Public University System, (sheila .henderson5@mycampus.apus.edu).

This book, written by William Deresiewicz and first copyrighted in 2014, is a hardbound book that covers the value of higher education. Although the book doesn't have any special features such as cartoons or illustrations, it is written in medium type with relatively short paragraphs, which makes it easy to read.

Dr. Deresiewicz used to be a professor at Yale and he writes this book about the system of elite education and what it does to kids. This book is written in a personal, conversational style that seems to have the author speaking directly to the reader. Clearly, it is a powerful critique of our present educational system, beginning with the way students are shepherded into elite schools and spanning some critical questions about college. The book is intended for anyone who is interested in education in general and our current college system.

This book is a forceful indictment of the current college system and what happens to kids who are on the fast track to success. Deresiewicz states that these students have learned how to please their teachers and coaches over the course of their school years and that the process has robbed themselves of introspective abilities that could benefit their stressed, often depressed, state of mind. He speaks forcefully about this, saying at one point, "They've learned to 'be a student,' not to use their minds." He says very few students are passionate about ideas. They are focused on success—getting "A"s—not on the thrill of learning and challenging the status quo.

In discussing the history of elite schools and how circumstances got to be the way they are, Deresiewicz looks to the industrial revolution and the wealth it created as the genesis of the elite school. He discusses the racism that developed as the gap between the wealthy and "the great unwashed" increased and how it impacted college enrollments. He says that the appearance of baby boomers on the college scene created another revolution, moving enrollments in elite colleges from aristocracy to meritocracy. He declares that the system that came out of the 1960s is the same one we are living with today.

The book is organized topically, from describing the "sheep" (the students), to self-examination to ask the question, "What is College For?," to schools and on to society as a whole. In answering the question of the purpose of college, Deresiewicz says that "return on investment" is the phrase talked about today. It is, in his opinion, all about getting a good job. He maintains that students don't hear about deeper questions such as whether jobs, financial security, and national prosperity are the things that matter. He encourages this type of questioning and posits that the first purpose of college is to teach its students to think—to be skeptical, to reach one's own conclusions, and to "find yourself." A little over half of the book is dedicated to describing how students are wronged by college, but then Deresiewicz gives the reader the answer to the school dilemma. And it is (drum roll, please): a four-year liberal arts education. Oh, with very good teachers. A liberal arts education will provide the skill of thinking, along with reading great books, according to Deresiewicz. Finally, he discusses the cost of the system of elite education to our society as a whole. He says that it brings back racial and fiscal inequality and cites lots of statistics to support his assertion. At last he attacks our political system as being elitist and calls for us to leave aristocracy and meritocracy behind as we try democracy.

I was with Dr. Deresiewicz right up until his answer to all the elite college system woes culminated in a liberal arts education. Really? Oh, with very good teachers. That should fix everything. While I agreed with many points in the book, I found his prescriptions to be simplistic at best and naïve at worst. He speaks passionately about his beliefs, which I admire, and backs them up with statistics. As a critical thinker, though, I know that statistics can be skewed, and looking at a topic through a specific lens can distort that topic. I wonder if that has what has happened to this author. In taking a hard look at elite colleges today, was his lens of "something is terribly wrong" sufficient to give the reader a skewed view of his topic?

I came away with the impression that this is one of those books that is great if you already agree with the author's basic premises. If you don't agree, or if you don't have the same context for the information he presents, it is an easy-to-read rant. The book does challenge some elitist views of race and economic standing and it is true that, in the United States today, the rich are getting richer and the middle class is getting poorer (and smaller). Whether a liberal arts education and democratizing colleges will solve those issues is difficult for me to believe.

Heaslip, R. J. (2014). *Managing Complex Projects and Programs: How to Improve Leadership of Complex Initiatives Using a Third-Generation Approach.* Hoboken, NJ: John Wiley & Sons. ISBN: 978-1-118-38301-8

Reviewed by S. Brook Henderson, American Public University System, (sheila. henderson5@mycampus.apus.edu)

Richard Heaslip wrote this book out of his own frustration. Trained as a research biochemical pharmacologist, he discovered that he didn't know anything about being a good project or program leader. As his career progressed, he needed to step into leadership roles in order to prosecute research programs. As the projects and programs grew in size and complexity, Dr. Heaslip's need to learn more about management as well as strategy grew apace. As he went on to assume an executive role, he became even more frustrated with trying to define project and program leader positions to interviewees; trying to articulate project and program leadership "best practices"; and realizing that project and program leadership education did not guarantee project/program success.

The book, then, is about "developing an advanced knowledge and understanding of what I will refer to as *programmatic science*." He goes on, then, to define programmatic science as a study of "managerial systems, principles, practices, and processes" that can be used to pursue organizational goals by using projects and programs. He says that programmatic science looks at what should be included in designing an approach to the management of projects and programs.

Heaslip begins by reviewing project management's history, including the assumptions that history has engendered. The industrial revolution begat organizations divided into functional specializations. We often call them "silos." Projects began by establishing cross-functional committees that represented the involved silos. They were temporary efforts organized to produce something unique. Workers were drawn from the various silos, or departments, and were expected to work in concert with equivalent workers from the other departments to achieve specific goals. A "project leader" would be appointed and off they would go. The mindset was that important projects could be planned and managed through controlled processes. This view was perfectly appropriate to the Industrial Age, Heaslip maintains, and responsibilities could be broken down into subcomponents with the execution of each as a specialty. Subsequent reassembling could produce the desired output. He calls this *first-generation programmatics*. The realistic result was that project and program leaders actually needed to be more flexible than the rigid process-driven model of the Industrial Age.

Second-generation programmatics developed in response to this need for flexibility, and the phase-gate approach to projects grew out of the need to learn and adapt. A phase gate is a period of work within a project or program that has a beginning and an end. At the end of the period a review is conducted to ensure that that phase of the project is complete and, if possible, functional. Several phases can be pursued at the same time, of course, but Heaslip remarks overall that this approach to project and program work has been well accepted by organizations. Large and complicated endeavors can be undertaken with some confidence, given the flexibility of this approach.

Other incremental approaches have been devised and used, including "agile" project management, which is a highly adaptive method of advancing a project or program toward its goal. Agile use of "just-in-time" planning can effect short, completed phases of a project. It can reduce the time wasted in continuous re-planning of complex projects. Agile project management, of course, has proved especially useful in the development of software. The increased autonomy of the project manager and the team to plan and replan has caused some distress for upper-level management, but overall the method has received general acceptance, according to Heaslip. He also asserts that these more flexible and adaptive styles of project leadership have reduced exasperation on the part of project leaders and teams of various types.

Heaslip's last foray into second-generation programmatic includes the elements of an improved project oversight model. He suggests that such a model should:

- Improve the abilities of organizations to manage their complex programmatic endeavors (using what we will call a third-generation programmatic approach).
- Fully embrace the use of first- and second-generation approaches when they are most appropriate.
- Clearly define the roles and responsibilities of the programmaticists under every generation of programmatic systems.
- Clearly define the relationships that should exist between programmaticists and governance committees—regardless of the numbers of "parties" in their oversight model.
- Minimize the amount of organizational complexity that needs to be managed.
- Address the pain and suffering of programmaticist-Exasperados. (p. 153)

Part 2 of the book, then, explains "the promise and practice of third-generation programmatics." Heaslip begins this journey with a description and discussion of complexity theory and the types of leadership that are needed for third-generation programmatics. He discusses that the three types of leadership he and others have learned are critical to complex projects and programs. First is enabling leadership that he sees as being the province of governing committees. Then he adds a layer of leadership he terms adaptive leadership (more about that in a minute), and finally he puts in administrative leadership, which is where he categorizes professional project management to be. His idea of adaptive leadership is the new information added.

The adaptive leadership concept issues from complexity leadership theory. Heaslip describes the theory thus: "Complexity leadership theory proposes that highly complex problems are best resolved by bringing together key stakeholders in an environment that allows them to leverage not only their individual knowledge, but also their individual leadership capabilities and styles." He sees adaptive leadership as a new role stemming from the theory that is "reflected in the actions that must be taken to adjust to new learning or tension." This type of leadership is not formalized in organizations, but arises from the need to solve complex problems and can take the form of an individual or a group, according to Heaslip. He uses this concept and description of adaptive leadership to springboard into a role he characterizes as "Programmaticist."

The programmaticist operates on a par with corporate executives, and Heaslip equates this role with the current literature on program management, which he says closely resembles adaptive leadership. He borrows a definition of program from a book of standards, *Managing Successful Programmes*, published by the Stationary Office, Norwich, UK. Its fourth edition was published in 2011, and the definition Heaslip borrows is, "a temporary, flexible organization created to coordinate, direct, and oversee the implementation of a set of related projects and activities in order to deliver outcomes and benefits related to the organization's strategic objectives," although he believes there is room for improvement in the definition. In Part 2 of the book, Heaslip redefines program management, the nature of a program, projects, and project management, and names a new field of study: programmatic sciences.

The final chapters of the book outline and discuss in detail third-generation programmatic and the programmatic sciences. These chapters look at the benefits of distinguishing project from programs and project management from program management and suggests a three-party system of leadership unique to third-generation programmatic. Heaslip discusses what it takes for an organization to grow from the current leadership system to the three-party system he advocates. He goes on to define the leadership competencies needed for programmaticists and discusses developing those competencies. Finally, he talks about what it takes for an organization to become a third-generation programmatics organization. These chapters are fairly long and quite detailed in their descriptions of these new ideas.

The book is divided into two parts: Professional Project and Program Management—Yesterday and Today, and the Promise and Practice of Third-Generation Programmatics. The first part has eight chapters. The second part has six. In its entirety, the book runs to 305 pages, including a 6-page index that is most helpful to the reader who is looking for something specific. The first part of the book is used to examine the challenges, problems, and difficulties with the current approaches to project and program management. The second part sets out to remedy these issues and to explain programmatic sciences in detail.

Richard J. Heaslip, PhD, comes from the pharmaceutical industry. That alone makes him an "outsider" looking in at project and program management from a distinctly different perspective. Before going out on his own as a consultant, he worked for the advancement of industry best practices in pharmaceutical program, project, portfolio, and performance management. He is recognized in the field of project and program management and was a contributor to the Project Management Institute's third edition of the *Standard for Program Management*. The book under review, *Managing Complex Projects and Programs*, came about as a result of his pharmaceutical career, teaching others about project and program management, and a good deal of research.

This book is an extremely valuable look at the current state of project and program management and is a compelling argument for a new science and a new view of the field. Heaslip's writing style is easy to follow, even though the subject matter is complex. Those who practice or have practiced in the field of project and program management will find this book intriguing and important. It brings a fresh view not borne of engineering or software development, and it is thorough and very well thought out. The book is worth reading by anyone who is concerned with the failure rate of projects in their organizations as well as by scholars who are looking for a new and different way to present information on the leadership that will be effective for projects and programs.

BOOKS RECEIVED

Daft, R. L. (2015). *Management* (12th ed.). Boston, MA: Cengage Learning. ISBN: 978-1285861982 (hardcover)

Gates, R. M. (2016). *A Passion for leadership: Lessons on change and reform from fifty years of public service*. New York: Knopf. ISBN: 987-0307959492 (hardcover)

Gordon, J., & Blanchard, K. (2014). *The carpenter: A Story about the greatest success strategies of all*. Hoboken, NJ: Wiley. ISBN: 978-0470888544 (hardcover)

Grenny, J., Patterson, K., Maxfield, D., McMillan, R., & Switzler, A. (2013). *Influencer: The new science of leading change* (2nd ed.). New York: McGraw Hill Education. ISBN: 978-0-07-180886-6 (hardcover)

Harvard Business Review. 2015. *HBR's 10 must reads*. Boston, MA: Harvard Business Review Press. ISBN: 978-16336690806 (paperback)

Heaslip, R. J. (2014). *Managing complex projects and programs: How to improve leadership of complex initiatives using a third-generation approach*. Hoboken, NJ: Wiley. ISBN: 978-1-118-38301-8

Mathis, R. L., & Jackson, J. H. (2016). *Human resource management* (15th ed.). Cincinnati, OH: Southwestern College Pub. ISBN: 978-1305500709 (hardcover)

Mello, J. A. (2014). *Strategic human resources management* (4th ed.). Cincinnati, OH: Southwestern College Pub. ISBN: 978-1285426792

Northhouse, P. G. (2015). *Leadership: Theory and practice* (7th ed.). Beverly Hills, CA: Sage. ISBN: 978-1483317533 (paperback)

Project Management Institute. (2013). *A guide to the project management body of knowledge*: (PEMBOK Guide) (5th ed.). Newtown Square, PA: Project Management Institute. ISBN: 978-1935589679 (softcover)

Rahim, A., (Ed.) (2016). *Management: Theory, research, and practice* (2nd ed.). San Diego, CA: Cognella Academic. ISBN: 978-1-60927-721-5 (softcover)

Rothaerme, F. (2014). *Strategic management concepts* (2nd ed.). New York: McGraw-Hill Education. ISBN: 978-0077645069 (hardcover)

Tarique, I., Briscoe, D. R., & Schuler, R. S. (2015). *International human resource management: Policies and practices* (5th ed.). New York: Routledge. ISBN: 978-0415710534 (paperback)